Computer Engineering

Computer Engineering

Henry Martin

Larsen & Keller
www.larsen-keller.com

Computer Engineering
Henry Martin
ISBN: 978-1-64172-381-7 (Hardback)

 Larsen & Keller

Published by Larsen and Keller Education,
5 Penn Plaza,
19th Floor,
New York, NY 10001, USA

Cataloging-in-Publication Data

Computer engineering / Henry Martin.
     p. cm.
Includes bibliographical references and index.
ISBN 978-1-64172-381-7
1. Computer engineering. 2. Computer architecture. 3. Computer organization.
4. Computer science. I. Martin, Henry.
TK7885 .C66 2020
004--dc23

For more information regarding Larsen and Keller Education and its products, please visit the publisher's website www.larsen-keller.com

TABLE OF CONTENTS

PREFACE

This book aims to help a broader range of students by exploring a wide variety of significant topics related to this discipline. It will help students in achieving a higher level of understanding of the subject and excel in their respective fields. This book would not have been possible without the unwavered support of my senior professors who took out the time to provide me feedback and help me with the process. I would also like to thank my family for their patience and support.

The branch of engineering, which is concerned with the development of computer hardware and software is referred to as computer engineering. It includes the integration of several fields of electronic engineering and computer science. It encompasses the areas such as electronic engineering, hardware-software integration and software design. It is involved in various aspects of computing such as the design of individual microcontrollers, personal computers, microprocessors, super computers, etc. The two major branches of computer engineering are computer hardware engineering and computer software engineering. Some of the specialties within this field are coding, cryptography, information protection, communications and wireless networks, compilers and operating systems, computational science and engineering, quantum computing, and embedded systems. This book contains some path-breaking studies in the field of computer engineering. Also included herein is a detailed explanation of the various concepts and applications of this field. Those in search of information to further their knowledge will be greatly assisted by this book.

A brief overview of the book contents is provided below:

Chapter – Introduction

A computer is a machine that is designed to execute applications and processes by combining hardware and software components. Supercomputer, mainframe computer, minicomputer, microcomputer, etc. are some of the types of computers. This chapter has been carefully written to provide an easy understanding of the characteristics and components of a computer system.

Chapter – Computer Architecture

Computer architecture refers to the set of methods that are used in the functioning and organization of a computer system. It includes parallel computer architecture, microarchitecture, system designs such as CPU, GPU, ALU, etc. This is an introductory chapter which will briefly introduce about these types of computer architecture.

Chapter – Computer Hardware

Computer hardware refers to the tangible parts of a computer system. Some of them are monitor, keyboard, mouse, hard drive, motherboard, video card, optical drive, etc. The topics elaborated in this chapter will help in gaining a better perspective about these components of computer hardware.

Chapter – Computer Software

Computer software is a set of programs and data that are designed to perform certain functions in a computer system. Software programming, programming paradigms, application software, etc. fall under its domain. This chapter closely examines about these computer hardware to provide an extensive understanding of the subject.

Chapter – Computer Networking

A group of computers connected with each other for sharing information and other resources is defined as a computer network. Network topology, network nodes, network security and network performance are studied under computer networking. This chapter delves into the subject of computer networking to provide an in-depth understanding of it.

Henry Martin

Introduction

1

- Computer
- Characteristics of a Computer
- Components of a Computer System
- Types of Computers

A computer is a machine that is designed to execute applications and processes by combining hardware and software components. Supercomputer, mainframe computer, minicomputer, microcomputer, etc. are some of the types of computers. This chapter has been carefully written to provide an easy understanding of the characteristics and components of a computer system.

Computer

Computer is a device for processing, storing, and displaying information. Computer once meant a person who did computations, but now the term almost universally refers to automated electronic machinery.

The first computers were used primarily for numerical calculations. However, as any information can be numerically encoded, people soon realized that computers are capable of general-purpose information processing. Their capacity to handle large amounts of data has extended the range and accuracy of weather forecasting. Their speed has allowed them to make decisions about routing telephone connections through a network and to control mechanical systems such as automobiles, nuclear reactors, and robotic surgical tools. They are also cheap enough to be embedded in everyday appliances and to make clothes dryers and rice cookers "smart." Computers have allowed us to pose and answer questions that could not be pursued before. These questions might be about DNA sequences in genes, patterns of activity in a consumer market, or all the uses of a word in texts that have been stored in a database. Increasingly, computers can also learn and adapt as they operate.

Computers also have limitations, some of which are theoretical. For example, there are undecidable propositions whose truth cannot be determined within a given set of rules, such as the logical structure of a computer. Because no universal algorithmic method can exist to identify such propositions, a computer asked to obtain the truth of such a proposition will (unless forcibly interrupted) continue indefinitely—a condition known as the "halting problem." Other limitations reflect current technology. Human minds are skilled at recognizing spatial patterns—easily distinguishing among human faces, for instance—but this is a difficult task for computers, which must process information sequentially, rather than grasping details overall at a glance. Another problematic area for computers involves natural language interactions. Because so much common knowledge and contextual information is assumed in ordinary human communication, researchers have yet to solve the problem of providing relevant information to general-purpose natural language programs.

Analog Computers

Analog computers use continuous physical magnitudes to represent quantitative information. At first they represented quantities with mechanical components, but after World War II voltages were used; by the 1960s digital computers had largely replaced them. Nonetheless, analog computers, and some hybrid digital-analog systems, continued in use through the 1960s in tasks such as aircraft and spaceflight simulation.

One advantage of analog computation is that it may be relatively simple to design and build an analog computer to solve a single problem. Another advantage is that analog computers can frequently represent and solve a problem in "real time"; that is, the computation proceeds at the same rate as the system being modeled by it. Their main disadvantages are that analog representations are limited in precision—typically a few decimal places but fewer in complex mechanisms—and general-purpose devices are expensive and not easily programmed.

Digital Computers

In contrast to analog computers, digital computers represent information in discrete form, generally as sequences of 0s and 1s (binary digits, or bits). The modern era of digital computers began in the late 1930s and early 1940s in the United States, Britain, and Germany. The first devices used switches operated by electromagnets (relays). Their programs were stored on punched paper tape or cards, and they had limited internal data storage.

Characteristics of a Computer

Basic characteristics about computer are:

- Speed: As you know computer can work very fast. It takes only few seconds for calculations that we take hours to complete. You will be surprised to know that computer can perform millions (1,000,000) of instructions and even more per second.

  Therefore, we determine the speed of computer in terms of microsecond (10-6 part of a second) or nanosecond (10 to the power -9 part of a second). From this you can imagine how fast your computer performs work.

- Accuracy: The degree of accuracy of computer is very high and every calculation is performed with the same accuracy. The accuracy level is 7.

  Determined on the basis of design of computer. The errors in computer are due to human and inaccurate data.

- Diligence: A computer is free from tiredness, lack of concentration, fatigue, etc. It can work for hours without creating any error. If millions of calculations are to be performed, a computer will perform every calculation with the same accuracy. Due to this capability it overpowers human being in routine type of work.

- Versatility: It means the capacity to perform completely different type of work. You may use your computer to prepare payroll slips. Next moment you may use it for inventory management or to prepare electric bills.

- Power of Remembering: Computer has the power of storing any amount of information or data. Any information can be stored and recalled as long as you require it, for any numbers of years. It depends entirely upon you how much data you want to store in a computer and when to lose or retrieve these data.

- No IQ: Computer is a dumb machine and it cannot do any work without instruction from the user. It performs the instructions at tremendous speed and with accuracy. It is you to decide what you want to do and in what sequence. So a computer cannot take its own decision as you can.

- No Feeling: It does not have feelings or emotion, taste, knowledge and experience. Thus it does not get tired even after long hours of work. It does not distinguish between users.

- Storage: The Computer has an in-built memory where it can store a large amount of data. You can also store data in secondary storage devices such as floppies, which can be kept outside your computer and can be carried to other computers.

Components of a Computer System

Conventional and assistive computer technologies are similar in that both employ the core concepts of input, information processing, and output. Understanding these concepts is essential to understanding how AT helps individuals with disabilities access a computer. Each system first must have a means to input information. This information is then processed. From the processed information, the computer produces some type of output. Input or output devices can be modified to provide access to individuals with disabilities who cannot use standard input or output devices. To provide a better understanding of input, output, and processing, these concepts are defined as follows.

- Input: The information entered into a computer system, examples include: typed text, mouse clicks, etc.

- Processing: The process of transforming input information into and output.

- Output: The visual, auditory, or tactile perceptions provided by the computer after processing the provided information. Examples include: text, images, sound, or video displayed on a monitor or through speaker as well as text or Braille from printers or embossers.

- Input Device: Any device that enters information into a computer from a external source. Examples include: keyboards, touch screens, mouse, trackballs, microphones, scanners, etc.

- Processing Device: The electronics that process or transform information provided as an input to a computer to an output. Examples include: the Central Processing Unit (CPU), operating systems (e.g. Windows, Apple software), microprocessors (e.g. Intel, Pentium), memory cards (RAM), graphic and other production application or programs (Adobe, Microsoft Word, etc).

- Output Device: A device used by a computer to communicate information in a usable form. Examples include: monitors, speakers, and printers, etc.

The following is an example showing how these three concepts work together: To access a website, the user opens an internet browser and, using the keyboard, enters a web address into the browser (input). The computer then uses that information to find the correct website (information processing)and the content of the desired site is displayed in the web browser (output).

AT for computer access can be applied by adapting either the input or output component of a computer system. Doing this provides an individual with a disability with a tool that utilizes his or her abilities to access a computer. An example of adapting an input device is providing an individual who does not have use of his or her hands with speech recognition software to enter text into a computer as opposed to a keyboard. As for adapting an output device, an individual with a visual impairment can use either a screen magnifier or screen reader to access output on a computer screen. Information processing, in terms of a computer, does not involve a human element and thus does not require assistive technology adaptations.

Types of Computers

Supercomputer

A supercomputer is the fastest computer in the world that can process a significant amount of data very quickly. The computing Performance of a "supercomputer" is measured very high as compared to a general purpose computer. The computing Performance of a supercomputer is measured in FLOPS (that is floating-point operations per second) instead of MIPS. The supercomputer consists of tens of thousands of processors which can perform billions and trillions of calculations per second, or you can say that supercomputers can deliver up to nearly a hundred quadrillions of FLOPS.

They have evolved from grid to cluster system of massively parallel computing. Cluster system computing means that machine uses multiple processors in one system instead of arrays of separate computers in a network.

These computers are most massive concerning size. A most powerful supercomputer can occupy few feet to hundreds of feet. The supercomputer price is very high, and they can vary from 2 lakh dollar to over 100 million dollars.

Supercomputers were introduced in the 1960s and developed by Seymour Cray with the Atlas at the University of Manchester. The Cray designed CDC 1604 which was the first supercomputer in the world, and it replaces vacuum tube with transistors.

The fastest supercomputer in the world was the Sunway TaihuLight, in the city of Wixu in China which is developed by China's National Research center of Parallel Computer Engineering & Technology (NRCPC), maintains its number 1 ranking for the first time, with a High-Performance Linpack (HPL) mark of 93.01 petaflops.

Characteristics of Supercomputer

- They can support more than a hundred users at a time.
- These machines are capable of handling the massive amount of calculations that are beyond the human capabilities, i.e., the human is unable to solve such extensive calculations.
- Many individuals can access supercomputers at the same time.
- These are the most expensive computers that can ever be made.

Features of Supercomputer

- They have more than 1 CPU (Central Processing Unit) which contains instructions so that it can interpret instructions and execute arithmetic and logical operations.
- The supercomputer can support extremely high computation speed of CPUs.
- They can operate on pairs of lists of numbers instead of pairs of numbers.
- They were used initially in applications related to national security, nuclear weapon design, and cryptography. But nowadays they are also employed by the aerospace, automotive and petroleum industries.

Uses of Supercomputer

- Supercomputers are not used for everyday tasks because of their superiority.

- Supercomputer handles those applications, which required the real-time processing. The uses are as follows:

- They're used for scientific simulations and research such as weather forecasting, meteorology, nuclear energy research, physics, and chemistry, as well as for extremely complex animated graphics. They are also used to interpret new diseases and predict illness behavior and treatment.

- The military uses supercomputers for testing new aircrafts, tanks, and weapons. They also use them to understand the effect on soldiers and wars. These machines are also used for encrypting the data.

- Scientists use them to test the impact of nuclear weapon detonation.

- Hollywood uses supercomputers for the creation of animations.

- In entertainment, supercomputers are used for online gaming.

Supercomputers help in stabilizing the game performance when a lot of users are playing the game.

Mainframe Computer

The definition and meaning of mainframe has shifted from its original reference to the main housing, or frame, that contained the central processing unit (CPU) of the computer. In those days, all computers were big-like the size of a garage and the frame for the CPU might have been as big as a walk-in closet. Now mainframe refers to the kind of large computer that runs an entire corporation.

While "large" can still mean as big as a room, most of today's "mainframes" are much smaller, although they're still quite a bit bigger than a personal computer or even a minicomputer. A mainframe has an enormous storage space on disk and tape (like thousands of kilobytes, measured in gigabytes), and an enormous amount of main memory. Theoretically, it works a lot faster than the fastest personal computer. A mainframe also costs big bucks, from half a million or so on up.

In today's world where all the business, transactions, communications are real time. So to perform all this task, a powerful computer require on the server side, which processes the instructions and provides the output in seconds. According to the usage of computers in today's world, we can categories computer in Supercomputer, Mainframe Computer, and Mini Computer and microcomputer categories. A mainframe computer is the fastest computer after supercomputer to execute complex and lengthy calculations. A mainframe computer is more powerful than Mini and Microcomputer, but less powerful than Supercomputer. A mainframe computer is used in the large organization.

A mainframe computer is a combination of memory (RAM) and many processors. It acts as a central processing unit for many workstations and terminals connected with it. A mainframe computer is used to process the large and huge amount of data in petabytes. It can control thousands of user 's. Name 'Mainframe' means that a frame for holding a number of processors and main memory. Mainframe computer plays a significant role in e-business where hundreds to thousands of people connect to a server to precede their request in a real time. Similarly, In banking, government, education system mainframe computer play a valuable role.

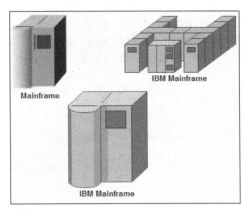

Mainframes are tended by special technicians who feed them the programs they run and who scramble around trying to fix them whenever they stop working, which is often. All mainframes are multi-tasking, multi-user machines, meaning they are designed so many different people can work on many different problems, all at the same time.

Mainframe computer initially created in early 1950's.Initially, the size was too big because of the vacuum tube. But after the invention of transistors main frame computer size get reduced.

Mainframes serve most often as information stores and processors. An army of smaller computers is connected to the mainframe. These smaller computers are not in the same room; they may be connected through phone lines across the world. Ordinary people in the company never touch the mainframe itself. Instead, they interact with the computer using a terminal, which is more or less a keyboard and a monitor connected to the mainframe with wires, or by modem over the phone lines. People use the smaller computers and get information from and send information to the mainframe.

IBM manufactured many mainframe computers for commercial, scientific and engineering use with different serial numbers. IBM manufactured 700 and 7000 series models with use of vacuum tube and transistors. In 1964, System/360 was manufactured for both commercial and scientific users. S/360 was the first computer to offer microcode. Microcode functionality makes the system modifiable without changing the computer. Now the customer can create their own application according to requirement. In 2000, Z-Series was introduced by IBM. Z-series computers are very powerful to process the instruction.

The difference between a minicomputer and a mainframe is arbitrary, and different people may use either term for the same machine. Even if you don't work for a large company, you might have contact with a mainframe: when you connect to an online information service or a commercial e-mail service from your personal computer, you are often connecting to a mainframe.

Components of Mainframe Computer

Mainframe computer provide reliable and secure process execution. Mainframe computer has some components to perform task.

CPU: CPU contains the processors, memory, control circuits, and interfaces for channels. A channel is an independent path between I/O devices and memory. This path is used for data movements and for controlling the computer components.

Controllers: Channels are used to connect devices with control units. Channel is also known as a bus. In Mainframe computer, the different control unit (internal circuit and logic) is used for different -different devices like tape, disk. Control unit is further connected with storage unit.

Cluster controller: Cluster controller is a device to connect channel terminal to host system. Cluster controls have two types:

Channel-attached cluster controllers and link-attached cluster controllers.

Cluster controllers provide advanced features like IBM Token Ring attachment interfaces, management, and monitoring.

I/O channels: During I/O connectivity, we used some term like IOCDS, ESCON, FICON, CHIPD's having unique definitions and purpose.

ICODS: ICODS stands for I/O control data set. It is a control file in I/O layer to translate physical I/O address into device address.

ESCON (Enterprise Systems Connection): This is a first IBM and vendor product for connecting more than one mainframe computer and with locally attached workstations. It is Fiber Optic channel to transfer the data with the maximum speed of 17 MByte/ s. We can extend the local to mainframe network up to 60 km. It has some limitations regarding speed and network area. To make it better IBM next version was FICON. FICON (fiber connector) is used to increase the transfer speed of ESCON channel. One Ficon connector is equal to eight ESCON connector.

Multiprocessors: Multiprocessors indicate that number of processors. Multiple processors in mainframe computer used some Prefix Storage Area to process the data (For error handling and interrupt handling).Using special instruction set processor can communicate with another processor using special instruction set.

The Advantage of Mainframe Computer

Mainframe computer has many advantages as well as disadvantages. From the last 50 years, there was a great revolution in mainframe computer in all field like size, processing speed, data transfer speed, security, and flexibility.

- Mainframe computer provides a great security against the attack of viruses, warm, spyware, malware. Encryption technique like file encryption, dataset and file encryption, network encryption, clustering encryption empower security.

- Mainframe computers are compatible with all types of software and hardware. Because different user connects with servers along with different hardware and software on their system. They can easily communicate with server-side without any interrupt.

- Mainframe computer deals with thousands of users to execute their instructions simultaneously and can store.

- Without disturbing process on the computer, we can add storage, processors or memory and extend its capability.

With some advantages, it has some disadvantages:

- A mainframe computer is expensive. It is not easy to purchase a mainframe as a comparison to the microcomputer. The microcomputer is handled by the single user, but mainframe handled many users. Installation is not easy.

Minicomputer

A minicomputer is also known as mini. It is a class of small computers that was introduced into the world in the mid-1960s. A minicomputer is a computer which has all the features of a large size computer, but its size is smaller than those. A minicomputer lies between the mainframe and the microcomputer because its size is smaller than the former one and larger than the latter one. A minicomputer is also called as a mid-range computer. Minicomputers are mainly multi-users systems where more than one user can work simultaneously. Mini computer examples: IBM's AS/400e, Honeywell200, TI-990.

Minicomputer can support multi-users at a time or you can say that minicomputer is a multi-processing system. Also, the power of processing of minicomputers is not larger than the power of mainframe and supercomputers. These minicomputers can do time-sharing, batch processing, and online processing.

Size of Minicomputer

The size of minicomputers can range from 12 inches in width to less than 7. This small size is especially attractive to students because they can use it anywhere they want.

History of Minicomputer

The term minicomputer was come to know in the 1960s and through that time only the small computers are made by making the use of transistors and core memory technologies. The first minicomputer which was developed was known as Digital Equipment Corporation, which was made by using transistors and it costs from the US $16000.

Types of Minicomputer

The types of minicomputer are- tablet PC, Desktop minicomputers, cell phones, notebooks, high-end mP3 players, etc.

Uses of Minicomputer

Each person using a minicomputer has their own *terminal* attached by wires or via a modem to the computer proper. (A terminal isn't a computer-it's basically just a keyboard and a monitor) The minicomputer spends a little bit of time on one person's task, then moves on to the next, and so on, juggling the work based on which jobs it thinks are most important. If you're the only one using a minicomputer, this can be one fast machine.

But once many users (people) are "on" the system, the thing begins to slow down-you may type something and then wait for a minute or more before you see a response on the screen. Minicomputers used to be the only option for companies. Now, many firms are turning to networks of personal computers to accomplish the same thing faster and cheaper.

They were used for three primary purposes:

Process Control

Minicomputers are primarily used by the companies for the manufacturing control of the process. Process Control has two primary functions- data acquisition and feedback.

Example: Factories make use of minicomputers to control the manufacturing process. If any problem appears in any part of the process, then it recognizes the change and made required adjustments.

Data Management

Minicomputers that we use for the data management can do any task regarding data like it can take, restore or generate data.

Communication

Minicomputers act as an interface between the human operator and a larger processor. The user can run operations such as error checking with the help of minicomputer and then can use the device for making adjustments also.

The other uses are as follows:

- They are also used for scientific computations.
- Used for business-transaction processing.
- Used for database management.
- Used for file handling
- Used for engineering computations.

Characteristics of a Minicomputer

- Its size is smaller than a mainframe or supercomputer.
- It is less expensive than mainframe or supercomputer.
- It is less powerful than mainframe or supercomputer and more powerful than microcomputers and workstations.
- It can do several tasks at once.
- It can be used by many people at one time.
- It is used by small enterprises.

Applications of Minicomputer

- Minicomputer was used in business accounting.

- A network of minicomputers can be created which allows a large library with its different-2 branches to build its own internal network and this network is more powerful than those handled by large-scale computer installations.

- It is used by the various sub-departments of the companies so that they can unload the task of mainframe computers.

- The areas where minicomputers have been traditionally applied in information handling are:

    ◦ Circulation.

    ◦ Cataloguing.

    ◦ Series control.

    ◦ Management.

    ◦ Acquisitions.

    ◦ Communications.

    ◦ Information retrieval.

Advantages of Minicomputer

- They are easy to use.

- They can fit anywhere.

- They are small and very portable.

- They are easy to carry.

- As compared to their size, they are fast.

- They hold a charge for a long time.

- They did not require a carefully controlled operational environment.

- They are more reliable.

Disadvantages of Minicomputer

- Some minicomputers don't have USB ports.

- Minicomputers do not have any CD/DVD drive.

- The user may not be familiar with the operating system.

- The keyboard can be small for fast typists.

- In this, generally, there is not much storage on board.

- It can be too small to do certain projects.

Microcomputer

A microcomputer is a complete computer on a small scale, designed for use by one person at a time. An antiquated term, a microcomputer is now primarily called a personal computer (PC), or a device based on a single-chip microprocessor. Common microcomputers include laptops and desktops. Beyond standard PCs, microcomputers also include some calculators, mobile phones, notebooks, workstations and embedded systems.

Smaller than a mainframe or minicomputer, a microcomputer uses a single integrated semiconductor chip for its central processing unit (CPU). They also contain memory in the form of read-only memory (ROM) and random access memory (RAM), input/output (I/O) ports, and a bus or system of interconnecting wires, all housed in a single unit usually referred to as a motherboard.

Common I/O devices include keyboards, monitors, printers and external storage.

The term microcomputer dates back to the 1970s. The advent of the Intel 4004 microprocessor in 1971, and later the Intel 8008 and Intel 8080 microprocessor in 1972 and 1974 respectively, paved the path to the creation of the microcomputer.

The first microcomputer was the Micral, released in 1973 by Réalisation d'Études Électroniques (R2E). Based on the Intel 8008, it was the first non-kit computer based on a microprocessor. In 1974, the Intel 8008-based MCM/70 microcomputer was released by Micro Computer Machines Inc. (later known as MCM Computers).

Though released after the Micral and MCM/70, the Altair 8800 is often considered the first successful commercial microcomputer. Released in 1974, it was designed by Micro Instrumentation Telemetry Systems (MITS) and was based on the Intel 8080 microprocessor. It retailed for around $400 in kit form, $600 assembled ($2,045 and $3,067 in 2018 dollars, respectively).

An Altair 8800 lies on display at the
Microsoft Visitor Center April 6, 2005 in Redmond, Wash.

As microprocessor chip design matured, so did the processing capacity of microcomputers. By the 1980s, microcomputers were being used for more than games and computer-based recreation, finding widespread use in personal computing, workstations and academia. By the 1990s, micro-computers were being produced as pocket-sized personal digital assistants (PDAs), and later came in the form of cellphones and portable music players.

Microcomputer Applications

Personal microcomputers are often used for education and entertainment. Beyond laptops and desktops, microcomputers can include video game consoles, computerized electronics and smartphones.

In the workplace, microcomputers have been used for applications including data and word processing, electronic spreadsheets, professional presentation and graphics programs, communications and database management systems. They have been used in business for tasks such as bookkeeping, inventory and communication; in medical settings to record and recall patient data, manage healthcare plans, complete schedule and for data processing; in financial institutions to record transactions, track billing, prepare financial statements and payrolls, and auditing; and in military applications for training devices, among other uses.

Microcomputers and IoT

The Raspberry Pi, a small, single-board computer, was once self-described as a microcontroller. Today used for internet of things (IoT) prototyping, education and applications, the Raspberry Pi and other single-board computers, such as those from Arduino, Intel and Particle, are more often described as microcontrollers than microcomputers. Microcomputers can be used for similar tasks in IoT applications as microcontrollers, however. Certain IoT devices, such as smart TVs, refrigerators and other connected appliances, are sometimes referred to as microcomputers.

The ascending hierarchy of general computer sizes is as follows:

- Embedded systems, which are fixed inside something and don't support direct human interaction but nonetheless meet all other criteria of microcomputers;

- Microcomputers;

- Workstations, formerly described as a more powerful personal computer for special applications;

- Minicomputers, now called mid-range servers;

- Mainframes, which are now usually referred to by manufacturers as large servers;

- Supercomputers, large servers, sometimes including systems of computers using parallel processing; and

- Parallel processing system, a system of interconnected computers that work on the same application together, sharing tasks that can be performed concurrently.

Microcomputers vs. Microcontrollers

A microcontroller is an integrated circuit (IC) designed to govern a specific operation in an embedded system. These single chips have onboard RAM, ROM and peripherals. Microcontrollers have been referred to as single microcomputers.

Microcomputers vs. Microprocessors

A microprocessor is a computer processor on a microchip that contains all or most CPU functions. Microprocessors do not have RAM, ROM or other peripherals. As such, microprocessors cannot perform standalone tasks. Rather, systems such as microcomputers, which contain microprocessors, can be programmed to perform functions on data by writing specific instructions for their microprocessors into their memory. A microcomputer can technically be described as the combination of a microprocessor and its peripheral I/O devices, circuitry and memory – just not on a single chip.

Microcomputers vs. Minicomputers

While microcomputers generally refer to laptops or desktops, minicomputers were a variety of computer primarily used in the 1960s to 1980s. Minicomputers were larger than microcomputers -- some stood more than 6 feet tall and weighted up to 700 pounds -- and boasted higher processing speeds at a significantly smaller size and price than mainframes and supercomputers available at the time. While microcomputers were often used at home and in the office, minicomputers were primarily found in academia, research labs and small companies, and they were used for word processing, accounting and teaching aids.

Digital Equipment Corporation's Programmed Data Processor-1, or PDP-1, was announced in 1960 and sold for $120,000 ($1,021,776 in 2018 dollars). Its descendent, the PDP-8, was introduced in 1965 and sold for nearly $18,500 ($148,022 in 2018 dollars). Considered one of the most successful minicomputers and first example of a commercial minicomputer, the 12-bit PDP-8 has been compared to the size of a small household refrigerator. Minicomputers did not contain microprocessors. In the 1980s, the minicomputer's prevalence declined as microprocessors became more powerful and available at lower cost. An antiquated term, minicomputers are often referred to as midrange computers.

Microcomputers vs. Mainframes

A mainframe computer is a high-performance computer used for large-scale computing purposes that require greater availability and security than small-scale machines can provide. Mainframes can process requests from a number of users simultaneously, whereas a microcomputer is designed to be used by one person at a time. As such, a mainframe computer can be described as a system that interconnects a number of microcomputers.

References

- Computer, technology: britannica.com, Retrieved 9 May, 2019
- What-are-characteristic-of-a-computer, introduction-to-computer, fundamental: ecomputernotes.com, Retrieved 8 August, 2019
- Supercomputer, introduction-to-computer, fundamental: ecomputernotes.com, Retrieved 28 April, 2019
- Mainframe, introduction-to-computer, fundamental: ecomputernotes.com, Retrieved 19 May, 2019
- Minicomputer, introduction-to-computer, fundamental: ecomputernotes.com, Retrieved 23 June, 2019
- Microcomputer, definition: techtarget.com, Retrieved 3 August, 2019

Computer Architecture 2

- **Parallel Computer Architecture**
- **System Design**
- **Microarchitecture**

Computer architecture refers to the set of methods that are used in the functioning and organization of a computer system. It includes parallel computer architecture, microarchitecture, system designs such as CPU, GPU, ALU, etc. This is an introductory chapter which will briefly introduce about these types of computer architecture.

The main components in a typical computer system are the processor, memory, input/output devices, and the communication channels that connect them.

The processor is the workhorse of the system; it is the component that executes a program by performing arithmetic and logical operations on data. It is the only component that creates new information by combining or modifying current information. In a typical system there will be only one processor, known at the central processing unit, or CPU. Modern high performance systems, for example vector processors and parallel processors, often have more than one processor. Systems with only one processor are serial processors, or, especially among computational scientists, scalar processors.

Memory is a passive component that simply stores information until it is requested by another part of the system. During normal operations it feeds instructions and data to the processor, and at other times it is the source or destination of data transferred by I/O devices. Information in a memory is accessed by its address. In programming language terms, one can view memory as a one-dimensional array M. A processor's request to the memory might be "send the instruction at location M" or a disk controller's request might be "store the following block of data in locations M through M."

Input/output (I/O) devices transfer information without altering it between the external world and one or more internal components. I/O devices can be secondary memories, for example disks and tapes, or devices used to communicate directly with users, such as video displays, keyboards, and mouses.

The communication channels that tie the system together can either be simple links that connect two devices or more complex switches that interconnect several components and allow any two of them to communicate at a given point in time. When a switch is configured to allow two devices to exchange information, all other devices that rely on the switch are *blocked*, i.e. they must wait until the switch can be reconfigured.

A common convention used in drawing simple "stick figures" of computer systems is the PMS notation. In a PMS diagram each major component is represented by a single letter, e.g. P for processor, M for memory, or S for switch. A subscript on a letter distinguished different types of components, e.g. M_p for primary memory and M_c for cache memory. Lines connecting two components represent links, and lines connecting more than two components represent a switch. Although they are primitive and might appear at first glance to be too simple, PMS diagrams convey quite a bit of information and have several advantages, not the least of which is they are independent of any particular manufacturer's notations.

As an example of a PMS diagram and a relatively simple computer architecture. The first thing one notices is a single communication channel, known as the *bus*, that connects all the other major components. Since the bus is a switch, only two of these components can communicate at any time. When the switch is configured for an I/O transfer, for example from main memory (M_p) to the disk (via K *disk*), the processor is unable to fetch data or instructions and remains idle. This organization is typical of personal computers and low end workstations; mainframes, supercomputers, and other high performance systems have much richer (and thus more expensive) structures for connecting I/O devices to internal main memory that allow the processor to keep working at full speed during I/O operations.

Parallel Computer Architecture

Parallel Computer Architecture is the method of organizing all the resources to maximize the performance and the programmability within the limits given by technology and the cost at any instance of time. It adds a new dimension in the development of computer system by using more and more number of processors.

In the last 50 years, there has been huge developments in the performance and capability of a computer system. This has been possible with the help of Very Large Scale Integration (VLSI) technology. VLSI technology allows a large number of components to be accommodated on a single chip and clock rates to increase. Therefore, more operations can be performed at a time, in parallel.

Parallel processing is also associated with data locality and data communication. Parallel Computer Architecture is the method of organizing all the resources to maximize the performance and the programmability within the limits given by technology and the cost at any instance of time.

Parallel computer architecture adds a new dimension in the development of computer system by using more and more number of processors. In principle, performance achieved by utilizing large number of processors is higher than the performance of a single processor at a given point of time.

Application Trends

With the advancement of hardware capacity, the demand for a well-performing application also increased, which in turn placed a demand on the development of the computer architecture.

Before the microprocessor era, high-performing computer system was obtained by exotic circuit technology and machine organization, which made them expensive. Now, highly performing computer system is obtained by using multiple processors, and most important and demanding applications are written as parallel programs. Thus, for higher performance both parallel architectures and parallel applications are needed to be developed.

Scientific and Engineering Computing

Parallel architecture has become indispensable in scientific computing (like physics, chemistry, biology, astronomy, etc.) and engineering applications (like reservoir modeling, airflow analysis, combustion efficiency, etc.). In almost all applications, there is a huge demand for visualization of computational output resulting in the demand for development of parallel computing to increase the computational speed.

Commercial Computing

In commercial computing (like video, graphics, databases, OLTP, etc.) also high speed computers are needed to process huge amount of data within a specified time. Desktop uses multithreaded programs that are almost like the parallel programs. This in turn demands to develop parallel architecture.

Technology Trends

With the development of technology and architecture, there is a strong demand for the development of high-performing applications. Experiments show that parallel computers can work much faster than utmost developed single processor. Moreover, parallel computers can be developed within the limit of technology and the cost.

The primary technology used here is VLSI technology. Therefore, nowadays more and more transistors, gates and circuits can be fitted in the same area. With the reduction of the basic VLSI feature size, clock rate also improves in proportion to it, while the number of transistors grows as the square. The use of many transistors at once (parallelism) can be expected to perform much better than by increasing the clock rate.

Technology trends suggest that the basic single chip building block will give increasingly large capacity. Therefore, the possibility of placing multiple processors on a single chip increases.

Architectural Trends

Development in technology decides what is feasible; architecture converts the potential of the technology into performance and capability. Parallelism and locality are two methods where larger volumes of resources and more transistors enhance the performance. However, these two methods compete for the same resources. When multiple operations are executed in parallel, the number of cycles needed to execute the program is reduced.

However, resources are needed to support each of the concurrent activities. Resources are also needed to allocate local storage. The best performance is achieved by an intermediate action plan that uses resources to utilize a degree of parallelism and a degree of locality.

Generally, the history of computer architecture has been divided into four generations having following basic technologies:

- Vacuum tubes.
- Transistors.
- Integrated circuits.
- VLSI.

Till 1985, the duration was dominated by the growth in bit-level parallelism. 4-bit microprocessors followed by 8-bit, 16-bit, and so on. To reduce the number of cycles needed to perform a full 32-bit operation, the width of the data path was doubled. Later on, 64-bit operations were introduced.

The growth in instruction-level-parallelism dominated the mid-80s to mid-90s. The RISC approach showed that it was simple to pipeline the steps of instruction processing so that on an average an instruction is executed in almost every cycle. Growth in compiler technology has made instruction pipelines more productive.

In mid-80s, microprocessor-based computers consisted of:

- An integer processing unit.
- A floating-point unit.
- A cache controller.
- SRAMs for the cache data.
- Tag storage.

As chip capacity increased, all these components were merged into a single chip. Thus, a single chip consisted of separate hardware for integer arithmetic, floating point operations, memory operations and branch operations. Other than pipelining individual instructions, it fetches multiple instructions at a time and sends them in parallel to different functional units whenever possible. This type of instruction level parallelism is called superscalar execution.

Convergence of Parallel Architectures

Parallel machines have been developed with several distinct architecture:

Communication Architecture

Parallel architecture enhances the conventional concepts of computer architecture with communication architecture. Computer architecture defines critical abstractions (like user-system boundary and hardware-software boundary) and organizational structure, whereas communication architecture defines the basic communication and synchronization operations. It also addresses the organizational structure.

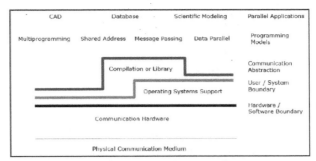

Physical Communication Medium.

Programming model is the top layer. Applications are written in programming model. Parallel programming models include:

- Shared address space.

- Message passing.

- Data parallel programming.

Shared address programming is just like using a bulletin board, where one can communicate with one or many individuals by posting information at a particular location, which is shared by all other individuals. Individual activity is coordinated by noting who is doing what task.

Message passing is like a telephone call or letters where a specific receiver receives information from a specific sender.

Data parallel programming is an organized form of cooperation. Here, several individuals perform an action on separate elements of a data set concurrently and share information globally.

Shared Memory

Shared memory multiprocessors are one of the most important classes of parallel machines. It gives better throughput on multiprogramming workloads and supports parallel programs.

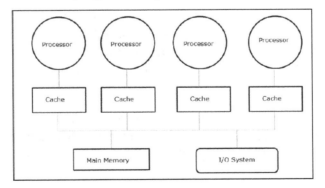

In this case, all the computer systems allow a processor and a set of I/O controller to access a collection of memory modules by some hardware interconnection. The memory capacity is increased by adding memory modules and I/O capacity is increased by adding devices to I/O controller or by adding additional I/O controller. Processing capacity can be increased by waiting for a faster processor to be available or by adding more processors.

All the resources are organized around a central memory bus. Through the bus access mechanism, any processor can access any physical address in the system. As all the processors are equidistant from all the memory locations, the access time or latency of all the processors is same on a memory location. This is called symmetric multiprocessor.

Message-passing Architecture

Message-passing architecture is also an important class of parallel machines. It provides communication among processors as explicit I/O operations. In this case, the communication is combined at the I/O level, instead of the memory system.

In message-passing architecture, user communication executed by using operating system or library calls that perform many lower level actions, which includes the actual communication operation. As a result, there is a distance between the programming model and the communication operations at the physical hardware level.

Send and receive is the most common user level communication operations in message-passing system. Send specifies a local data buffer (which is to be transmitted) and a receiving remote processor. Receive specifies a sending process and a local data buffer in which the transmitted data will be placed. In send operation, an identifier or a tag is attached to the message and the receiving operation specifies the matching rule like a specific tag from a specific processor or any tag from any processor.

The combination of a send and a matching receive completes a memory-to-memory copy. Each end specifies its local data address and a pair wise synchronization event.

Convergence

Development of the hardware and software has faded the clear boundary between the shared memory and message passing camps. Message passing and a shared address space represents two distinct programming models; each gives a transparent paradigm for sharing, synchronization and communication. However, the basic machine structures have converged towards a common organization.

Data Parallel Processing

Another important class of parallel machine is variously called – processor arrays, data parallel architecture and single-instruction-multiple-data machines. The main feature of the programming model is that operations can be executed in parallel on each element of a large regular data structure (like array or matrix).

Data parallel programming languages are usually enforced by viewing the local address space of a group of processes, one per processor, forming an explicit global space. As all the processors communicate together and there is a global view of all the operations, so either a shared address space or message passing can be used.

Fundamental Design Issues

Development of programming model only cannot increase the efficiency of the computer nor can the development of hardware alone do it. However, development in computer architecture can make the difference in the performance of the computer. We can understand the design problem by focusing on how programs use a machine and which basic technologies are provided.

Communication Abstraction

Communication abstraction is the main interface between the programming model and the system implementation. It is like the instruction set that provides a platform so that the same program can run correctly on many implementations. Operations at this level must be simple.

Communication abstraction is like a contract between the hardware and software, which allows each other the flexibility to improve without affecting the work.

Programming Model Requirements

A parallel program has one or more threads operating on data. A parallel programming model defines what data the threads can name, which operations can be performed on the named data, and which order is followed by the operations.

To confirm that the dependencies between the programs are enforced, a parallel program must coordinate the activity of its threads.

Parallel Computer Architecture - Models

Parallel processing has been developed as an effective technology in modern computers to meet the demand for higher performance, lower cost and accurate results in real-life applications. Concurrent events are common in today's computers due to the practice of multiprogramming, multiprocessing, or multicomputing.

Modern computers have powerful and extensive software packages. To analyze the development of the performance of computers, first we have to understand the basic development of hardware and software.

- Computer Development Milestones: There is two major stages of development of computer - mechanical or electromechanical parts. Modern computers evolved after the introduction of electronic components. High mobility electrons in electronic computers replaced the operational parts in mechanical computers. For information transmission, electric signal which travels almost at the speed of a light replaced mechanical gears or levers.

- Elements of Modern computers: A modern computer system consists of computer hardware, instruction sets, application programs, system software and user interface.

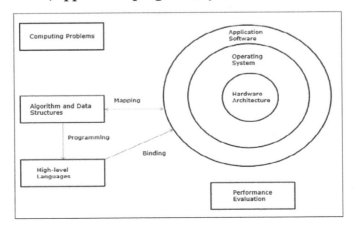

The computing problems are categorized as numerical computing, logical reasoning, and transaction processing. Some complex problems may need the combination of all the three processing modes.

- Evolution of computer architecture: In last four decades, computer architecture has gone through revolutionary changes. We started with Von Neumann architecture and now we have multicomputers and multiprocessors.

- Performance of a computer system: Performance of a computer system depends both on machine capability and program behavior. Machine capability can be improved with better hardware technology, advanced architectural features and efficient resource management. Program behavior is unpredictable as it is dependent on application and run-time conditions.

Multiprocessors and Multicomputers

Here, we will discuss two types of parallel computers:

- Multiprocessors
- Multicomputers

Shared-memory Multicomputers

Three most common shared memory multiprocessors models are:

Uniform Memory Access (UMA)

In this model, all the processors share the physical memory uniformly. All the processors have equal access time to all the memory words. Each processor may have a private cache memory. Same rule is followed for peripheral devices.

When all the processors have equal access to all the peripheral devices, the system is called a symmetric multiprocessor. When only one or a few processors can access the peripheral devices, the system is called an asymmetric multiprocessor.

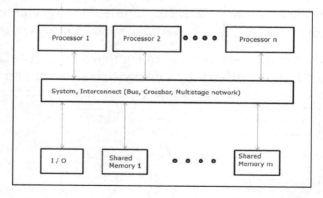

Non-uniform Memory Access (NUMA)

In NUMA multiprocessor model, the access time varies with the location of the memory word. Here, the shared memory is physically distributed among all the processors, called local memories. The collection of all local memories forms a global address space which can be accessed by all the processors.

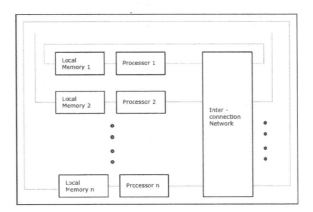

Cache Only Memory Architecture (COMA)

The COMA model is a special case of the NUMA model. Here, all the distributed main memories are converted to cache memories.

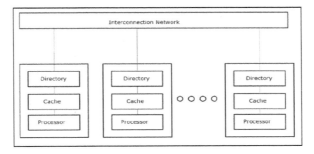

Distributed-memory Multicomputers: A distributed memory multicomputer system consists of multiple computers, known as nodes, inter-connected by message passing network. Each node acts as an autonomous computer having a processor, a local memory and sometimes I/O devices. In this case, all local memories are private and are accessible only to the local processors. This is why, the traditional machines are called no-remote-memory-access (NORMA) machines.

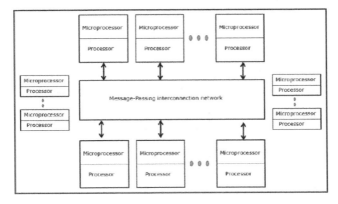

Multivector and SIMD Computers

Here, we will discuss supercomputers and parallel processors for vector processing and data parallelism.

Vector Supercomputers

In a vector computer, a vector processor is attached to the scalar processor as an optional feature. The host computer first loads program and data to the main memory. Then the scalar control unit decodes all the instructions. If the decoded instructions are scalar operations or program operations, the scalar processor executes those operations using scalar functional pipelines.

On the other hand, if the decoded instructions are vector operations then the instructions will be sent to vector control unit.

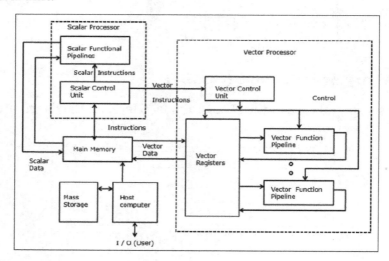

SIMD Supercomputers

In SIMD computers, 'N' number of processors are connected to a control unit and all the processors have their individual memory units. All the processors are connected by an interconnection network.

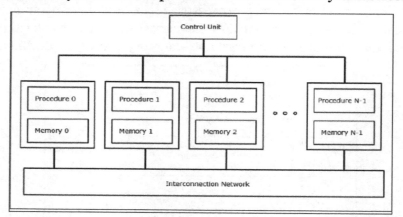

PRAM and VLSI Models

The ideal model gives a suitable framework for developing parallel algorithms without considering the physical constraints or implementation details.

The models can be enforced to obtain theoretical performance bounds on parallel computers or to evaluate VLSI complexity on chip area and operational time before the chip is fabricated.

Parallel Random-access Machines

Sheperdson and Sturgis modeled the conventional Uniprocessor computers as random-access-machines (RAM). Fortune and Wyllie developed a parallel random-access-machine (PRAM) model for modeling an idealized parallel computer with zero memory access overhead and synchronization.

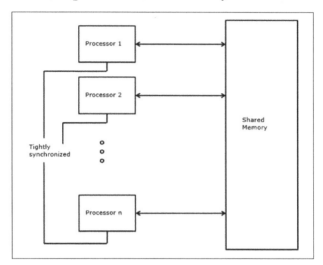

An N-processor PRAM has a shared memory unit. This shared memory can be centralized or distributed among the processors. These processors operate on a synchronized read-memory, write-memory and compute cycle. So, these models specify how concurrent read and write operations are handled.

Following are the possible memory update operations :

- Exclusive read (ER): In this method, in each cycle only one processor is allowed to read from any memory location.

- Exclusive write (EW): In this method, at least one processor is allowed to write into a memory location at a time.

- Concurrent read (CR): It allows multiple processors to read the same information from the same memory location in the same cycle.

- Concurrent write (CW): It allows simultaneous write operations to the same memory location. To avoid write conflict some policies are set up.

VLSI Complexity Model

Parallel computers use VLSI chips to fabricate processor arrays, memory arrays and large-scale switching networks.

Nowadays, VLSI technologies are 2-dimensional. The size of a VLSI chip is proportional to the amount of storage (memory) space available in that chip.

We can calculate the space complexity of an algorithm by the chip area (A) of the VLSI chip implementation of that algorithm. If T is the time (latency) needed to execute the algorithm, then A.T gives an upper bound on the total number of bits processed through the chip (or I/O). For certain computing, there exists a lower bound, f(s), such that:

$$A.T^2 >= O(f(s))$$

Where A=chip area and T=time

Architectural Development Tracks

The evolution of parallel computers I spread along the following tracks:

- Multiple Processor Tracks
  - Multiprocessor track
  - Multicomputer track
- Multiple data track
  - Vector track
  - SIMD track
- Multiple threads track
  - Multithreaded track
  - Dataflow track

In multiple processor track, it is assumed that different threads execute concurrently on different processors and communicate through shared memory (multiprocessor track) or message passing (multicomputer track) system.

In multiple data track, it is assumed that the same code is executed on the massive amount of data. It is done by executing same instructions on a sequence of data elements (vector track) or through the execution of same sequence of instructions on a similar set of data (SIMD track).

In multiple threads track, it is assumed that the interleaved execution of various threads on the same processor to hide synchronization delays among threads executing on different processors. Thread interleaving can be coarse (multithreaded track) or fine (dataflow track).

Processor in Parallel System

In the 80's, a special purpose processor was popular for making multicomputers called Transputer. A transputer consisted of one core processor, a small SRAM memory, a DRAM main memory interface and four communication channels, all on a single chip. To make a parallel computer communication, channels were connected to form a network of Transputers. But it has a lack of computational power and hence couldn't meet the increasing demand of parallel applications. This problem was solved by the development of RISC processors and it was cheap also.

Modern parallel computer uses microprocessors which use parallelism at several levels like instruction-level parallelism and data level parallelism.

High Performance Processors

RISC and RISCy processors dominate today's parallel computers market. Characteristics of traditional RISC are:

- Has few addressing modes.

- Has a fixed format for instructions, usually 32 or 64 bits.

- Has dedicated load/store instructions to load data from memory to register and store data from register to memory.

- Arithmetic operations are always performed on registers.

- Uses pipelining.

Most of the microprocessors these days are superscalar, i.e. in a parallel computer multiple instruction pipelines are used. Therefore, superscalar processors can execute more than one instruction at the same time. Effectiveness of superscalar processors is dependent on the amount of instruction-level parallelism (ILP) available in the applications. To keep the pipelines filled, the instructions at the hardware level are executed in a different order than the program order.

Many modern microprocessors use super pipelining approach. In super pipelining, to increase the clock frequency, the work done within a pipeline stage is reduced and the number of pipeline stages is increased.

Very Large Instruction Word (VLIW) Processors

These are derived from horizontal microprogramming and superscalar processing. Instructions in VLIW processors are very large. The operations within a single instruction are executed in parallel and are forwarded to the appropriate functional units for execution. So, after fetching a VLIW instruction, its operations are decoded. Then the operations are dispatched to the functional units in which they are executed in parallel.

Vector Processors

Vector processors are co-processor to general-purpose microprocessor. Vector processors are generally register-register or memory-memory. A vector instruction is fetched and decoded and then a certain operation is performed for each element of the operand vectors, whereas in a normal processor a vector operation needs a loop structure in the code. To make it more efficient, vector processors chain several vector operations together, i.e., the result from one vector operation are forwarded to another as operand.

Caching

Caches are important element of high-performance microprocessors. After every 18 months, speed of microprocessors become twice, but DRAM chips for main memory cannot compete with this speed. So, caches are introduced to bridge the speed gap between the processor and memory.

A cache is a fast and small SRAM memory. Many more caches are applied in modern processors like Translation Look-aside Buffers (TLBs) caches, instruction and data caches, etc.

Direct Mapped Cache

In direct mapped caches, a 'modulo' function is used for one-to-one mapping of addresses in the main memory to cache locations. As same cache entry can have multiple main memory blocks mapped to it, the processor must be able to determine whether a data block in the cache is the data block that is actually needed. This identification is done by storing a tag together with a cache block.

Fully Associative Cache

A fully associative mapping allows for placing a cache block anywhere in the cache. By using some replacement policy, the cache determines a cache entry in which it stores a cache block. Fully associative caches have flexible mapping, which minimizes the number of cache-entry conflicts. Since a fully associative implementation is expensive, these are never used large scale.

Set-associative Cache

A set-associative mapping is a combination of a direct mapping and a fully associative mapping. In this case, the cache entries are subdivided into cache sets. As in direct mapping, there is a fixed mapping of memory blocks to a set in the cache. But inside a cache set, a memory block is mapped in a fully associative manner.

Cache Strategies

Other than mapping mechanism, caches also need a range of strategies that specify what should happen in the case of certain events. In case of (set-) associative caches, the cache must determine which cache block is to be replaced by a new block entering the cache.

Some well-known replacement strategies are:

- First-In First Out (FIFO)
- Least Recently Used (LRU)

Multiprocessors and Multicomputers

Multiprocessor System Interconnects

Parallel processing needs the use of efficient system interconnects for fast communication among the Input/Output and peripheral devices, multiprocessors and shared memory.

Hierarchical Bus Systems

A hierarchical bus system consists of a hierarchy of buses connecting various systems and sub-systems/components in a computer. Each bus is made up of a number of signal, control, and power lines. Different buses like local buses, backplane buses and I/O buses are used to perform different interconnection functions.

Local buses are the buses implemented on the printed-circuit boards. A backplane bus is a printed circuit on which many connectors are used to plug in functional boards. Buses which connect input/output devices to a computer system are known as I/O buses.

Crossbar Switch and Multiport Memory

Switched networks give dynamic interconnections among the inputs and outputs. Small or medium size systems mostly use crossbar networks. Multistage networks can be expanded to the larger systems, if the increased latency problem can be solved.

Both crossbar switch and multiport memory organization is a single-stage network. Though a single stage network is cheaper to build, but multiple passes may be needed to establish certain connections. A multistage network has more than one stage of switch boxes. These networks should be able to connect any input to any output.

Multistage and Combining Networks

Multistage networks or multistage interconnection networks are a class of high-speed computer networks which is mainly composed of processing elements on one end of the network and memory elements on the other end, connected by switching elements.

These networks are applied to build larger multiprocessor systems. This includes Omega Network, Butterfly Network and many more.

Multicomputers

Multicomputers are distributed memory MIMD architectures. The following diagram shows a conceptual model of a multicomputer :

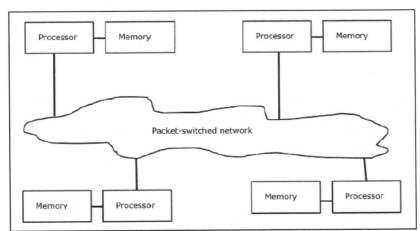

Multicomputers are message-passing machines which apply packet switching method to exchange data. Here, each processor has a private memory, but no global address space as a processor can access only its own local memory. So, communication is not transparent: here programmers have to explicitly put communication primitives in their code.

Having no globally accessible memory is a drawback of multicomputers. This can be solved by using the following two schemes:

- Virtual Shared Memory (VSM).

- Shared Virtual Memory (SVM).

In these schemes, the application programmer assumes a big shared memory which is globally addressable. If required, the memory references made by applications are translated into the message-passing paradigm.

Virtual Shared Memory (VSM)

VSM is a hardware implementation. So, the virtual memory system of the Operating System is transparently implemented on top of VSM. So, the operating system thinks it is running on a machine with a shared memory.

Shared Virtual Memory (SVM)

SVM is a software implementation at the Operating System level with hardware support from the Memory Management Unit (MMU) of the processor. Here, the unit of sharing is Operating System memory pages.

If a processor addresses a particular memory location, the MMU determines whether the memory page associated with the memory access is in the local memory or not. If the page is not in the memory, in a normal computer system it is swapped in from the disk by the Operating System. But, in SVM, the Operating System fetches the page from the remote node which owns that particular page.

Three Generations of Multicomputers

Design Choices in the Past

While selecting a processor technology, a multicomputer designer chooses low-cost medium grain processors as building blocks. Majority of parallel computers are built with standard off-the-shelf microprocessors. Distributed memory was chosen for multi-computers rather than using shared memory, which would limit the scalability. Each processor has its own local memory unit.

For interconnection scheme, multicomputers have message passing, point-to-point direct networks rather than address switching networks. For control strategy, designer of multi-computers choose the asynchronous MIMD, MPMD, and SMPD operations. Caltech's Cosmic Cube is the first of the first generation multi-computers.

Present and Future Development

The next generation computers evolved from medium to fine grain multicomputers using a globally shared virtual memory. Second generation multi-computers are still in use at present. But using better processor like i386, i860, etc. second generation computers have developed a lot.

Third generation computers are the next generation computers where VLSI implemented nodes will be used. Each node may have a 14-MIPS processor, 20-Mbytes/s routing channels and 16 Kbytes of RAM integrated on a single chip.

The Intel Paragon System

Previously, homogeneous nodes were used to make hypercube multicomputers, as all the functions were given to the host. So, this limited the I/O bandwidth. Thus to solve large-scale problems efficiently or with high throughput, these computers could not be used. The Intel Paragon System was designed to overcome this difficulty. It turned the multicomputer into an application server with multiuser access in a network environment.

Message Passing Mechanisms

Message passing mechanisms in a multicomputer network needs special hardware and software support. Here, we will discuss some schemes.

Message-routing Schemes

In multicomputer with store and forward routing scheme, packets are the smallest unit of information transmission. In wormhole–routed networks, packets are further divided into flits. Packet length is determined by the routing scheme and network implementation, whereas the flit length is affected by the network size.

In Store and forward routing, packets are the basic unit of information transmission. In this case, each node uses a packet buffer. A packet is transmitted from a source node to a destination node through a sequence of intermediate nodes. Latency is directly proportional to the distance between the source and the destination.

In wormhole routing, the transmission from the source node to the destination node is done through a sequence of routers. All the flits of the same packet are transmitted in an inseparable sequence in a pipelined fashion. In this case, only the header flit knows where the packet is going.

Deadlock and Virtual Channels

A virtual channel is a logical link between two nodes. It is formed by flit buffer in source node and receiver node, and a physical channel between them. When a physical channel is allocated for a pair, one source buffer is paired with one receiver buffer to form a virtual channel.

When all the channels are occupied by messages and none of the channel in the cycle is freed, a deadlock situation will occur. To avoid this a deadlock avoidance scheme has to be followed.

Cache Coherence and Synchronization

The Cache Coherence Problem

In a multiprocessor system, data inconsistency may occur among adjacent levels or within the same level of the memory hierarchy. For example, the cache and the main memory may have inconsistent copies of the same object.

As multiple processors operate in parallel, and independently multiple caches may possess different copies of the same memory block, this creates cache coherence problem. Cache coherence schemes help to avoid this problem by maintaining a uniform state for each cached block of data.

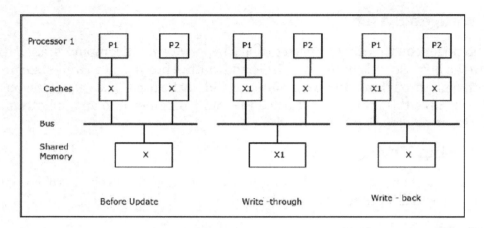

Let X be an element of shared data which has been referenced by two processors, P1 and P2. In the beginning, three copies of X are consistent. If the processor P1 writes a new data X1 into the cache, by using write-through policy, the same copy will be written immediately into the shared memory. In this case, inconsistency occurs between cache memory and the main memory. When a write-back policy is used, the main memory will be updated when the modified data in the cache is replaced or invalidated.

In general, there are three sources of inconsistency problem:

- Sharing of writable data.

- Process migration.

- I/O activity.

Snoopy Bus Protocols

Snoopy protocols achieve data consistency between the cache memory and the shared memory through a bus-based memory system. Write-invalidate and write-update policies are used for maintaining cache consistency.

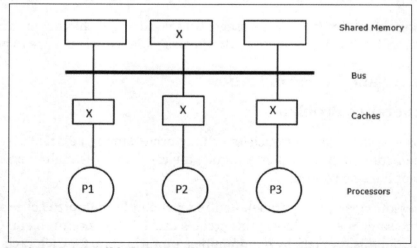

Consistent copies of block X are in shared memory and three processor caches.

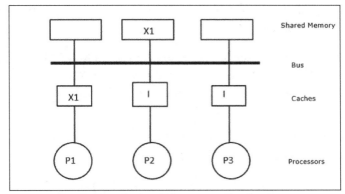

After a write invalidate operation by P1.

In this case, we have three processors P1, P2, and P3 having a consistent copy of data element 'X' in their local cache memory and in the shared memory. Processor P1 writes X1 in its cache memory using write-invalidate protocol. So, all other copies are invalidated via the bus. It is denoted by 'I'. Invalidated blocks are also known as dirty, i.e. they should not be used. The write-update protocol updates all the cache copies via the bus. By using write back cache, the memory copy is also updated.

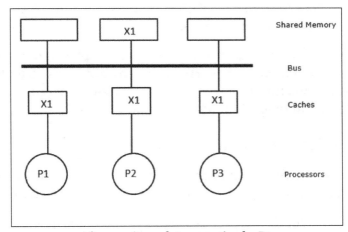

After a write update operation by P1.

Cache Events and Actions

Following events and actions occur on the execution of memory-access and invalidation commands:

- Read-miss: When a processor wants to read a block and it is not in the cache, a read-miss occurs. This initiates a bus-read operation. If no dirty copy exists, then the main memory that has a consistent copy, supplies a copy to the requesting cache memory. If a dirty copy exists in a remote cache memory, that cache will restrain the main memory and send a copy to the requesting cache memory. In both the cases, the cache copy will enter the valid state after a read miss.

- Write-hit: If the copy is in dirty or reserved state, write is done locally and the new state is dirty. If the new state is valid, write-invalidate command is broadcasted to all the caches, invalidating their copies. When the shared memory is written through, the resulting state is reserved after this first write.

- Write-miss: If a processor fails to write in the local cache memory, the copy must come either from the main memory or from a remote cache memory with a dirty block. This is done by sending a read-invalidate command, which will invalidate all cache copies. Then the local copy is updated with dirty state.

- Read-hit: Read-hit is always performed in local cache memory without causing a transition of state or using the snoopy bus for invalidation.

- Block replacement: When a copy is dirty, it is to be written back to the main memory by block replacement method. However, when the copy is either in valid or reserved or invalid state, no replacement will take place.

Directory-based Protocols

By using a multistage network for building a large multiprocessor with hundreds of processors, the snoopy cache protocols need to be modified to suit the network capabilities. Broadcasting being very expensive to perform in a multistage network, the consistency commands is sent only to those caches that keep a copy of the block. This is the reason for development of directory-based protocols for network-connected multiprocessors.

In a directory-based protocols system, data to be shared are placed in a common directory that maintains the coherence among the caches. Here, the directory acts as a filter where the processors ask permission to load an entry from the primary memory to its cache memory. If an entry is changed the directory either updates it or invalidates the other caches with that entry.

Hardware Synchronization Mechanisms

Synchronization is a special form of communication where instead of data control, information is exchanged between communicating processes residing in the same or different processors.

Multiprocessor systems use hardware mechanisms to implement low-level synchronization operations. Most multiprocessors have hardware mechanisms to impose atomic operations such as memory read, write or read-modify-write operations to implement some synchronization primitives. Other than atomic memory operations, some inter-processor interrupts are also used for synchronization purposes.

Cache Coherency in Shared Memory Machines

Maintaining cache coherency is a problem in multiprocessor system when the processors contain local cache memory. Data inconsistency between different caches easily occurs in this system.

The major concern areas are:

- Sharing of writable data.

- Process migration.

- I/O activity.

Sharing of Writable Data

When two processors (P1 and P2) have same data element (X) in their local caches and one process (P1) writes to the data element (X), as the caches are write-through local cache of P1, the main memory is also updated. Now when P2 tries to read data element (X), it does not find X because the data element in the cache of P2 has become outdated.

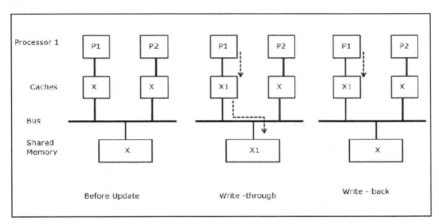

Process Migration

In the first stage, cache of P1 has data element X, whereas P2 does not have anything. A process on P2 first writes on X and then migrates to P1. Now, the process starts reading data element X, but as the processor P1 has outdated data the process cannot read it. So, a process on P1 writes to the data element X and then migrates to P2. After migration, a process on P2 starts reading the data element X but it finds an outdated version of X in the main memory.

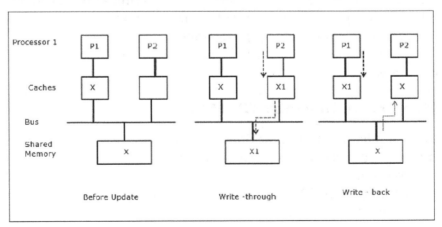

I/O Activity

As illustrated in the figure, an I/O device is added to the bus in a two-processor multiprocessor architecture. In the beginning, both the caches contain the data element X. When the I/O device receives a new element X, it stores the new element directly in the main memory. Now, when either P1 or P2 (assume P1) tries to read element X it gets an outdated copy. So, P1 writes to element X. Now, if I/O device tries to transmit X it gets an outdated copy.

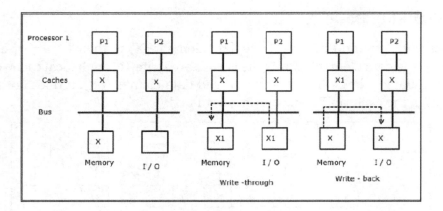

Uniform Memory Access (UMA)

Uniform Memory Access (UMA) architecture means the shared memory is the same for all processors in the system. Popular classes of UMA machines, which are commonly used for (file-) servers, are the so-called Symmetric Multiprocessors (SMPs). In an SMP, all system resources like memory, disks, other I/O devices, etc. are accessible by the processors in a uniform manner.

Non-uniform Memory Access (NUMA)

In NUMA architecture, there are multiple SMP clusters having an internal indirect/shared network, which are connected in scalable message-passing network. So, NUMA architecture is logically shared physically distributed memory architecture.

In a NUMA machine, the cache-controller of a processor determines whether a memory reference is local to the SMP's memory or it is remote. To reduce the number of remote memory accesses, NUMA architectures usually apply caching processors that can cache the remote data. But when caches are involved, cache coherency needs to be maintained. So these systems are also known as CC-NUMA (Cache Coherent NUMA).

Cache Only Memory Architecture (COMA)

COMA machines are similar to NUMA machines, with the only difference that the main memories of COMA machines act as direct-mapped or set-associative caches. The data blocks are hashed to a location in the DRAM cache according to their addresses. Data that is fetched remotely is actually stored in the local main memory. Moreover, data blocks do not have a fixed home location, they can freely move throughout the system.

COMA architectures mostly have a hierarchical message-passing network. A switch in such a tree contains a directory with data elements as its sub-tree. Since data has no home location, it must be explicitly searched for. This means that a remote access requires a traversal along the switches in the tree to search their directories for the required data. So, if a switch in the network receives multiple requests from its subtree for the same data, it combines them into a single request which is sent to the parent of the switch. When the requested data returns, the switch sends multiple copies of it down its subtree.

COMA versus CC-NUMA

Following are the differences between COMA and CC-NUMA:

- COMA tends to be more flexible than CC-NUMA because COMA transparently supports the migration and replication of data without the need of the OS.

- COMA machines are expensive and complex to build because they need non-standard memory management hardware and the coherency protocol is harder to implement.

- Remote accesses in COMA are often slower than those in CC-NUMA since the tree network needs to be traversed to find the data.

Interconnection Network Design

An interconnection network in a parallel machine transfers information from any source node to any desired destination node. This task should be completed with as small latency as possible. It should allow a large number of such transfers to take place concurrently. Moreover, it should be inexpensive as compared to the cost of the rest of the machine.

The network is composed of links and switches, which helps to send the information from the source node to the destination node. A network is specified by its topology, routing algorithm, switching strategy, and flow control mechanism.

Organizational Structure

Interconnection networks are composed of following three basic components:

- Links: A link is a cable of one or more optical fibers or electrical wires with a connector at each end attached to a switch or network interface port. Through this, an analog signal is transmitted from one end, received at the other to obtain the original digital information stream.

- Switches: A switch is composed of a set of input and output ports, an internal "cross-bar" connecting all input to all output, internal buffering, and control logic to effect the input-output connection at each point in time. Generally, the number of input ports is equal to the number of output ports.

- Network Interfaces: The network interface behaves quite differently than switch nodes and may be connected via special links. The network interface formats the packets and constructs the routing and control information. It may have input and output buffering, compared to a switch. It may perform end-to-end error checking and flow control. Hence, its cost is influenced by its processing complexity, storage capacity, and number of ports.

Interconnection Network

Interconnection networks are composed of switching elements. Topology is the pattern to connect the individual switches to other elements, like processors, memories and other switches. A network allows exchange of data between processors in the parallel system.

- Direct connection networks: Direct networks have point-to-point connections between neighboring nodes. These networks are static, which means that the point-to-point connections are fixed. Some examples of direct networks are rings, meshes and cubes.

- Indirect connection networks: Indirect networks have no fixed neighbors. The communication topology can be changed dynamically based on the application demands. Indirect networks can be subdivided into three parts: bus networks, multistage networks and crossbar switches.

  ○ Bus networks: A bus network is composed of a number of bit lines onto which a number of resources are attached. When busses use the same physical lines for data and addresses, the data and the address lines are time multiplexed. When there are multiple bus-masters attached to the bus, an arbiter is required.

  ○ Multistage networks: A multistage network consists of multiple stages of switches. It is composed of 'axb' switches which are connected using a particular interstage connection pattern (ISC). Small 2x2 switch elements are a common choice for many multistage networks. The number of stages determine the delay of the network. By choosing different interstage connection patterns, various types of multistage network can be created.

  ○ Crossbar switches: A crossbar switch contains a matrix of simple switch elements that can switch on and off to create or break a connection. Turning on a switch element in the matrix, a connection between a processor and a memory can be made. Crossbar switches are non-blocking, that is all communication permutations can be performed without blocking.

Evaluating Design Trade-offs in Network Topology

If the main concern is the routing distance, then the dimension has to be maximized and a hypercube made. In store-and-forward routing, assuming that the degree of the switch and the number of links were not a significant cost factor, and the numbers of links or the switch degree are the main costs, the dimension has to be minimized and a mesh built.

In worst case traffic pattern for each network, it is preferred to have high dimensional networks where all the paths are short. In patterns where each node is communicating with only one or two nearby neighbors, it is preferred to have low dimensional networks, since only a few of the dimensions are actually used.

Routing

The routing algorithm of a network determines which of the possible paths from source to destination is used as routes and how the route followed by each particular packet is determined. Dimension order routing limits the set of legal paths so that there is exactly one route from each source to each destination. The one obtained by first traveling the correct distance in the high-order dimension, then the next dimension and so on.

Routing Mechanisms

Arithmetic, source-based port select, and table look-up are three mechanisms that high-speed switches use to determine the output channel from information in the packet header. All of these mechanisms are simpler than the kind of general routing computations implemented in traditional LAN and WAN routers. In parallel computer networks, the switch needs to make the routing decision for all its inputs in every cycle, so the mechanism needs to be simple and fast.

Deterministic Routing

A routing algorithm is deterministic if the route taken by a message is determined exclusively by its source and destination, and not by other traffic in the network. If a routing algorithm only selects shortest paths toward the destination, it is minimal, otherwise it is non-minimal.

Deadlock Freedom

Deadlock can occur in a various situations. When two nodes attempt to send data to each other and each begins sending before either receives, a 'head-on' deadlock may occur. Another case of deadlock occurs, when there are multiple messages competing for resources within the network.

The basic technique for proving a network is deadlock free, is to clear the dependencies that can occur between channels as a result of messages moving through the networks and to show that there are no cycles in the overall channel dependency graph; hence there is no traffic patterns that can lead to a deadlock. The common way of doing this is to number the channel resources such that all routes follow a particular increasing or decreasing sequences, so that no dependency cycles arise.

Switch Design

Design of a network depends on the design of the switch and how the switches are wired together. The degree of the switch, its internal routing mechanisms, and its internal buffering decides what topologies can be supported and what routing algorithms can be implemented. Like any other hardware component of a computer system, a network switch contains data path, control, and storage.

Ports

The total number of pins is actually the total number of input and output ports times the channel width. As the perimeter of the chip grows slowly compared to the area, switches tend to be pin limited.

Internal Datapath

The datapath is the connectivity between each of the set of input ports and every output port. It is generally referred to as the internal cross-bar. A non-blocking cross-bar is one where each input port can be connected to a distinct output in any permutation simultaneously.

Channel Buffers

The organization of the buffer storage within the switch has an important impact on the switch performance. Traditional routers and switches tend to have large SRAM or DRAM buffers external to the switch fabric, while in VLSI switches the buffering is internal to the switch and comes out of the same silicon budget as the datapath and the control section. As the chip size and density increases, more buffering is available and the network designer has more options, but still the buffer real-estate comes at a prime choice and its organization is important.

Flow Control

When multiple data flows in the network attempt to use the same shared network resources at the same time, some action must be taken to control these flows. If we don't want to lose any data, some of the flows must be blocked while others proceed.

The problem of flow control arises in all networks and at many levels. But it is qualitatively different in parallel computer networks than in local and wide area networks. In parallel computers, the network traffic needs to be delivered about as accurately as traffic across a bus and there are a very large number of parallel flows on very small-time scale.

Latency Tolerance

The speed of microprocessors has increased by more than a factor of ten per decade, but the speed of commodity memories (DRAMs) has only doubled, i.e., access time is halved. Therefore, the latency of memory access in terms of processor clock cycles grow by a factor of six in 10 years. Multiprocessors intensified the problem.

In bus-based systems, the establishment of a high-bandwidth bus between the processor and the memory tends to increase the latency of obtaining the data from the memory. When the memory is physically distributed, the latency of the network and the network interface is added to that of the accessing the local memory on the node.

Latency usually grows with the size of the machine, as more nodes imply more communication relative to computation, more jump in the network for general communication, and likely more contention. The main goal of hardware design is to reduce the latency of the data access while maintaining high, scalable bandwidth.

How latency tolerance is handled is best understood by looking at the resources in the machine and how they are utilized. From the processor point of view, the communication architecture from one node to another can be viewed as a pipeline. The stages of the pipeline include network interfaces at the source and destination, as well as in the network links and switches along the way. There are also stages in the communication assist, the local memory/cache system, and the main processor, depending on how the architecture manages communication.

The utilization problem in the baseline communication structure is either the processor or the communication architecture is busy at a given time, and in the communication pipeline only one stage is busy at a time as the single word being transmitted makes its way from source to destination. The aim in latency tolerance is to overlap the use of these resources as much as possible.

Latency Tolerance in Explicit Message Passing

The actual transfer of data in message-passing is typically sender-initiated, using a send operation. A receive operation does not in itself motivate data to be communicated, but rather copies data from an incoming buffer into the application address space. Receiver-initiated communication is done by issuing a request message to the process that is the source of the data. The process then sends the data back via another send.

A synchronous send operation has communication latency equal to the time it takes to communicate all the data in the message to the destination, and the time for receive processing, and the time for an acknowledgment to be returned. The latency of a synchronous receive operation is its processing overhead; which includes copying the data into the application, and the additional latency if the data has not yet arrived. We would like to hide these latencies, including overheads if possible, at both ends.

Latency Tolerance in a Shared Address Space

The baseline communication is through reads and writes in a shared address space. For convenience, it is called read-write communication. Receiver-initiated communication is done with read operations that result in data from another processor's memory or cache being accessed. If there is no caching of shared data, sender-initiated communication may be done through writes to data that are allocated in remote memories.

With cache coherence, the effect of writes is more complex: either writes leads to sender or receiver-initiated communication depends on the cache coherence protocol. Either receiver-initiated or sender-initiated, the communication in a hardware-supported read writes shared address space is naturally fine-grained, which makes tolerance latency very important.

Block Data Transfer in a Shared Address Space

In a shared address space, either by hardware or software the coalescing of data and the initiation of block transfers can be done explicitly in the user program or transparently by the system. Explicit block transfers are initiated by executing a command similar to a send in the user program. The send command is explained by the communication assist, which transfers the data in a pipelined manner from the source node to the destination. At the destination, the communication assist pulls the data words in from the network interface and stores them in the specified locations.

There are two prime differences from send-receive message passing, both of which arise from the fact that the sending process can directly specify the program data structures where the data is to be placed at the destination, since these locations are in the shared address space.

Proceeding Past Long-latency Events in a Shared Address Space

If the memory operation is made non-blocking, a processor can proceed past a memory operation to other instructions. For writes, this is usually quite simple to implement if the write is put in a write buffer, and the processor goes on while the buffer takes care of issuing the write to the memory system and tracking its completion as required. The difference is that unlike a write, a read is generally followed very soon by an instruction that needs the value returned by the read.

Pre-communication in a Shared Address Space

Pre-communication is a technique that has already been widely adopted in commercial microprocessors, and its importance is likely to increase in the future. A prefetch instruction does not replace the actual read of the data item, and the prefetch instruction itself must be non-blocking, if it is to achieve its goal of hiding latency through overlap.

In this case, as shared data is not cached, the prefetched data is brought into a special hardware structure called a prefetch buffer. When the word is actually read into a register in the next iteration, it is read from the head of the prefetch buffer rather than from memory. If the latency to hide were much bigger than the time to compute single loop iteration, we would prefetch several iterations ahead and there would potentially be several words in the prefetch buffer at a time.

Multithreading in a Shared Address Space

In terms of hiding different types of latency, hardware-supported multithreading is perhaps the versatile technique. It has the following conceptual advantages over other approaches:

- It requires no special software analysis or support.

- As it is invoked dynamically, it can handle unpredictable situations, like cache conflicts, etc. just as well as predictable ones.

- Like prefetching, it does not change the memory consistency model since it does not reorder accesses within a thread.

- While the previous techniques are targeted at hiding memory access latency, multithreading can potentially hide the latency of any long-latency event just as easily, as long as the event can be detected at runtime. This includes synchronization and instruction latency as well.

This trend may change in future, as latencies are becoming increasingly longer as compared to processor speeds. Also with more sophisticated microprocessors that already provide methods that can be extended for multithreading, and with new multithreading techniques being developed to combine multithreading with instruction-level parallelism, this trend certainly seems to be undergoing some change in future.

System Design

Systems design is the process of defining the architecture, modules, interfaces, and data for a system to satisfy specified requirements. Systems design could be seen as the application of systems theory to product development. There is some overlap with the disciplines of systems analysis, systems architecture and systems engineering.

If the broader topic of product development "blends the perspective of marketing, design, and manufacturing into a single approach to product development," then design is the act of taking the marketing information and creating the design of the product to be manufactured. Systems design is therefore the process of defining and developing systems to satisfy specified requirements of the user.

Until the 1990s, systems design had a crucial and respected role in the data processing industry. In the 1990s, standardization of hardware and software resulted in the ability to build modular systems. The increasing importance of software running on generic platforms has enhanced the discipline of software engineering.

Architectural Design

The architectural design of a system emphasizes the design of the system architecture that describes the structure, behavior and more views of that system and analysis.

Logical Design

The logical design of a system pertains to an abstract representation of the data flows, inputs and outputs of the system. This is often conducted via modelling, using an over-abstract (and sometimes graphical) model of the actual system. In the context of systems, designs are included. Logical design includes entity-relationship diagrams (ER diagrams).

Physical Design

The physical design relates to the actual input and output processes of the system. This is explained in terms of how data is input into a system, how it is verified/authenticated, how it is processed, and how it is displayed. In physical design, the following requirements about the system are decided.

- Input requirement,

- Output requirements,

- Storage requirements,

- Processing requirements,

- System control and backup or recovery.

Put another way, the physical portion of system design can generally be broken down into three sub-tasks:

- User Interface Design,

- Data Design,

- Process Design.

User Interface Design is concerned with how users add information to the system and with how the system presents information back to them. Data Design is concerned with how the data is represented and stored within the system. Finally, Process Design is concerned with how data moves through the system, and with how and where it is validated, secured and/or transformed as it flows into, through and out of the system. At the end of the system design phase, documentation describing the three sub-tasks is produced and made available for use in the next phase.

Physical design, in this context, does not refer to the tangible physical design of an information system. To use an analogy, a personal computer's physical design involves input via a keyboard, processing within the CPU, and output via a monitor, printer, etc. It would not concern the actual layout of the tangible hardware, which for a PC would be a monitor, CPU, motherboard, hard drive, modems, video/graphics cards, USB slots, etc. It involves a detailed design of a user and a product database structure processor and a control processor. The H/S personal specification is developed for the proposed system.

Related Disciplines

Benchmarking: This is an effort to evaluate how current systems perform.

Computer programming and debugging in the software world, or detailed design in the consumer, enterprise or commercial world - specifies the final system components.

Design: designers will produce one or more 'models' of what they see a system eventually looking like, with ideas from the analysis section either used or discarded. A document will be produced with a description of the system, but nothing is specific – they might say 'touchscreen' or 'GUI operating system', but not mention any specific brands.

Requirements analysis: Analyzes the needs of the end users or customers.

System architecture: Creates a blueprint for the design with the necessary structure and behavior specifications for the hardware, software, people and data resources. In many cases, multiple architectures are evaluated before one is selected.

System testing: Evaluates the system's actual functionality in relation to expected or intended functionality, including all integration aspects.

Alternative Design Methodologies

Rapid Application Development (RAD)

Rapid application development (RAD) is a methodology in which a system designer produces prototypes for an end-user. The end-user reviews the prototype, and offers feedback on its suitability. This process is repeated until the end-user is satisfied with the final system.

Joint Application Design (JAD)

Joint application design (JAD) is a methodology which evolved from RAD, in which a system designer consults with a group consisting of the following parties:

- Executive sponsor,
- System designer,
- Managers of the system.

JAD involves a number of stages, in which the group collectively develops an agreed pattern for the design and implementation of the system.

CPU

A central processing unit (CPU), also called a central processor or main processor, is the electronic circuitry within a computer that carries out the instructions of a computer program by performing the basic arithmetic, logic, controlling, and input/output (I/O) operations specified by the instructions. The computer industry has used the term "central processing unit" at least since the early 1960s. Traditionally, the term "CPU" refers to a processor, more specifically to its processing unit and control unit (CU), distinguishing these core elements of a computer from external components such as main memory and I/O circuitry.

The form, design, and implementation of CPUs have changed over the course of their history, but their fundamental operation remains almost unchanged. Principal components of a CPU include the arithmetic logic unit (ALU) that performs arithmetic and logic operations, processor registers that supply operands to the ALU and store the results of ALU operations, and a control unit that orchestrates the fetching (from memory) and execution of instructions by directing the coordinated operations of the ALU, registers and other components.

Most modern CPUs are microprocessors, where the CPU is contained on a single metal-oxide-semiconductor (MOS) integrated circuit (IC) chip. An IC that contains a CPU may also contain memory, peripheral interfaces, and other components of a computer; such integrated devices are variously called microcontrollers or systems on a chip (SoC). Some computers employ a multi-core processor, which is a single chip containing two or more CPUs called "cores"; in that context, one can speak of such single chips as "sockets".

Array processors or vector processors have multiple processors that operate in parallel, with no unit considered central. There also exists the concept of virtual CPUs which are an abstraction of dynamical aggregated computational resources.

An Intel 80486DX2 CPU, as seen from above.

Bottom side of an Intel 80486DX2, showing its pins.

Operation

The fundamental operation of most CPUs, regardless of the physical form they take, is to execute a sequence of stored instructions that is called a program. The instructions to be executed are kept in some kind of computer memory. Nearly all CPUs follow the fetch, decode and execute steps in their operation, which are collectively known as the instruction cycle.

After the execution of an instruction, the entire process repeats, with the next instruction cycle normally fetching the next-in-sequence instruction because of the incremented value in the program counter. If a jump instruction was executed, the program counter will be modified to contain the address of the instruction that was jumped to and program execution continues normally. In more complex CPUs, multiple instructions can be fetched, decoded and executed simultaneously.

Some instructions manipulate the program counter rather than producing result data directly; such instructions are generally called "jumps" and facilitate program behavior like loops, conditional program execution (through the use of a conditional jump), and existence of functions. In some processors, some other instructions change the state of bits in a "flags" register. These flags can be used to influence how a program behaves, since they often indicate the outcome of various operations. For example, in such processors a "compare" instruction evaluates two values and sets or clears bits in the flags register to indicate which one is greater or whether they are equal; one of these flags could then be used by a later jump instruction to determine program flow.

Fetch

The first step, fetch, involves retrieving an instruction (which is represented by a number or sequence of numbers) from program memory. The instruction's location (address) in program memory is determined by a program counter (PC), which stores a number that identifies the address of the next instruction to be fetched. After an instruction is fetched, the PC is incremented by the length of the instruction so that it will contain the address of the next instruction in the sequence. Often, the instruction to be fetched must be retrieved from relatively slow memory, causing the CPU to stall while waiting for the instruction to be returned. This issue is largely addressed in modern processors by caches and pipeline architectures.

Decode

The instruction that the CPU fetches from memory determines what the CPU will do. In the decode step, performed by the circuitry known as the *instruction decoder*, the instruction is converted into signals that control other parts of the CPU.

The way in which the instruction is interpreted is defined by the CPU's instruction set architecture (ISA). Often, one group of bits (that is, a "field") within the instruction, called the opcode, indicates which operation is to be performed, while the remaining fields usually provide supplemental information required for the operation, such as the operands. Those operands may be specified as a constant value (called an immediate value), or as the location of a value that may be a processor register or a memory address, as determined by some addressing mode.

In some CPU designs the instruction decoder is implemented as a hardwired, unchangeable circuit. In others, a microprogram is used to translate instructions into sets of CPU configuration signals that are applied sequentially over multiple clock pulses. In some cases the memory that stores the microprogram is rewritable, making it possible to change the way in which the CPU decodes instructions.

Execute

After the fetch and decode steps, the execute step is performed. Depending on the CPU architecture, this may consist of a single action or a sequence of actions. During each action, various parts of the CPU are electrically connected so they can perform all or part of the desired operation and then the action is completed, typically in response to a clock pulse. Very often the results are written to an internal CPU register for quick access by subsequent instructions. In other cases results may be written to slower, but less expensive and higher capacity main memory.

For example, if an addition instruction is to be executed, the arithmetic logic unit (ALU) inputs are connected to a pair of operand sources (numbers to be summed), the ALU is configured to perform an addition operation so that the sum of its operand inputs will appear at its output, and the ALU output is connected to storage (e.g., a register or memory) that will receive the sum. When the clock pulse occurs, the sum will be transferred to storage and, if the resulting sum is too large (i.e., it is larger than the ALU's output word size), an arithmetic overflow flag will be set.

Structure and Implementation

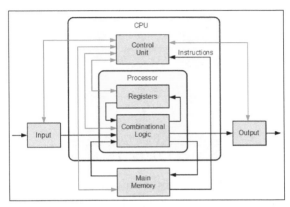

Block diagram of a basic uniprocessor-CPU computer. Black lines indicate data flow, whereas red lines indicate control flow; arrows indicate flow directions.

Hardwired into a CPU's circuitry is a set of basic operations it can perform, called an instruction set. Such operations may involve, for example, adding or subtracting two numbers, comparing two numbers, or jumping to a different part of a program. Each basic operation is represented by a particular combination of bits, known as the machine language opcode; while executing instructions in a machine language program, the CPU decides which operation to perform by "decoding" the opcode. A complete machine language instruction consists of an opcode and, in many cases, additional bits that specify arguments for the operation (for example, the numbers to be summed in the case of an addition operation). Going up the complexity scale, a machine language program is a collection of machine language instructions that the CPU executes.

The actual mathematical operation for each instruction is performed by a combinational logic circuit within the CPU's processor known as the arithmetic logic unit or ALU. In general, a CPU executes an instruction by fetching it from memory, using its ALU to perform an operation, and then storing the result to memory. Beside the instructions for integer mathematics and logic operations, various other machine instructions exist, such as those for loading data from memory and storing it back, branching operations, and mathematical operations on floating-point numbers performed by the CPU's floating-point unit (FPU).

Control Unit

The control unit (CU) is a component of the CPU that directs the operation of the processor. It tells the computer's memory, arithmetic and logic unit and input and output devices how to respond to the instructions that have been sent to the processor.

It directs the operation of the other units by providing timing and control signals. Most computer resources are managed by the CU. It directs the flow of data between the CPU and the other devices.

John von Neumann included the control unit as part of the von Neumann architecture. In modern computer designs, the control unit is typically an internal part of the CPU with its overall role and operation unchanged since its introduction.

Arithmetic Logic Unit

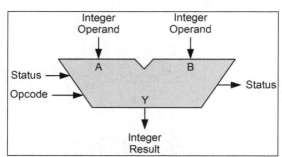

Symbolic representation of an ALU and its input and output signals.

The arithmetic logic unit (ALU) is a digital circuit within the processor that performs integer arithmetic and bitwise logic operations. The inputs to the ALU are the data words to be operated on (called operands), status information from previous operations, and a code from the control unit indicating which operation to perform. Depending on the instruction being executed, the operands may come from internal CPU registers or external memory, or they may be constants generated by the ALU itself.

When all input signals have settled and propagated through the ALU circuitry, the result of the performed operation appears at the ALU's outputs. The result consists of both a data word, which may be stored in a register or memory, and status information that is typically stored in a special, internal CPU register reserved for this purpose.

Address Generation Unit

Address generation unit (AGU), sometimes also called address computation unit (ACU), is an execution unit inside the CPU that calculates addresses used by the CPU to access main memory. By having address calculations handled by separate circuitry that operates in parallel with the rest of the CPU, the number of CPU cycles required for executing various machine instructions can be reduced, bringing performance improvements.

While performing various operations, CPUs need to calculate memory addresses required for fetching data from the memory; for example, in-memory positions of array elements must be calculated before the CPU can fetch the data from actual memory locations. Those address-generation calculations involve different integer arithmetic operations, such as addition, subtraction, modulo operations, or bit shifts. Often, calculating a memory address involves more than one general-purpose machine instruction, which do not necessarily decode and execute quickly. By incorporating an AGU into a CPU design, together with introducing specialized instructions that use the AGU, various address-generation calculations can be offloaded from the rest of the CPU, and can often be executed quickly in a single CPU cycle.

Capabilities of an AGU depend on a particular CPU and its architecture. Thus, some AGUs implement and expose more address-calculation operations, while some also include more advanced specialized instructions that can operate on multiple operands at a time. Furthermore, some CPU architectures include multiple AGUs so more than one address-calculation operation can be executed simultaneously, bringing further performance improvements by capitalizing on the superscalar nature of advanced CPU designs. For example, Intel incorporates multiple AGUs into its Sandy Bridge and Haswell microarchitectures, which increase bandwidth of the CPU memory subsystem by allowing multiple memory-access instructions to be executed in parallel.

Memory Management Unit (MMU)

Most high-end microprocessors (in desktop, laptop, server computers) have a memory management unit, translating logical addresses into physical RAM addresses, providing memory protection and paging abilities, useful for virtual memory. Simpler processors, especially microcontrollers, usually don't include an MMU.

Cache

A CPU cache is a hardware cache used by the central processing unit (CPU) of a computer to reduce the average cost (time or energy) to access data from the main memory. A cache is a smaller, faster memory, closer to a processor core, which stores copies of the data from frequently used main memory locations. Most CPUs have different independent caches, including instruction and data caches, where the data cache is usually organized as a hierarchy of more cache levels (L1, L2, L3, L4, etc.).

All modern (fast) CPUs (with few specialized exceptions) have multiple levels of CPU caches. The first CPUs that used a cache had only one level of cache; unlike later level 1 caches, it was not split into L1d (for data) and L1i (for instructions). Almost all current CPUs with caches have a split L1 cache. They also have L2 caches and, for larger processors, L3 caches as well. The L2 cache is usually not split and acts as a common repository for the already split L1 cache. Every core of a multi-core processor has a dedicated L2 cache and is usually not shared between the cores. The L3 cache, and higher-level caches, are shared between the cores and are not split. An L4 cache is currently uncommon, and is generally on dynamic random-access memory (DRAM), rather than on static random-access memory (SRAM), on a separate die or chip. That was also the case historically with L1, while bigger chips have allowed integration of it and generally all cache levels, with the possible exception of the last level. Each extra level of cache tends to be bigger and be optimized differently.

Other types of caches exist (that are not counted towards the "cache size" of the most important caches mentioned above), such as the translation lookaside buffer (TLB) that is part of the memory management unit (MMU) that most CPUs have.

Caches are generally sized in powers of two: 4, 8, 16 etc. KiB or MiB (for larger non-L1) sizes, although the IBM z13 has a 96 KiB L1 instruction cache.

Clock Rate

Most CPUs are synchronous circuits, which means they employ a clock signal to pace their sequential operations. The clock signal is produced by an external oscillator circuit that generates a consistent number of pulses each second in the form of a periodic square wave. The frequency of the clock pulses determines the rate at which a CPU executes instructions and, consequently, the faster the clock, the more instructions the CPU will execute each second.

To ensure proper operation of the CPU, the clock period is longer than the maximum time needed for all signals to propagate (move) through the CPU. In setting the clock period to a value well above the worst-case propagation delay, it is possible to design the entire CPU and the way it moves data around the "edges" of the rising and falling clock signal. This has the advantage of simplifying the CPU significantly, both from a design perspective and a component-count perspective. However, it also carries the disadvantage that the entire CPU must wait on its slowest elements, even though some portions of it are much faster. This limitation has largely been compensated for by various methods of increasing CPU parallelism.

However, architectural improvements alone do not solve all of the drawbacks of globally synchronous CPUs. For example, a clock signal is subject to the delays of any other electrical signal. Higher clock rates in increasingly complex CPUs make it more difficult to keep the clock signal in phase (synchronized) throughout the entire unit. This has led many modern CPUs to require multiple identical clock signals to be provided to avoid delaying a single signal significantly enough to cause the CPU to malfunction. Another major issue, as clock rates increase dramatically, is the amount of heat that is dissipated by the CPU. The constantly changing clock causes many components to switch regardless of whether they are being used at that time. In general, a component that is switching uses more energy than an element in a static state. Therefore, as clock rate increases, so does energy consumption, causing the CPU to require more heat dissipation in the form of CPU cooling solutions.

One method of dealing with the switching of unneeded components is called clock gating, which involves turning off the clock signal to unneeded components (effectively disabling them). However, this is often regarded as difficult to implement and therefore does not see common usage outside of very low-power designs. One notable recent CPU design that uses extensive clock gating is the IBM PowerPC-based Xenon used in the Xbox 360; that way, power requirements of the Xbox 360 are greatly reduced. Another method of addressing some of the problems with a global clock signal is the removal of the clock signal altogether. While removing the global clock signal makes the design process considerably more complex in many ways, asynchronous (or clockless) designs carry marked advantages in power consumption and heat dissipation in comparison with similar synchronous designs. While somewhat uncommon, entire asynchronous CPUs have been built without using a global clock signal. Two notable examples of this are the ARM compliant AMULET and the MIPS R3000 compatible MiniMIPS.

Rather than totally removing the clock signal, some CPU designs allow certain portions of the device to be asynchronous, such as using asynchronous ALUs in conjunction with superscalar pipelining to achieve some arithmetic performance gains. While it is not altogether clear whether totally asynchronous designs can perform at a comparable or better level than their synchronous counterparts, it is evident that they do at least excel in simpler math operations. This, combined with their excellent power consumption and heat dissipation properties, makes them very suitable for embedded computers.

Integer Range

Every CPU represents numerical values in a specific way. For example, some early digital computers represented numbers as familiar decimal (base 10) numeral system values, and others have employed more unusual representations such as ternary (base three). Nearly all modern CPUs represent numbers in binary form, with each digit being represented by some two-valued physical quantity such as a "high" or "low" voltage.

32s	16s	8s	4s	2s	1s
1	0	1	0	0	0

A six-bit word containing the binary encoded representation of decimal value 40. Most modern CPUs employ word sizes that are a power of two, for example 8, 16, 32 or 64 bits.

Related to numeric representation is the size and precision of integer numbers that a CPU can represent. In the case of a binary CPU, this is measured by the number of bits (significant digits of a binary encoded integer) that the CPU can process in one operation, which is commonly called word size, bit width, data path width, integer precision, or integer size. A CPU's integer size determines the range of integer values it can directly operate on. For example, an 8-bit CPU can directly manipulate integers represented by eight bits, which have a range of 256 (2^8) discrete integer values.

Integer range can also affect the number of memory locations the CPU can directly address (an address is an integer value representing a specific memory location). For example, if a binary CPU uses 32 bits to represent a memory address then it can directly address 2^{32} memory locations. To circumvent this limitation and for various other reasons, some CPUs use mechanisms (such as bank switching) that allow additional memory to be addressed.

CPUs with larger word sizes require more circuitry and consequently are physically larger, cost more and consume more power (and therefore generate more heat). As a result, smaller 4- or 8-bit microcontrollers are commonly used in modern applications even though CPUs with much larger word sizes (such as 16, 32, 64, even 128-bit) are available. When higher performance is required, however, the benefits of a larger word size (larger data ranges and address spaces) may outweigh the disadvantages. A CPU can have internal data paths shorter than the word size to reduce size and cost. For example, even though the IBM System/360 instruction set was a 32-bit instruction set, the System/360 Model 30 and Model 40 had 8-bit data paths in the arithmetic logical unit, so that a 32-bit add required four cycles, one for each 8 bits of the operands, and, even though the Motorola 68000 series instruction set was a 32-bit instruction set, the Motorola 68000 and Motorola 68010 had 16-bit data paths in the arithmetic logical unit, so that a 32-bit add required two cycles.

To gain some of the advantages afforded by both lower and higher bit lengths, many instruction sets have different bit widths for integer and floating-point data, allowing CPUs implementing that instruction set to have different bit widths for different portions of the device. For example, the IBM System/360 instruction set was primarily 32 bit, but supported 64-bit floating point values to facilitate greater accuracy and range in floating point numbers. The System/360 Model 65 had an 8-bit adder for decimal and fixed-point binary arithmetic and a 60-bit adder for floating-point arithmetic. Many later CPU designs use similar mixed bit width, especially when the processor is meant for general-purpose usage where a reasonable balance of integer and floating point capability is required.

Parallelism

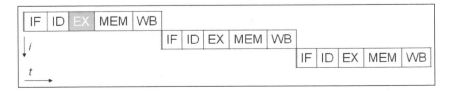

Model of a subscalar CPU, in which it takes fifteen clock cycles to complete three instructions.

The description of the basic operation of a CPU offered in the previous section describes the simplest form that a CPU can take. This type of CPU, usually referred to as *subscalar*, operates on and executes one instruction on one or two pieces of data at a time, that is less than one instruction per clock cycle (IPC < 1).

This process gives rise to an inherent inefficiency in subscalar CPUs. Since only one instruction is executed at a time, the entire CPU must wait for that instruction to complete before proceeding to the next instruction. As a result, the subscalar CPU gets "hung up" on instructions which take more than one clock cycle to complete execution. Even adding a second execution unit does not improve performance much; rather than one pathway being hung up, now two pathways are hung up and the number of unused transistors is increased. This design, wherein the CPU's execution resources can operate on only one instruction at a time, can only possibly reach scalar performance (one instruction per clock cycle, IPC = 1). However, the performance is nearly always subscalar (less than one instruction per clock cycle, IPC < 1).

Attempts to achieve scalar and better performance have resulted in a variety of design methodologies that cause the CPU to behave less linearly and more in parallel. When referring to parallelism in CPUs, two terms are generally used to classify these design techniques:

Instruction-level parallelism (ILP), which seeks to increase the rate at which instructions are executed within a CPU (that is, to increase the use of on-die execution resources); task-level parallelism (TLP), which purposes to increase the number of threads or processes that a CPU can execute simultaneously.

Each methodology differs both in the ways in which they are implemented, as well as the relative effectiveness they afford in increasing the CPU's performance for an application.

Instruction-level Parallelism

Basic five-stage pipeline. In the best case scenario, this pipeline can sustain a completion rate of one instruction per clock cycle.

One of the simplest methods used to accomplish increased parallelism is to begin the first steps of instruction fetching and decoding before the prior instruction finishes executing. This is the simplest form of a technique known as instruction pipelining, and is used in almost all modern general-purpose CPUs. Pipelining allows more than one instruction to be executed at any given time by breaking down the execution pathway into discrete stages. This separation can be compared to an assembly line, in which an instruction is made more complete at each stage until it exits the execution pipeline and is retired.

Pipelining does, however, introduce the possibility for a situation where the result of the previous operation is needed to complete the next operation; a condition often termed data dependency conflict. To cope with this, additional care must be taken to check for these sorts of conditions and delay a portion of the instruction pipeline if this occurs. Naturally, accomplishing this requires additional circuitry, so pipelined processors are more complex than subscalar ones (though not very significantly so). A pipelined processor can become very nearly scalar, inhibited only by pipeline stalls (an instruction spending more than one clock cycle in a stage).

IF	ID	EX	MEM	WB				
IF	ID	EX	MEM	WB				
	IF	ID	EX	MEM	WB			
	IF	ID	EX	MEM	WB			
		IF	ID	EX	MEM	WB		
		IF	ID	EX	MEM	WB		
			IF	ID	EX	MEM	WB	
			IF	ID	EX	MEM	WB	
				IF	ID	EX	MEM	WB
				IF	ID	EX	MEM	WB

A simple superscalar pipeline. By fetching and dispatching two instructions at a time, a maximum of two instructions per clock cycle can be completed.

Further improvement upon the idea of instruction pipelining led to the development of a method that decreases the idle time of CPU components even further. Designs that are said to be superscalar include a long instruction pipeline and multiple identical execution units, such as load-store units, arithmetic-logic units, floating-point units and address generation units. In a superscalar pipeline, multiple instructions are read and passed to a dispatcher, which decides whether or not the instructions can be executed in parallel (simultaneously). If so they are dispatched to available execution units, resulting in the ability for several instructions to be executed simultaneously. In general, the more instructions a superscalar CPU is able to dispatch simultaneously to waiting execution units, the more instructions will be completed in a given cycle.

Most of the difficulty in the design of a superscalar CPU architecture lies in creating an effective dispatcher. The dispatcher needs to be able to quickly and correctly determine whether instructions can be executed in parallel, as well as dispatch them in such a way as to keep as many execution units busy as possible. This requires that the instruction pipeline is filled as often as possible and gives rise to the need in superscalar architectures for significant amounts of CPU cache. It also makes hazard-avoiding techniques like branch prediction, speculative execution, register renaming, out-of-order execution and transactional memory crucial to maintaining high levels of performance. By attempting to predict which branch (or path) a conditional instruction will take, the CPU can minimize the number of times that the entire pipeline must wait until a conditional instruction is completed. Speculative execution often provides modest performance increases by executing portions of code that may not be needed after a conditional operation completes. Out-of-order execution somewhat rearranges the order in which instructions are executed to reduce delays due to data dependencies. Also in case of single instruction stream, multiple data stream—a case when a lot of data from the same type has to be processed — modern processors can disable parts of the pipeline so that when a single instruction is executed many times, the CPU skips the fetch and decode phases and thus greatly increases performance on certain occasions, especially in highly monotonous program engines such as video creation software and photo processing.

In the case where a portion of the CPU is superscalar and part is not, the part which is not suffers a performance penalty due to scheduling stalls. The Intel P5 Pentium had two superscalar ALUs which could accept one instruction per clock cycle each, but its FPU could not accept one instruction per clock cycle. Thus the P5 was integer superscalar but not floating point superscalar. Intel's successor to the P5 architecture, P6, added superscalar capabilities to its floating point features, and therefore afforded a significant increase in floating point instruction performance.

Both simple pipelining and superscalar design increase a CPU's ILP by allowing a single processor to complete execution of instructions at rates surpassing one instruction per clock cycle. Most modern CPU designs are at least somewhat superscalar, and nearly all general purpose CPUs designed in the last decade are superscalar. In later years some of the emphasis in designing high-ILP computers has been moved out of the CPU's hardware and into its software interface, or ISA. The strategy of the very long instruction word (VLIW) causes some ILP to become implied directly by the software, reducing the amount of work the CPU must perform to boost ILP and thereby reducing the design's complexity.

Task-level Parallelism

Another strategy of achieving performance is to execute multiple threads or processes in parallel. This area of research is known as parallel computing. In Flynn's taxonomy, this strategy is known as multiple instruction stream, multiple data stream (MIMD).

One technology used for this purpose was multiprocessing (MP). The initial flavor of this technology is known as symmetric multiprocessing (SMP), where a small number of CPUs share a coherent view of their memory system. In this scheme, each CPU has additional hardware to maintain a constantly up-to-date view of memory. By avoiding stale views of memory, the CPUs can cooperate on the same program and programs can migrate from one CPU to another. To increase the number of cooperating CPUs beyond a handful, schemes such as non-uniform memory access (NUMA) and directory-based coherence protocols were introduced in the 1990s. SMP systems are limited to a small number of CPUs while NUMA systems have been built with thousands of processors. Initially, multiprocessing was built using multiple discrete CPUs and boards to implement the interconnect between the processors. When the processors and their interconnect are all implemented on a single chip, the technology is known as chip-level multiprocessing (CMP) and the single chip as a multi-core processor.

It was later recognized that finer-grain parallelism existed with a single program. A single program might have several threads (or functions) that could be executed separately or in parallel. Some of the earliest examples of this technology implemented input/output processing such as direct memory access as a separate thread from the computation thread. A more general approach to this technology was introduced in the 1970s when systems were designed to run multiple computation threads in parallel. This technology is known as multi-threading (MT). This approach is considered more cost-effective than multiprocessing, as only a small number of components within a

CPU is replicated to support MT as opposed to the entire CPU in the case of MP. In MT, the execution units and the memory system including the caches are shared among multiple threads. The downside of MT is that the hardware support for multithreading is more visible to software than that of MP and thus supervisor software like operating systems have to undergo larger changes to support MT. One type of MT that was implemented is known as temporal multithreading, where one thread is executed until it is stalled waiting for data to return from external memory. In this scheme, the CPU would then quickly context switch to another thread which is ready to run, the switch often done in one CPU clock cycle, such as the UltraSPARC T1. Another type of MT is simultaneous multithreading, where instructions from multiple threads are executed in parallel within one CPU clock cycle.

For several decades from the 1970s to early 2000s, the focus in designing high performance general purpose CPUs was largely on achieving high ILP through technologies such as pipelining, caches, superscalar execution, out-of-order execution, etc. This trend culminated in large, power-hungry CPUs such as the Intel Pentium 4. By the early 2000s, CPU designers were thwarted from achieving higher performance from ILP techniques due to the growing disparity between CPU operating frequencies and main memory operating frequencies as well as escalating CPU power dissipation owing to more esoteric ILP techniques.

CPU designers then borrowed ideas from commercial computing markets such as transaction processing, where the aggregate performance of multiple programs, also known as throughput computing, was more important than the performance of a single thread or process.

This reversal of emphasis is evidenced by the proliferation of dual and more core processor designs and notably, Intel's newer designs resembling its less superscalar P6 architecture. Late designs in several processor families exhibit CMP, including the x86-64 Opteron and Athlon 64 X2, the SPARC UltraSPARC T1, IBM POWER4 and POWER5, as well as several video game console CPUs like the Xbox 360's triple-core PowerPC design, and the PlayStation 3's 7-core Cell microprocessor.

Data Parallelism

A less common but increasingly important paradigm of processors (and indeed, computing in general) deals with data parallelism. The processors discussed earlier are all referred to as some type of scalar device. As the name implies, vector processors deal with multiple pieces of data in the context of one instruction. This contrasts with scalar processors, which deal with one piece of data for every instruction. Using Flynn's taxonomy, these two schemes of dealing with data are generally referred to as single instruction stream, multiple data stream (SIMD) and single instruction stream, single data stream (SISD), respectively. The great utility in creating processors that deal with vectors of data lies in optimizing tasks that tend to require the same operation (for example, a sum or a dot product) to be performed on a large set of data. Some classic examples of these types of tasks include multimedia applications (images, video and sound), as well as many types of scientific and engineering tasks. Whereas a scalar processor must complete the entire process of fetching, decoding and executing each instruction and value in a set of data, a vector processor can perform a single operation on a comparatively large set of data with one instruction. This is only possible when the application tends to require many steps which apply one operation to a large set of data.

Most early vector processors, such as the Cray-1, were associated almost exclusively with scientific research and cryptography applications. However, as multimedia has largely shifted to digital media, the need for some form of SIMD in general-purpose processors has become significant. Shortly after inclusion of floating-point units started to become commonplace in general-purpose processors, specifications for and implementations of SIMD execution units also began to appear for general-purpose processors. Some of these early SIMD specifications - like HP's Multimedia Acceleration eXtensions (MAX) and Intel's MMX - were integer-only. This proved to be a significant impediment for some software developers, since many of the applications that benefit from SIMD primarily deal with floating-point numbers. Progressively, developers refined and remade these early designs into some of the common modern SIMD specifications, which are usually associated with one ISA. Some notable modern examples include Intel's SSE and the PowerPC-related AltiVec (also known as VMX).

Virtual CPUs

Cloud computing can involve subdividing CPU operation into virtual central processing units (vCPUs).

A host is the virtual equivalent of a physical machine, on which a virtual system is operating. When there are several physical machines operating in tandem and managed as a whole, the grouped computing and memory resources form a cluster. In some systems, it is possible to dynamically add and remove from a cluster. Resources available at a host and cluster level can be partitioned out into resources pools with fine granularity.

Performance

The performance or speed of a processor depends on, among many other factors, the clock rate (generally given in multiples of hertz) and the instructions per clock (IPC), which together are the factors for the instructions per second (IPS) that the CPU can perform. Many reported IPS values have represented "peak" execution rates on artificial instruction sequences with few branches, whereas realistic workloads consist of a mix of instructions and applications, some of which take longer to execute than others. The performance of the memory hierarchy also greatly affects processor performance, an issue barely considered in MIPS calculations. Because of these problems, various standardized tests, often called "benchmarks" for this purpose—such as SPECint—have been developed to attempt to measure the real effective performance in commonly used applications.

Processing performance of computers is increased by using multi-core processors, which essentially is plugging two or more individual processors (called cores in this sense) into one integrated circuit. Ideally, a dual core processor would be nearly twice as powerful as a single core processor. In practice, the performance gain is far smaller, only about 50%, due to imperfect software algorithms and implementation. Increasing the number of cores in a processor (i.e. dual-core, quad-core, etc.) increases the workload that can be handled. This means that the processor can now handle numerous asynchronous events, interrupts, etc. which can take a toll on the CPU when overwhelmed. These cores can be thought of as different floors in a processing plant, with each floor handling a different task. Sometimes, these cores will handle the same tasks as cores adjacent to them if a single core is not enough to handle the information.

Due to specific capabilities of modern CPUs, such as simultaneous multithreading and uncore, which involve sharing of actual CPU resources while aiming at increased utilization, monitoring performance levels and hardware use gradually became a more complex task. As a response, some CPUs implement additional hardware logic that monitors actual use of various parts of a CPU and provides various counters accessible to software; an example is Intel's Performance Counter Monitor technology.

GPU

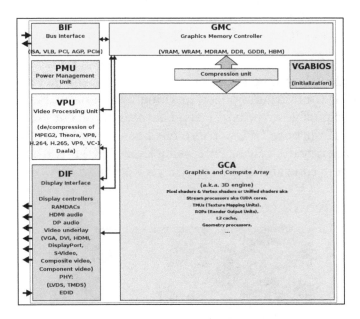

Components of a GPU

A graphics processing unit (GPU) is a specialized electronic circuit designed to rapidly manipulate and alter memory to accelerate the creation of images in a frame buffer intended for output to a display device. GPUs are used in embedded systems, mobile phones, personal computers, work-stations, and game consoles. Modern GPUs are very efficient at manipulating computer graphics and image processing. Their highly parallel structure makes them more efficient than general-pur-pose central processing units (CPUs) for algorithms that process large blocks of data in parallel. In a personal computer, a GPU can be present on a video card or embedded on the motherboard. In certain CPUs, they are embedded on the CPU die.

The term "GPU" was coined by Sony in reference to the PlayStation console's Toshiba-designed Sony GPU in 1994. The term was popularized by Nvidia in 1999, who marketed the GeForce 256 as "the world's first GPU". It was presented as a "single-chip processor with integrated transform, lighting, triangle setup/clipping, and rendering engines". Rival ATI Technologies coined the term "visual processing unit" or VPU with the release of the Radeon 9700 in 2002.

Computational Functions

Modern GPUs use most of their transistors to do calculations related to 3D computer graph-ics. In addition to the 3D hardware, today's GPUs include basic 2D acceleration and frame-buffer capabilities (usually with a VGA compatibility mode). Newer cards such as AMD/ATI

HD5000-HD7000 even lack 2D acceleration; it has to be emulated by 3D hardware. GPUs were initially used to accelerate the memory-intensive work of texture mapping and rendering polygons, later adding units to accelerate geometric calculations such as the rotation and translation of vertices into different coordinate systems. Recent developments in GPUs include support for programmable shaders which can manipulate vertices and textures with many of the same operations supported by CPUs, oversampling and interpolation techniques to reduce aliasing, and very high-precision color spaces. Because most of these computations involve matrix and vector operations, engineers and scientists have increasingly studied the use of GPUs for non-graphical calculations; they are especially suited to other embarrassingly parallel problems.

With the emergence of deep learning, the importance of GPUs has increased. In research done by Indigo, it was found that while training deep learning neural networks, GPUs can be 250 times faster than CPUs. The explosive growth of Deep Learning in recent years has been attributed to the emergence of general purpose GPUs. There has been some level of competition in this area with ASICs, most prominently the Tensor Processing Unit (TPU) made by Google. However, ASICs require changes to existing code and GPUs are still very popular.

GPU Accelerated Video Decoding

The ATI HD5470 GPU (above) features UVD 2.1 which enables it to decode AVC and VC-1 video formats.

Most GPUs made since 1995 support the YUV color space and hardware overlays, important for digital video playback, and many GPUs made since 2000 also support MPEG primitives such as motion compensation and iDCT. This process of hardware accelerated video decoding, where portions of the video decoding process and video post-processing are offloaded to the GPU hardware, is commonly referred to as "GPU accelerated video decoding", "GPU assisted video decoding", "GPU hardware accelerated video decoding" or "GPU hardware assisted video decoding".

More recent graphics cards even decode high-definition video on the card, offloading the central processing unit. The most common APIs for GPU accelerated video decoding are DxVA for Microsoft Windows operating system and VDPAU, VAAPI, XvMC, and XvBA for Linux-based and UNIX-like operating systems. All except XvMC are capable of decoding videos encoded with MPEG-1, MPEG-2, MPEG-4 ASP (MPEG-4 Part 2), MPEG-4 AVC (H.264 / DivX 6), VC-1, WMV3/WMV9, Xvid / OpenDivX (DivX 4), and DivX 5 codecs, while XvMC is only capable of decoding MPEG-1 and MPEG-2.

Video Decoding Processes that can be Accelerated

The video decoding processes that can be accelerated by today's modern GPU hardware are:

- Motion compensation (mocomp).

- Inverse discrete cosine transform (iDCT).

- Inverse telecine 3:2 and 2:2 pull-down correction.

- Inverse modified discrete cosine transform (iMDCT).

- In-loop deblocking filter.

- Intra-frame prediction.

- Inverse quantization (IQ).

- Variable-length decoding (VLD), more commonly known as slice-level acceleration.

- Spatial-temporal deinterlacing and automatic interlace/progressive source detection.

- Bitstream processing (Context-adaptive variable-length coding/Context-adaptive binary arithmetic coding) and perfect pixel positioning.

GPU Forms

Dedicated Graphics Cards

The GPUs of the most powerful class typically interface with the motherboard by means of an expansion slot such as PCI Express (PCIe) or Accelerated Graphics Port (AGP) and can usually be replaced or upgraded with relative ease, assuming the motherboard is capable of supporting the upgrade. A few graphics cards still use Peripheral Component Interconnect (PCI) slots, but their bandwidth is so limited that they are generally used only when a PCIe or AGP slot is not available.

A dedicated GPU is not necessarily removable, nor does it necessarily interface with the motherboard in a standard fashion. The term "dedicated" refers to the fact that dedicated graphics cards have RAM that is dedicated to the card's use, not to the fact that *most* dedicated GPUs are removable. Further, this RAM is usually specially selected for the expected serial workload of the graphics card. Sometimes, systems with dedicated, *discrete* GPUs were called "DIS" systems, as opposed to "UMA" systems. Dedicated GPUs for portable computers are most commonly interfaced through a non-standard and often proprietary slot due to size and weight constraints. Such ports may still be considered PCIe or AGP in terms of their logical host interface, even if they are not physically interchangeable with their counterparts.

Technologies such as SLI by Nvidia and CrossFire by AMD allow multiple GPUs to draw images simultaneously for a single screen, increasing the processing power available for graphics.

Integrated Graphics Processing Unit

Integrated graphics processing unit (IGPU), Integrated graphics, shared graphics solutions, integrated graphics processors (IGP) or unified memory architecture (UMA) utilize a portion of a computer's system RAM rather than dedicated graphics memory. IGPs can be integrated onto the motherboard as part of the chipset, or on the same die with the CPU (like AMD APU or Intel HD Graphics). On certain motherboards, AMD's IGPs can use dedicated sideport memory. This is a separate fixed block of high performance memory that is dedicated for use by the GPU. In early 2007, computers with integrated graphics account for about 90% of all PC shipments. They are less costly to implement than dedicated graphics processing, but tend to be less capable. Historically, integrated processing was considered unfit to play 3D games or run graphically intensive programs but could run less intensive programs such as Adobe Flash. Examples of such IGPs would be offerings from SiS and VIA circa 2004. However, modern integrated graphics processors such as AMD Accelerated Processing Unit and Intel HD Graphics are more than capable of handling 2D graphics or low stress 3D graphics.

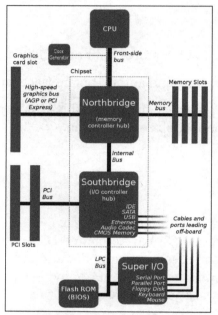

The position of an integrated GPU in a northbridge/southbridge system layout

An ASRock motherboard with integrated graphics, which has HDMI, VGA and DVI outs.

Since the GPU computations are extremely memory-intensive, integrated processing may find itself competing with the CPU for the relatively slow system RAM, as it has minimal or no dedicated video memory. IGPs can have up to 29.856 GB/s of memory bandwidth from system RAM, whereas a graphics card may have up to 264 GB/s of bandwidth between its RAM and GPU core. This memory bus bandwidth can limit the performance of the GPU, though multi-channel memory can mitigate this deficiency. Older integrated graphics chipsets lacked hardware transform and lighting, but newer ones include it.

Hybrid Graphics Processing

This newer class of GPUs competes with integrated graphics in the low-end desktop and notebook markets. The most common implementations of this are ATI's HyperMemory and Nvidia's TurboCache.

Hybrid graphics cards are somewhat more expensive than integrated graphics, but much less expensive than dedicated graphics cards. These share memory with the system and have a small dedicated memory cache, to make up for the high latency of the system RAM. Technologies within PCI Express can make this possible. While these solutions are sometimes advertised as having as much as 768MB of RAM, this refers to how much can be shared with the system memory.

Stream Processing and General Purpose GPUs (GPGPU)

It is becoming increasingly common to use a general purpose graphics processing unit (GPGPU) as a modified form of stream processor (or a vector processor), running compute kernels. This concept turns the massive computational power of a modern graphics accelerator's shader pipeline into general-purpose computing power, as opposed to being hard wired solely to do graphical operations. In certain applications requiring massive vector operations, this can yield several orders of magnitude higher performance than a conventional CPU. The two largest discrete GPU designers, AMD and Nvidia, are beginning to pursue this approach with an array of applications. Both Nvidia and AMD have teamed with Stanford University to create a GPU-based client for the Folding@home distributed computing project, for protein folding calculations. In certain circumstances, the GPU calculates forty times faster than the CPUs traditionally used by such applications.

GPGPU can be used for many types of embarrassingly parallel tasks including ray tracing. They are generally suited to high-throughput type computations that exhibit data-parallelism to exploit the wide vector width SIMD architecture of the GPU.

Furthermore, GPU-based high performance computers are starting to play a significant role in large-scale modelling. Three of the 10 most powerful supercomputers in the world take advantage of GPU acceleration.

GPU supports API extensions to the C programming language such as OpenCL and OpenMP. Furthermore, each GPU vendor introduced its own API which only works with their cards, AMD APP SDK and CUDA from AMD and Nvidia, respectively. These technologies allow specified functions called compute kernels from a normal C program to run on the GPU's stream processors. This makes it possible for C programs to take advantage of a GPU's ability to operate on large buffers in parallel, while still using the CPU when appropriate. CUDA is also the first API to allow CPU-based applications to directly access the resources of a GPU for more general purpose computing without the limitations of using a graphics API.

Since 2005 there has been interest in using the performance offered by GPUs for evolutionary computation in general, and for accelerating the fitness evaluation in genetic programming in particular. Most approaches compile linear or tree programs on the host PC and transfer the executable to the GPU to be run. Typically the performance advantage is only obtained by running the single active program simultaneously on many example problems in parallel, using the GPU's SIMD architecture. However, substantial acceleration can also be obtained by not compiling the programs, and instead transferring them to the GPU, to be interpreted there. Acceleration can then be obtained by either interpreting multiple programs simultaneously, simultaneously running multiple example problems, or combinations of both. A modern GPU can readily simultaneously interpret hundreds of thousands of very small programs.

Some modern workstation GPUs, such as the Nvidia Quadro workstation cards using the Volta and Turing architectures, feature dedicating processing cores for tensor-based deep learning applications. In Nvidia's current series of GPUs these cores are called Tensor Cores. These GPUs usually have significant FLOPS performance increases, utilizing 4x4 matrix multiplication and division, resulting in hardware performance up to 128 TFLOPS in some applications. These tensor cores are also supposed to appear in consumer cards running the Turing architecture, and possibly in the Navi series of consumer cards from AMD.

External GPU (eGPU)

An external GPU is a graphics processor located outside of the housing of the computer. External graphics processors are sometimes used with laptop computers. Laptops might have a substantial amount of RAM and a sufficiently powerful central processing unit (CPU), but often lack a powerful graphics processor, and instead have a less powerful but more energy-efficient on-board graphics chip. On-board graphics chips are often not powerful enough for playing the latest games, or for other graphically intensive tasks, such as editing video.

Therefore, it is desirable to be able to attach a GPU to some external bus of a notebook. PCI Express is the only bus commonly used for this purpose. The port may be, for example, an Express-Card or mPCIe port (PCIe ×1, up to 5 or 2.5 Gbit/s respectively) or a Thunderbolt 1, 2, or 3 port (PCIe ×4, up to 10, 20, or 40 Gbit/s respectively). Those ports are only available on certain notebook systems.

Official vendor support for External GPUs has gained traction recently. One notable milestone was Apple's decision to officially support External GPUs with mac OS High Sierra 10.13.4. There are also several major hardware vendors (HP, Alienware, Razer) releasing Thunderbolt 3 eGPU enclosures. This support has continued to fuel eGPU implementations by enthusiasts.

In 2013, 438.3 million GPUs were shipped globally and the forecast for 2014 was 414.2 million.

ALU

An arithmetic logic unit (ALU) is a combinational digital electronic circuit that performs arithmetic and bitwise operations on integer binary numbers. This is in contrast to a floating-point unit (FPU), which operates on floating point numbers. An ALU is a fundamental building block of many types of computing circuits, including the central processing unit (CPU) of computers, FPUs, and graphics processing units (GPUs). A single CPU, FPU or GPU may contain multiple ALUs.

The inputs to an ALU are the data to be operated on, called operands, and a code indicating the operation to be performed; the ALU's output is the result of the performed operation. In many designs, the ALU also has status inputs or outputs, or both, which convey information about a previous operation or the current operation, respectively, between the ALU and external status registers.

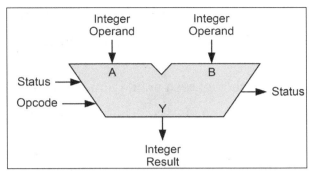

A symbolic representation of an ALU and its input and output signals, indicated by arrows pointing into or out of the ALU, respectively. Each arrow represents one or more signals. Control signals enter from the left and status signals exit on the right; data flows from top to bottom.

Signals

An ALU has a variety of input and output nets, which are the electrical conductors used to convey digital signals between the ALU and external circuitry. When an ALU is operating, external circuits apply signals to the ALU inputs and, in response, the ALU produces and conveys signals to external circuitry via its outputs.

Data

A basic ALU has three parallel data buses consisting of two input operands (*A* and *B*) and a result output (*Y*). Each data bus is a group of signals that conveys one binary integer number. Typically, the A, B and Y bus widths (the number of signals comprising each bus) are identical and match the native word size of the external circuitry (e.g., the encapsulating CPU or other processor).

Opcode

The *opcode* input is a parallel bus that conveys to the ALU an operation selection code, which is an enumerated value that specifies the desired arithmetic or logic operation to be performed by the ALU. The opcode size (its bus width) determines the maximum number of different operations the ALU can perform; for example, a four-bit opcode can specify up to sixteen different ALU operations. Generally, an ALU opcode is not the same as a machine language opcode, though in some cases it may be directly encoded as a bit field within a machine language opcode.

Status

Outputs

The status outputs are various individual signals that convey supplemental information about the result of the current ALU operation. General-purpose ALUs commonly have status signals such as:

- *Carry-out*, which conveys the carry resulting from an addition operation, the borrow resulting from a subtraction operation, or the overflow bit resulting from a binary shift operation.

- Zero, which indicates all bits of Y are logic zero.

- Negative, which indicates the result of an arithmetic operation is negative.

- Overflow, which indicates the result of an arithmetic operation has exceeded the numeric range of Y.

- Parity, which indicates whether an even or odd number of bits in Y are logic one.

At the end of each ALU operation, the status output signals are usually stored in external registers to make them available for future ALU operations (e.g., to implement multiple-precision arithmetic) or for controlling conditional branching. The collection of bit registers that store the status outputs are often treated as a single, multi-bit register, which is referred to as the "status register" or "condition code register".

Inputs

The status inputs allow additional information to be made available to the ALU when performing an operation. Typically, this is a single "carry-in" bit that is the stored carry-out from a previous ALU operation.

Circuit Operation

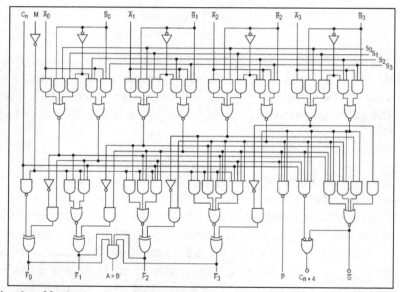

The combinational logic circuitry of the 74181 integrated circuit, which is a simple four-bit ALU.

An ALU is a combinational logic circuit, meaning that its outputs will change asynchronously in response to input changes. In normal operation, stable signals are applied to all of the ALU inputs and, when enough time (known as the "propagation delay") has passed for the signals to propagate through the ALU circuitry, the result of the ALU operation appears at the ALU outputs. The external circuitry connected to the ALU is responsible for ensuring the stability of ALU input signals throughout the operation, and for allowing sufficient time for the signals to propagate through the ALU before sampling the ALU result.

In general, external circuitry controls an ALU by applying signals to its inputs. Typically, the external circuitry employs sequential logic to control the ALU operation, which is paced by a clock signal of a sufficiently low frequency to ensure enough time for the ALU outputs to settle under worst-case conditions.

For example, a CPU begins an ALU addition operation by routing operands from their sources (which are usually registers) to the ALU's operand inputs, while the control unit simultaneously applies a value to the ALU's opcode input, configuring it to perform addition. At the same time, the CPU also routes the ALU result output to a destination register that will receive the sum. The ALU's input signals, which are held stable until the next clock, are allowed to propagate through the ALU and to the destination register while the CPU waits for the next clock. When the next clock arrives, the destination register stores the ALU result and, since the ALU operation has completed, the ALU inputs may be set up for the next ALU operation.

Functions

A number of basic arithmetic and bitwise logic functions are commonly supported by ALUs. Basic, general purpose ALUs typically include these operations in their repertoires:

Arithmetic Operations

- Add: A and B are summed and the sum appears at Y and carry-out.

- Add with carry: A, B and carry-in are summed and the sum appears at Y and carry-out.

- Subtract: B is subtracted from A (or vice versa) and the difference appears at Y and carry-out. For this function, carry-out is effectively a "borrow" indicator. This operation may also be used to compare the magnitudes of A and B; in such cases the Y output may be ignored by the processor, which is only interested in the status bits (particularly zero and negative) that result from the operation.

- Subtract with borrow: B is subtracted from A (or vice versa) with borrow (carry-in) and the difference appears at Y and carry-out (borrow out).

- Two's complement (negate): A (or B) is subtracted from zero and the difference appears at Y.

- Increment: A (or B) is increased by one and the resulting value appears at Y.

- Decrement: A (or B) is decreased by one and the resulting value appears at Y.

- Pass through: all bits of A (or B) appear unmodified at Y. This operation is typically used to determine the parity of the operand or whether it is zero or negative, or to load the operand into a processor register.

Bitwise Logical Operations

- AND: the bitwise AND of A and B appears at Y.

- OR: the bitwise OR of A and B appears at Y.

- Exclusive-OR: the bitwise XOR of A and B appears at Y.

- Ones' complement: all bits of A (or B) are inverted and appear at Y.

Bit Shift Operations

Bit shift examples for an eight-bit ALU		
Type	Left	Right

Arithmetic shift	MSB ... LSB
	7 6 5 4 3 2 1 0
	`0 0 0 1 0 1 1 1`
	↓↓↓↓↓↓↓↓
	`0 0 1 0 1 1 1 0` ← `0`
		MSB ... LSB
		7 6 5 4 3 2 1 0
		`1 0 0 1 0 1 1 1`
		↓↓↓↓↓↓↓↓
		`1 1 0 0 1 0 1 1`

Logical shift	MSB ... LSB
	7 6 5 4 3 2 1 0
	`0 0 0 1 0 1 1 1`
	↓↓↓↓↓↓↓↓
	`0 0 1 0 1 1 1 0` ← `0`
		MSB ... LSB
		7 6 5 4 3 2 1 0
		`0 0 0 1 0 1 1 1`
		↓↓↓↓↓↓↓↓
		`0` → `0 0 0 0 1 0 1 1`

Rotate	MSB ... LSB
	7 6 5 4 3 2 1 0
	`0 0 0 1 0 1 1 1`
	↓↓↓↓↓↓↓↓
	`0 0 1 0 1 1 1 0`
		MSB ... LSB
		7 6 5 4 3 2 1 0
		`0 0 0 1 0 1 1 1`
		↓↓↓↓↓↓↓↓
		`1 0 0 0 1 0 1 1`

Rotate through carry	MSB ... LSB
	7 6 5 4 3 2 1 0 C
	`0 0 0 1 0 1 1 1` `1`
	↓↓↓↓↓↓↓↓
	`0 0 1 0 1 1 1 0` `0`
		MSB ... LSB
		7 6 5 4 3 2 1 0 C
		`0 0 0 1 0 1 1 1` `1`
		↓↓↓↓↓↓↓↓
		`1 0 0 0 1 0 1 1` `1`

ALU shift operations cause operand A (or B) to shift left or right (depending on the opcode) and the shifted operand appears at Y. Simple ALUs typically can shift the operand by only one bit position, whereas more complex ALUs employ barrel shifters that allow them to shift the operand by an arbitrary number of bits in one operation. In all single-bit shift operations, the bit shifted out of the operand appears on carry-out; the value of the bit shifted into the operand depends on the type of shift.

- Arithmetic shift: The operand is treated as a two's complement integer, meaning that the most significant bit is a "sign" bit and is preserved.

- Logical shift: A logic zero is shifted into the operand. This is used to shift unsigned integers.

- Rotate: The operand is treated as a circular buffer of bits so its least and most significant bits are effectively adjacent.

- Rotate through carry: The carry bit and operand are collectively treated as a circular buffer of bits.

Applications

Multiple-precision Arithmetic

In integer arithmetic computations, multiple-precision arithmetic is an algorithm that operates on integers which are larger than the ALU word size. To do this, the algorithm treats each operand as an ordered collection of ALU-size fragments, arranged from most-significant (MS) to least-significant (LS) or vice versa. For example, in the case of an 8-bit ALU, the 24-bit integer 0x123456 would be treated as a collection of three 8-bit fragments: 0x12 (MS), 0x34, and 0x56 (LS). Since the size of a fragment exactly matches the ALU word size, the ALU can directly operate on this "piece" of operand.

The algorithm uses the ALU to directly operate on particular operand fragments and thus generate a corresponding fragment (a "partial") of the multi-precision result. Each partial, when generated, is written to an associated region of storage that has been designated for the multiple-precision result. This process is repeated for all operand fragments so as to generate a complete collection of partials, which is the result of the multiple-precision operation.

In arithmetic operations (e.g., addition, subtraction), the algorithm starts by invoking an ALU operation on the operands' LS fragments, thereby producing both a LS partial and a carry out bit. The algorithm writes the partial to designated storage, whereas the processor's state machine typically stores the carry out bit to an ALU status register. The algorithm then advances to the next fragment of each operand's collection and invokes an ALU operation on these fragments along with the stored carry bit from the previous ALU operation, thus producing another (more significant) partial and a carry out bit. As before, the carry bit is stored to the status register and the partial is written to designated storage. This process repeats until all operand fragments have been processed, resulting in a complete collection of partials in storage, which comprise the multi-precision arithmetic result.

In multiple-precision shift operations, the order of operand fragment processing depends on the shift direction. In left-shift operations, fragments are processed LS first because the LS bit of each partial—which is conveyed via the stored carry bit—must be obtained from the MS bit of the previously left-shifted, less-significant operand. Conversely, operands are processed MS first in right-shift operations because the MS bit of each partial must be obtained from the LS bit of the previously right-shifted, more-significant operand.

In bitwise logical operations (e.g., logical AND, logical OR), the operand fragments may be processed in any arbitrary order because each partial depends only on the corresponding operand fragments (the stored carry bit from the previous ALU operation is ignored).

Complex Operations

Although an ALU can be designed to perform complex functions, the resulting higher circuit complexity, cost, power consumption and larger size makes this impractical in many cases. Consequently, ALUs are often limited to simple functions that can be executed at very high speeds (i.e., very short propagation delays), and the external processor circuitry is responsible for performing complex functions by orchestrating a sequence of simpler ALU operations.

For example, computing the square root of a number might be implemented in various ways, depending on ALU complexity:

- Calculation in a single clock: A very complex ALU that calculates a square root in one operation.

- Calculation pipeline: A group of simple ALUs that calculates a square root in stages, with intermediate results passing through ALUs arranged like a factory production line. This circuit can accept new operands before finishing the previous ones and produces results as fast as the very complex ALU, though the results are delayed by the sum of the propagation delays of the ALU stages.

- Iterative calculation: A simple ALU that calculates the square root through several steps under the direction of a control unit.

The implementations above transition from fastest and most expensive to slowest and least costly. The square root is calculated in all cases, but processors with simple ALUs will take longer to perform the calculation because multiple ALU operations must be performed.

Implementation

An ALU is usually implemented either as a stand-alone integrated circuit (IC), such as the 74181, or as part of a more complex IC. In the latter case, an ALU is typically instantiated by synthesizing it from a description written in VHDL, Verilog or some other hardware description language. For example, the following VHDL code describes a very simple 8-bit ALU:

```
entity alu is

port ( -- the alu connections to external circuitry:

 A : in  signed(7 downto 0);   -- operand A

 B : in  signed(7 downto 0);   -- operand B

 OP : in  unsigned(2 downto 0); -- opcode

 Y : out signed(7 downto 0));  -- operation result

end alu;
architecture behavioral of alu is

begin

 case OP is  -- decode the opcode and perform the operation:

  when "000" =>  Y <= A + B;   -- add

  when "001" =>  Y <= A - B;   -- subtract

  when "010" =>  Y <= A - 1;   -- decrement

  when "011" =>  Y <= A + 1;   -- increment
```

when "100" => Y <= not A;   -- 1's complement

when "101" => Y <= A and B; -- bitwise AND

when "110" => Y <= A or B; -- bitwise OR

when "111" => Y <= A xor B; -- bitwise XOR

when others => Y <= (others => 'X');

 end case;

end behavioral.

Processor Register

In computer architecture, a processor register is a quickly accessible location available to a computer's central processing unit (CPU). Registers usually consist of a small amount of fast storage, although some registers have specific hardware functions, and may be read-only or write-only. Registers are typically addressed by mechanisms other than main memory, but may in some cases be assigned a memory address e.g. DEC PDP-10, ICT 1900.

Almost all computers, whether load/store architecture or not, load data from a larger memory into registers where it is used for arithmetic operations and is manipulated or tested by machine instructions. Manipulated data is then often stored back to main memory, either by the same instruction or by a subsequent one. Modern processors use either static or dynamic RAM as main memory, with the latter usually accessed via one or more cache levels.

Processor registers are normally at the top of the memory hierarchy, and provide the fastest way to access data. The term normally refers only to the group of registers that are directly encoded as part of an instruction, as defined by the instruction set. However, modern high-performance CPUs often have duplicates of these "architectural registers" in order to improve performance via register renaming, allowing parallel and speculative execution. Modern x86 design acquired these techniques around 1995 with the releases of Pentium Pro, Cyrix 6x86, Nx586, and AMD K5.

When a computer program accesses the same data repeatedly, this is called locality of reference. Holding frequently used values in registers can be critical to a program's performance. Register allocation is performed either by a compiler in the code generation phase, or manually by an assembly language programmer.

Register Size

Registers are normally measured by the number of bits they can hold, for example, an "8-bit register", "32-bit register" or a "64-bit register" or even more. In some instruction sets, the registers can operate in various modes breaking down its storage memory into smaller ones (32-bit into four 8-bit one for instance) to which multiple data (vector, or one dimensional array of data) can be loaded and operated upon at the same time. Typically it is implemented by adding extra registers that map their memory into bigger one. Processors that have the ability to execute single instruction on multiple data are called vector processors.

Types of Registers

A processor often contains several kinds of registers, which can be classified according to their content or instructions that operate on them:

- User-accessible registers can be read or written by machine instructions. The most common division of user-accessible registers is into data registers and address registers.

  - Data registers can hold numeric data values such as integer and, in some architectures, floating-point values, as well as characters, small bit arrays and other data. In some older and low end CPUs, a special data register, known as the accumulator, is used implicitly for many operations.

  - Address registers hold addresses and are used by instructions that indirectly access primary memory.

    - Some processors contain registers that may only be used to hold an address or only to hold numeric values (in some cases used as an index register whose value is added as an offset from some address); others allow registers to hold either kind of quantity. A wide variety of possible addressing modes, used to specify the effective address of an operand, exist.

    - The stack pointer is used to manage the run-time stack. Rarely, other data stacks are addressed by dedicated address registers.

  - General-purpose registers (GPRs) can store both data and addresses, i.e., they are combined data/address registers and rarely the register file is unified to include floating point as well.

  - Status registers hold truth values often used to determine whether some instruction should or should not be executed.

  - Floating-point registers (FPRs) store floating point numbers in many architectures.

  - Constant registers hold read-only values such as zero, one, or pi.

  - Vector registers hold data for vector processing done by SIMD instructions (Single Instruction, Multiple Data).

  - Special-purpose registers (SPRs) hold program state; they usually include the program counter, also called the instruction pointer, and the status register; the program counter and status register might be combined in a program status word (PSW) register. The aforementioned stack pointer is sometimes also included in this group. Embedded microprocessors can also have registers corresponding to specialized hardware elements.

  - In some architectures, model-specific registers (also called machine-specific registers) store data and settings related to the processor itself. Because their meanings are attached to the design of a specific processor, they cannot be expected to remain standard between processor generations.

  - Memory Type Range Registers (MTRRs).

- Internal registers: Registers not accessible by instructions, used internally for processor operations.

  - Instruction register, holding the instruction currently being executed.

  - Registers related to fetching information from RAM, a collection of storage registers located on separate chips from the CPU:

    - Memory buffer register (MBR), also known as Memory data register (MDR).

    - Memory address register (MAR).

- Architectural register: The registers visible to software defined by an architecture may not correspond to the physical hardware, if there is register renaming being performed by underlying hardware.

Hardware registers are similar, but occur outside CPUs.

In some architectures (such as SPARC and MIPS), the first or last register in the integer register file is a pseudo-register in a way that it is hardwired to always return zero when read (mostly to simplify indexing modes), and it cannot be overwritten. In Alpha this is also done for the floating-point register file. As a result of this, register files are commonly quoted as having one register more than how many of them are actually usable; for example, 32 registers are quoted when only 31 of them fit within the above definition of a register.

Control Unit

The control unit (CU) is a component of a computer's central processing unit (CPU) that directs the operation of the processor. It tells the computer's memory, arithmetic and logic unit and input and output devices how to respond to the instructions that have been sent to the processor.

It directs the operation of the other units by providing timing and control signals. Most computer resources are managed by the CU. It directs the flow of data between the CPU and the other devices. John von Neumann included the control unit as part of the von Neumann architecture. In modern computer designs, the control unit is typically an internal part of the CPU with its overall role and operation unchanged since its introduction.

Functions of the Control Unit

The Control unit (CU) is digital circuitry contained within the processor that coordinates the sequence of data movements into, out of, and between a processor's many sub-units. The result of these routed data movements through various digital circuits (sub-units) within the processor produces the manipulated data expected by a software instruction (loaded earlier, likely from memory). It controls (conducts) data flow inside the processor and additionally provides several external control signals to the rest of the computer to further direct data and instructions to/from processor external destinations (i.e. memory).

Examples of devices that require a CU are CPUs and graphics processing units (GPUs). The CU receives external instructions or commands which it converts into a sequence of control signals that the CU applies to the data path to implement a sequence of register-transfer level operations.

More precisely, the Control Unit (CU) is generally a sizable collection of complex digital circuitry interconnecting and directing the many execution units (i.e. ALU, data buffers, registers) contained within a CPU. The CU is normally the first CPU unit to accept from an externally stored computer program a single instruction (based on the CPU's instruction set). The CU then decodes this individual instruction into several sequential steps (fetching addresses/data from registers/memory, managing execution ([i.e. data sent to the ALU or I/O]), and storing the resulting data back into registers/memory) that controls and coordinates the CPU's inner works to properly manipulate the data. The design of these sequential steps is based on the needs of each instruction and can range in number of steps, the order of execution, and which units are enabled.

Thus by only using a program of set instructions in memory, the CU will configure all the CPU's data flows as needed to manipulate the data correctly between instructions. This results in a computer that could run a complete program and require no human intervention to make hardware changes between instructions (as had to be done when using only punch cards for computations before stored programmed computers with CUs were invented). These detailed steps from the CU dictate which of the CPU's interconnecting hardware control signals to enable/disable or which CPU units are selected/de-selected and the unit's proper order of execution as required by the instruction's operation to produce the desired manipulated data. Additionally, the CU's orderly hardware coordination properly sequences these control signals, then configures the many hardware units comprising the CPU, directing how data should also be moved, changed, and stored outside the CPU (i.e. memory) according to the instruction's objective.

Depending on the type of instruction entering the CU, the order and number of sequential steps produced by the CU could vary the selection and configuration of which parts of the CPU's hardware are utilized to achieve the instruction's objective (mainly moving, storing, and modifying data within the CPU). This one feature, that efficiently uses just software instructions to control/select/configure a computer's CPU hardware (via the CU) and eventually manipulates a program's data, is a significant reason most modern computers are flexible and universal when running various programs. As compared to some 1930s or 1940s computers without a proper CU, they often required rewiring their hardware when changing programs. This CU instruction decode process is then repeated when the Program Counter is incremented to the next stored program address and the new instruction enters the CU from that address, and so on until the programs end.

Other more advanced forms of Control Units manage the translation of instructions (but not the data containing portion) into several micro-instructions and the CU manages the scheduling of the micro-instructions between the selected execution units to which the data is then channeled and changed according to the execution unit's function (i.e., ALU contains several functions). On some processors, the Control Unit may be further broken down into additional units, such as an instruction unit or scheduling unit to handle scheduling, or a retirement unit to deal with results coming from the instruction pipeline. Again, the Control Unit orchestrates the main functions of the CPU: carrying out stored instructions in the software program, then directing the flow of data throughout the computer based upon these instructions (roughly likened to how traffic lights will systematically control the flow of cars [containing data] to different locations within the traffic grid (CPU), until it parks at the desired parking spot [memory address/register]. The car occupants [data] then go into the building [execution unit] and come back changed in some way, then get back into the car and return to another location via the controlled traffic grid).

Hardwired Control Unit

Hardwired control units are implemented through use of combinational logic units, featuring a finite number of gates that can generate specific results based on the instructions that were used to invoke those responses. Hardwired control units are generally faster than the microprogrammed designs.

Their design uses a fixed architecture—it requires changes in the wiring if the instruction set is modified or changed. This architecture is preferred in reduced instruction set computers (RISC) as they use a simpler instruction set.

A controller that uses this approach can operate at high speed; however, it has little flexibility, and the complexity of the instruction set it can implement is limited.

The hardwired approach has become less popular as computers have evolved. Previously, control units for CPUs used ad-hoc logic, and they were difficult to design.

Microprogram Control Unit

The idea of microprogramming was introduced by Maurice Wilkes in 1951 as an intermediate level to execute computer program instructions. Microprograms were organized as a sequence of microinstructions and stored in special control memory. The algorithm for the microprogram control unit, unlike the hardwired control unit, is usually specified by flowchart description. The main advantage of the microprogram control unit is the simplicity of its structure. Outputs of the controller are organized in microinstructions and they can be easily replaced.

Memory Organization

A memory unit is the collection of storage units or devices together. The memory unit stores the binary information in the form of bits. Generally, memory/storage is classified into 2 categories:

Volatile Memory: This loses its data, when power is switched off.

Non-Volatile Memory: This is a permanent storage and does not lose any data when power is switched off.

Memory Hierarchy

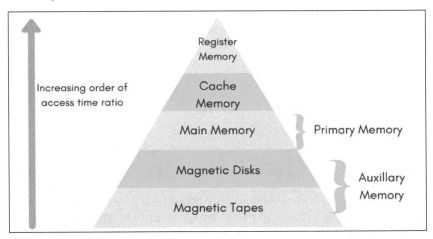

The total memory capacity of a computer can be visualized by hierarchy of components. The memory hierarchy system consists of all storage devices contained in a computer system from the slow Auxiliary Memory to fast Main Memory and to smaller Cache memory.

Auxillary memory access time is generally 1000 times that of the main memory, hence it is at the bottom of the hierarchy.

The main memory occupies the central position because it is equipped to communicate directly with the CPU and with auxiliary memory devices through Input/output processor (I/O).

When the program not residing in main memory is needed by the CPU, they are brought in from auxiliary memory. Programs not currently needed in main memory are transferred into auxiliary memory to provide space in main memory for other programs that are currently in use.

The cache memory is used to store program data which is currently being executed in the CPU. Approximate access time ratio between cache memory and main memory is about 1 to 7~10.

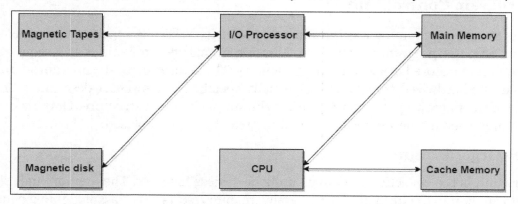

Memory Access Methods

Each memory type, is a collection of numerous memory locations. To access data from any memory, first it must be located and then the data is read from the memory location. Following are the methods to access information from memory locations:

Random Access: Main memories are random access memories, in which each memory location has a unique address. Using this unique address any memory location can be reached in the same amount of time in any order.

Sequential Access: This methods allows memory access in a sequence or in order.

Direct Access: In this mode, information is stored in tracks, with each track having a separate read/write head.

Main Memory

The memory unit that communicates directly within the CPU, Auxillary memory and Cache memory, is called main memory. It is the central storage unit of the computer system. It is a large and fast memory used to store data during computer operations. Main memory is made up of RAM and ROM, with RAM integrated circuit chips holing the major share.

RAM: Random Access Memory.

DRAM: Dynamic RAM, is made of capacitors and transistors, and must be refreshed every 10~100 ms. It is slower and cheaper than SRAM.

SRAM: Static RAM, has a six transistor circuit in each cell and retains data, until powered off.

NVRAM: Non-Volatile RAM, retains its data, even when turned off. Example: Flash memory.

ROM: Read Only Memory, is non-volatile and is more like a permanent storage for information. It also stores the bootstrap loader program, to load and start the operating system when computer is turned on. PROM(Programmable ROM), EPROM(Erasable PROM) and EEPROM(Electrically Erasable PROM) are some commonly used ROMs.

Auxiliary Memory

Devices that provide backup storage are called auxiliary memory. For example: Magnetic disks and tapes are commonly used auxiliary devices. Other devices used as auxiliary memory are magnetic drums, magnetic bubble memory and optical disks.

It is not directly accessible to the CPU, and is accessed using the Input/Output channels.

Cache Memory

The data or contents of the main memory that are used again and again by CPU, are stored in the cache memory so that we can easily access that data in shorter time.

Whenever the CPU needs to access memory, it first checks the cache memory. If the data is not found in cache memory then the CPU moves onto the main memory. It also transfers block of recent data into the cache and keeps on deleting the old data in cache to accomodate the new one.

Hit Ratio

The performance of cache memory is measured in terms of a quantity called hit ratio. When the CPU refers to memory and finds the word in cache it is said to produce a hit. If the word is not found in cache, it is in main memory then it counts as a miss.

The ratio of the number of hits to the total CPU references to memory is called hit ratio.

Hit Ratio = Hit/(Hit + Miss).

Associative Memory

It is also known as content addressable memory (CAM). It is a memory chip in which each bit position can be compared. In this the content is compared in each bit cell which allows very fast table lookup. Since the entire chip can be compared, contents are randomly stored without considering addressing scheme. These chips have less storage capacity than regular memory chips.

Microarchitecture

In computer engineering, microarchitecture, also called computer organization and sometimes abbreviated as µarch or uarch, is the way a given instruction set architecture (ISA) is implemented in a particular processor. A given ISA may be implemented with different microarchitectures; implementations may vary due to different goals of a given design or due to shifts in technology.

Computer architecture is the combination of microarchitecture and instruction set architecture.

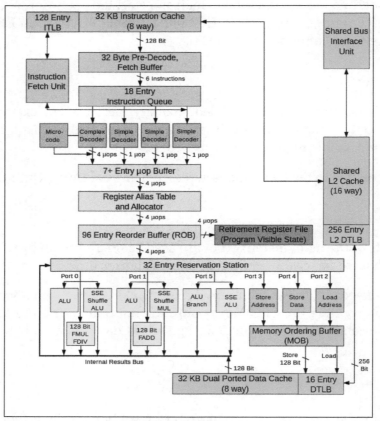

Intel Core microarchitecture.

Relation to Instruction Set Architecture

The ISA is roughly the same as the programming model of a processor as seen by an assembly language programmer or compiler writer. The ISA includes the execution model, processor registers, address and data formats among other things. The microarchitecture includes the constituent parts of the processor and how these interconnect and interoperate to implement the ISA.

The microarchitecture of a machine is usually represented as (more or less detailed) diagrams that describe the interconnections of the various microarchitectural elements of the machine, which may be anything from single gates and registers, to complete arithmetic logic units (ALUs) and even larger elements. These diagrams generally separate the datapath (where data is placed) and the control path (which can be said to steer the data).

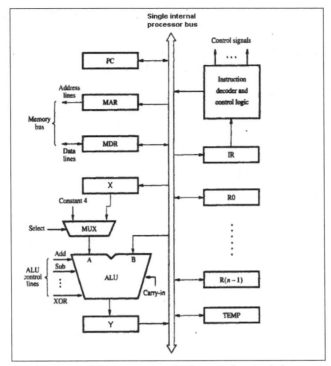

A microarchitecture organized around a single bus.

The person designing a system usually draws the specific microarchitecture as a kind of data flow diagram. Like a block diagram, the microarchitecture diagram shows microarchitectural elements such as the arithmetic and logic unit and the register file as a single schematic symbol. Typically, the diagram connects those elements with arrows, thick lines and thin lines to distinguish between three-state buses (which require a three-state buffer for each device that drives the bus), unidirectional buses (always driven by a single source, such as the way the address bus on simpler computers is always driven by the memory address register), and individual control lines. Very simple computers have a single data bus organization – they have a single three-state bus. The diagram of more complex computers usually shows multiple three-state buses, which help the machine do more operations simultaneously.

Each microarchitectural element is in turn represented by a schematic describing the interconnections of logic gates used to implement it. Each logic gate is in turn represented by a circuit diagram describing the connections of the transistors used to implement it in some particular logic family. Machines with different microarchitectures may have the same instruction set architecture, and thus be capable of executing the same programs. New microarchitectures and/or circuitry solutions, along with advances in semiconductor manufacturing, are what allows newer generations of processors to achieve higher performance while using the same ISA.

In principle, a single microarchitecture could execute several different ISAs with only minor changes to the microcode.

Aspects of Microarchitecture

The pipelined datapath is the most commonly used datapath design in microarchitecture today. This technique is used in most modern microprocessors, microcontrollers, and DSPs. The pipelined architecture allows multiple instructions to overlap in execution, much like an assembly line. The pipeline includes several different stages which are fundamental in microarchitecture designs. Some of these stages include instruction fetch, instruction decode, execute, and write back. Some architectures include other stages such as memory access. The design of pipelines is one of the central microarchitectural tasks.

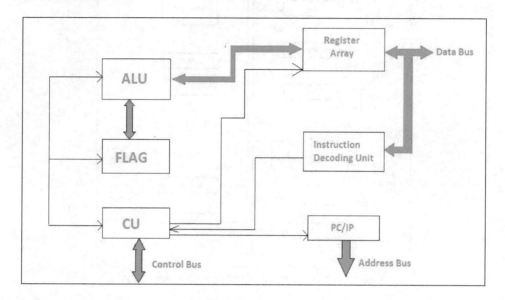

Execution units are also essential to microarchitecture. Execution units include arithmetic logic units (ALU), floating point units (FPU), load/store units, branch prediction, and SIMD. These units perform the operations or calculations of the processor. The choice of the number of execution units, their latency and throughput is a central microarchitectural design task. The size, latency, throughput and connectivity of memories within the system are also microarchitectural decisions.

System-level design decisions such as whether or not to include peripherals, such as memory controllers, can be considered part of the microarchitectural design process. This includes decisions on the performance-level and connectivity of these peripherals.

Unlike architectural design, where achieving a specific performance level is the main goal, microarchitectural design pays closer attention to other constraints. Since microarchitecture design decisions directly affect what goes into a system, attention must be paid to issues such as chip area/cost, power consumption, logic complexity, ease of connectivity, manufacturability, ease of debugging, and testability.

Microarchitectural Concepts

Instruction Cycles

In general, all CPUs, single-chip microprocessors or multi-chip implementations run programs by performing the following steps:

- Read an instruction and decode it.

- Find any associated data that is needed to process the instruction.

- Process the instruction.

- Write the results out.

The instruction cycle is repeated continuously until the power is turned off.

Multicycle Microarchitecture

Historically, the earliest computers were multicycle designs. The smallest, least-expensive computers often still use this technique. Multicycle architectures often use the least total number of logic elements and reasonable amounts of power. They can be designed to have deterministic timing and high reliability. In particular, they have no pipeline to stall when taking conditional branches or interrupts. However, other microarchitectures often perform more instructions per unit time, using the same logic family. When discussing "improved performance," an improvement is often relative to a multicycle design.

In a multicycle computer, the computer does the four steps in sequence, over several cycles of the clock. Some designs can perform the sequence in two clock cycles by completing successive stages on alternate clock edges, possibly with longer operations occurring outside the main cycle. For example, stage one on the rising edge of the first cycle, stage two on the falling edge of the first cycle, etc.

In the control logic, the combination of cycle counter, cycle state (high or low) and the bits of the instruction decode register determine exactly what each part of the computer should be doing. To design the control logic, one can create a table of bits describing the control signals to each part of the computer in each cycle of each instruction. Then, this logic table can be tested in a software simulation running test code. If the logic table is placed in a memory and used to actually run a real computer, it is called a microprogram. In some computer designs, the logic table is optimized into the form of combinational logic made from logic gates, usually using a computer program that optimizes logic. Early computers used ad-hoc logic design for control until Maurice Wilkes invented this tabular approach and called it microprogramming.

Increasing Execution Speed

Complicating this simple-looking series of steps is the fact that the memory hierarchy, which includes caching, main memory and non-volatile storage like hard disks (where the program instructions and data reside), has always been slower than the processor itself. Step (2) often introduces a lengthy (in CPU terms) delay while the data arrives over the computer bus. A considerable amount of research has been put into designs that avoid these delays as much as possible. Over the years, a central goal was to execute more instructions in parallel, thus increasing the effective execution speed of a program. These efforts introduced complicated logic and circuit structures. Initially, these techniques could only be implemented on expensive mainframes or supercomputers due to the amount of circuitry needed for these techniques. As semiconductor manufacturing progressed, more and more of these techniques could be implemented on a single semiconductor chip.

Instruction Set Choice

Instruction sets have shifted over the years, from originally very simple to sometimes very complex (in various respects). In recent years, load-store architectures, VLIW and EPIC types have been in fashion. Architectures that are dealing with data parallelism include SIMD and Vectors. Some labels used to denote classes of CPU architectures are not particularly descriptive, especially so the CISC label; many early designs retroactively denoted "CISC" are in fact significantly simpler than modern RISC processors (in several respects).

However, the choice of instruction set architecture may greatly affect the complexity of implementing high-performance devices. The prominent strategy, used to develop the first RISC processors, was to simplify instructions to a minimum of individual semantic complexity combined with high encoding regularity and simplicity. Such uniform instructions were easily fetched, decoded and executed in a pipelined fashion and a simple strategy to reduce the number of logic levels in order to reach high operating frequencies; instruction cache-memories compensated for the higher operating frequency and inherently low code density while large register sets were used to factor out as much of the (slow) memory accesses as possible.

Instruction Pipelining

One of the first, and most powerful, techniques to improve performance is the use of instruction pipelining. Early processor designs would carry out all of the steps above for one instruction before moving onto the next. Large portions of the circuitry were left idle at any one step; for instance, the instruction decoding circuitry would be idle during execution and so on.

Pipelining improves performance by allowing a number of instructions to work their way through the processor at the same time. In the same basic example, the processor would start to decode (step 1) a new instruction while the last one was waiting for results. This would allow up to four instructions to be "in flight" at one time, making the processor look four times as fast. Although any one instruction takes just as long to complete (there are still four steps) the CPU as a whole "retires" instructions much faster.

RISC makes pipelines smaller and much easier to construct by cleanly separating each stage of the instruction process and making them take the same amount of time—one cycle. The processor as a whole operates in an assembly line fashion, with instructions coming in one side and results out the other. Due to the reduced complexity of the classic RISC pipeline, the pipelined core and an instruction cache could be placed on the same size die that would otherwise fit the core alone on a CISC design. This was the real reason that RISC was faster. Early designs like the SPARC and MIPS often ran over 10 times as fast as Intel and Motorola CISC solutions at the same clock speed and price.

Pipelines are by no means limited to RISC designs. By 1986 the top-of-the-line VAX implementation (VAX 8800) was a heavily pipelined design, slightly predating the first commercial MIPS and SPARC designs. Most modern CPUs (even embedded CPUs) are now pipelined, and microcoded CPUs with no pipelining are seen only in the most area-constrained embedded processors. Large CISC machines, from the VAX 8800 to the modern Pentium 4 and Athlon, are implemented with both microcode and pipelines. Improvements in pipelining and caching are the two major microarchitectural advances that have enabled processor performance to keep pace with the circuit technology on which they are based.

Cache

It was not long before improvements in chip manufacturing allowed for even more circuitry to be placed on the die, and designers started looking for ways to use it. One of the most common was to add an ever-increasing amount of cache memory on-die. Cache is simply very fast memory. It can be accessed in a few cycles as opposed to many needed to "talk" to main memory. The CPU includes a cache controller which automates reading and writing from the cache. If the data is already in the cache it simply "appears", whereas if it is not the processor is "stalled" while the cache controller reads it in.

RISC designs started adding cache in the mid-to-late 1980s, often only 4 KB in total. This number grew over time, and typical CPUs now have at least 512 KB, while more powerful CPUs come with 1 or 2 or even 4, 6, 8 or 12 MB, organized in multiple levels of a memory hierarchy. Generally speaking, more cache means more performance, due to reduced stalling.

Caches and pipelines were a perfect match for each other. Previously, it didn't make much sense to build a pipeline that could run faster than the access latency of off-chip memory. Using on-chip cache memory instead, meant that a pipeline could run at the speed of the cache access latency, a much smaller length of time. This allowed the operating frequencies of processors to increase at a much faster rate than that of off-chip memory.

Branch Prediction

One barrier to achieving higher performance through instruction-level parallelism stems from pipeline stalls and flushes due to branches. Normally, whether a conditional branch will be taken isn't known until late in the pipeline as conditional branches depend on results coming from a register. From the time that the processor's instruction decoder has figured out that it has encountered a conditional branch instruction to the time that the deciding register value can be read out, the pipeline needs to be stalled for several cycles, or if it's not and the branch is taken, the pipeline needs to be flushed. As clock speeds increase the depth of the pipeline increases with it, and some modern processors may have 20 stages or more. On average, every fifth instruction executed is a branch, so without any intervention, that's a high amount of stalling.

Techniques such as branch prediction and speculative execution are used to lessen these branch penalties. Branch prediction is where the hardware makes educated guesses on whether a particular branch will be taken. In reality one side or the other of the branch will be called much more often than the other. Modern designs have rather complex statistical prediction systems, which watch the results of past branches to predict the future with greater accuracy. The guess allows the hardware to prefetch instructions without waiting for the register read. Speculative execution is a further enhancement in which the code along the predicted path is not just prefetched but also executed before it is known whether the branch should be taken or not. This can yield better performance when the guess is good, with the risk of a huge penalty when the guess is bad because instructions need to be undone.

Superscalar

Even with all of the added complexity and gates needed to support the concepts outlined above, improvements in semiconductor manufacturing soon allowed even more logic gates to be used.

In the outline above the processor processes parts of a single instruction at a time. Computer programs could be executed faster if multiple instructions were processed simultaneously. This is what superscalar processors achieve, by replicating functional units such as ALUs. The replication of functional units was only made possible when the die area of a single-issue processor no longer stretched the limits of what could be reliably manufactured. By the late 1980s, superscalar designs started to enter the market place.

In modern designs it is common to find two load units, one store (many instructions have no results to store), two or more integer math units, two or more floating point units, and often a SIMD unit of some sort. The instruction issue logic grows in complexity by reading in a huge list of instructions from memory and handing them off to the different execution units that are idle at that point. The results are then collected and re-ordered at the end.

Out-of-order Execution

The addition of caches reduces the frequency or duration of stalls due to waiting for data to be fetched from the memory hierarchy, but does not get rid of these stalls entirely. In early designs a *cache miss* would force the cache controller to stall the processor and wait. Of course there may be some other instruction in the program whose data *is* available in the cache at that point. Out-of-order execution allows that ready instruction to be processed while an older instruction waits on the cache, then re-orders the results to make it appear that everything happened in the programmed order. This technique is also used to avoid other operand dependency stalls, such as an instruction awaiting a result from a long latency floating-point operation or other multi-cycle operations.

Register Renaming

Register renaming refers to a technique used to avoid unnecessary serialized execution of program instructions because of the reuse of the same registers by those instructions. Suppose we have two groups of instruction that will use the same register. One set of instructions is executed first to leave the register to the other set, but if the other set is assigned to a different similar register, both sets of instructions can be executed in parallel (or) in series.

Multiprocessing and Multithreading

Computer architects have become stymied by the growing mismatch in CPU operating frequencies and DRAM access times. None of the techniques that exploited instruction-level parallelism (ILP) within one program could make up for the long stalls that occurred when data had to be fetched from main memory. Additionally, the large transistor counts and high operating frequencies needed for the more advanced ILP techniques required power dissipation levels that could no longer be cheaply cooled. For these reasons, newer generations of computers have started to exploit higher levels of parallelism that exist outside of a single program or program thread.

This trend is sometimes known as throughput computing. This idea originated in the mainframe market where online transaction processing emphasized not just the execution speed of one transaction, but the capacity to deal with massive numbers of transactions. With transaction-based applications such as network routing and web-site serving greatly increasing in the last decade, the computer industry has re-emphasized capacity and throughput issues.

One technique of how this parallelism is achieved is through multiprocessing systems, computer systems with multiple CPUs. Once reserved for high-end mainframes and supercomputers, small-scale (2–8) multiprocessors servers have become commonplace for the small business market. For large corporations, large scale (16–256) multiprocessors are common. Even personal computers with multiple CPUs have appeared since the 1990s.

With further transistor size reductions made available with semiconductor technology advances, multi-core CPUs have appeared where multiple CPUs are implemented on the same silicon chip. Initially used in chips targeting embedded markets, where simpler and smaller CPUs would allow multiple instantiations to fit on one piece of silicon. By 2005, semiconductor technology allowed dual high-end desktop CPUs *CMP* chips to be manufactured in volume. Some designs, such as Sun Microsystems' UltraSPARC T1 have reverted to simpler (scalar, in-order) designs in order to fit more processors on one piece of silicon.

Another technique that has become more popular recently is multithreading. In multithreading, when the processor has to fetch data from slow system memory, instead of stalling for the data to arrive, the processor switches to another program or program thread which is ready to execute. Though this does not speed up a particular program/thread, it increases the overall system throughput by reducing the time the CPU is idle.

Conceptually, multithreading is equivalent to a context switch at the operating system level. The difference is that a multithreaded CPU can do a thread switch in one CPU cycle instead of the hundreds or thousands of CPU cycles a context switch normally requires. This is achieved by replicating the state hardware (such as the register file and program counter) for each active thread.

A further enhancement is simultaneous multithreading. This technique allows superscalar CPUs to execute instructions from different programs/threads simultaneously in the same cycle.

References

- Denny atkin. "computer shopper: the right gpu for you". Archived from the original on 2007-05-06. Retrieved 2007-05-15

- Wiśniewski, remigiusz (2009). Synthesis of compositional microprogram control units for programmable devices. Zielona góra: university of zielona góra. P. 153. Isbn 978-83-7481-293-1

- Parallel-computer-architecture-introduction, parallel-computer-architecture: tutorialspoint.com Retrieved 12 April, 2019

- What is computer performance?. The national academies press. 2011. Doi:10.17226/12980. Isbn 978-0-309-15951-7. Retrieved may 16, 2016

- Moskowitz, sanford l. (2016). Advanced materials innovation: managing global technology in the 21st century. John wiley & sons. Pp. 165–167. Isbn 9780470508923

- Memory-organization, computer-architecture: studytonight.com, Retrieved 1 June, 2019

- Micro-programmed versus hardwired control units;". Www.cs.binghamton.edu. Archived from the original on 2017-04-30. Retrieved 2017-02-17

Computer Hardware

- **Power Supply Unit**
- **Motherboard**
- **Input Devices**
- **Output Devices**
- **Storage Devices**
- **Hardware Upgrade**

Computer hardware refers to the tangible parts of a computer system. Some of them are monitor, keyboard, mouse, hard drive, motherboard, video card, optical drive, etc. The topics elaborated in this chapter will help in gaining a better perspective about these components of computer hardware.

Computer hardware is a collective term used to describe any of the physical components of an analog or digital computer. The term hardware distinguishes the tangible aspects of a computing device from software, which consists of written instructions that tell physical components what to do.

Computer hardware can be categorized as having either internal or external components. Internal components include items such as the motherboard, central processing unit (CPU), random access memory (RAM), hard drive, optical drive, heat sink, power supply, transistors, chips, graphics processing unit (GPU), network interface card (NIC) and Universal Serial Bus (USB) ports. These components collectively process or store the instructions delivered by the program or operating system (OS).

External components, also called peripheral components, are those items that are often connected to the computer in order to control either its input or output. Common input components include a mouse, keyboard, microphone, camera, touchpad, stylus, joystick, scanner, USB flash drive or memory card. Monitors, printers, speakers, headphones and earphones/earbuds are all examples of output computer hardware components. All these hardware devices are designed to either provide instructions to the software or render results from its execution.

Internal Hardware Components

This computer hardware chart illustrates what typical internal computer hardware components look like.

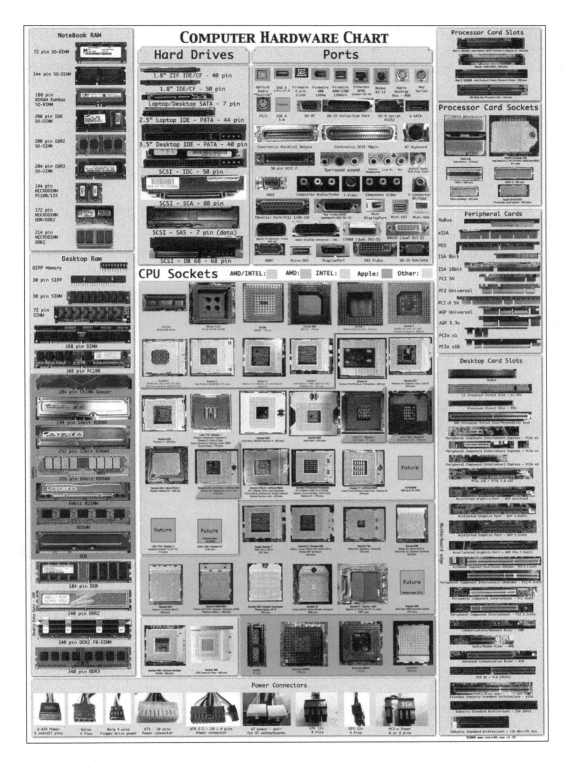

External Hardware Components

External hardware components are called *peripherals*. Peripherals include input devices, such as a mouse or keyboard; output devices, such as a monitor or printer; and external storage devices, such as a hard drive or USB card.

Other common external hardware components include microphones, monitors, speakers, headphones, digital cameras, touchpads, stylus pens, joysticks, scanners and memory cards. All these hardware devices are designed to either provide instructions to the software or render the results from its execution.

Hardware Virtualization

Hardware virtualization is the abstraction of physical computing resources from the software that uses the resources. This is made possible by a virtual machine (VM) manager called a *hypervisor*. Essentially, the hypervisor creates virtual versions of internal hardware so that resources can be shared and used more efficiently. In cloud computing, hardware virtualization is often associated with infrastructure as a service (IaaS).

IaaS is a delivery model for providing hardware resources over high-speed internet. In the IaaS model, a cloud provider hosts hardware components that are traditionally present in an on-premises data center, including servers, storage and networking hardware, but unlike a hardware as a service (HaaS) provider, an IaaS provider will also host the software that makes virtualization possible. Typically, an IaaS provider also supplies a range of services to accompany infrastructure components. These can include detailed billing, monitoring, log access, security, load balancing and clustering, as well as storage resiliency, such as backup, replication and recovery.

Power Supply Unit

A power supply unit, commonly abbreviated as PSU, does more than just supply your computer with power. It is the point where power enters your system from an external power source and is then allocated by the motherboard to individual component hardware. Not all power supplies are made equally however, and without the right wattage PSU your system will fail to work.

A modern computer will generally need a PSU that's rated between 500W – 850W to effectively power all hardware, although the size of the PSU will depend entirely on the power consumption of the system. Computers that are used for highly intensive tasks such as graphic design or gaming will require more powerful components and thus will need a bigger PSU to cater to this additional need.

Without the right amount of power, components won't be able to run effectively and the computer might experience crashes or simply fail to boot at all. It's recommended to have a power supply that more than covers your system usage. Not only do you guard yourself against system failure, you also future-proof yourself against needing a new PSU when you upgrade to more powerful PC components.

Understanding your computer and its hardware components can prove very useful when the time comes to upgrade or replace any parts, or when building a computer. Should a problem arise with the internal workings of your computer, you will have a better understanding of the importance of each component, the need for them to be in good working condition and how to go about solving any issues.

Motherboard

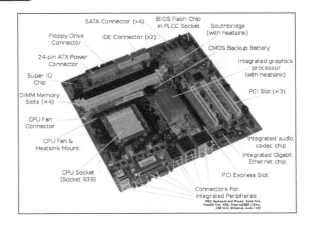

Motherboard for desktop personal computer, showing the typical components and interfaces that are found on a motherboard. This model was made by Intel in 2008 and follows the microATX layout (known as the "form factor") usually employed for desktop computers. It is designed to work with Intel's Pentium Dual-Core, Core 2 Duo, Pentium D, Pentium 4 and Celeron processor.

A motherboard (sometimes alternatively known as the mainboard, main circuit board, system board, baseboard, planar board or logic board, or colloquially, a mobo) is the main printed circuit board (PCB) found in general purpose computers and other expandable systems. It holds, and allows, communication between many of the crucial electronic components of a system, such as the central processing unit (CPU) and memory, and provides connectors for other peripherals. Unlike a backplane, a motherboard usually contains significant sub-systems such as the central processor, the chipset's input/output and memory controllers, interface connectors, and other components integrated for general purpose use and applications.

Motherboard specifically refers to a PCB with expansion capability and as the name suggests, this board is often referred to as the "mother" of all components attached to it, which often include peripherals, interface cards, and daughtercards: sound cards, video cards, network cards, hard drives, or other forms of persistent storage; TV tuner cards, cards providing extra USB or FireWire slots and a variety of other custom components.

Similarly, the term mainboard is applied to devices with a single board and no additional expansions or capability, such as controlling boards in laser printers, televisions, washing machines, mobile phones and other embedded systems with limited expansion abilities.

Design

The Octek Jaguar V motherboard from 1993. This board has few onboard peripherals, as evidenced by the 6 slots provided for ISA cards and the lack of other built-in external interface connectors. Note the large AT keyboard connector at the back right is its only peripheral interface.

The motherboard of a Samsung Galaxy SII; almost all functions of the device are integrated into a very small board.

A motherboard provides the electrical connections by which the other components of the system communicate. Unlike a backplane, it also contains the central processing unit and hosts other subsystems and devices.

A typical desktop computer has its microprocessor, main memory, and other essential components connected to the motherboard. Other components such as external storage, controllers for video display and sound, and peripheral devices may be attached to the motherboard as plug-in cards or via cables; in modern microcomputers it is increasingly common to integrate some of these peripherals into the motherboard itself.

An important component of a motherboard is the microprocessor's supporting chipset, which provides the supporting interfaces between the CPU and the various buses and external components. This chipset determines, to an extent, the features and capabilities of the motherboard.

Modern motherboards include:

- Sockets (or slots) in which one or more microprocessors may be installed. In the case of CPUs in ball grid array packages, such as the VIA C3, the CPU is directly soldered to the motherboard.

- Memory Slots into which the system's main memory is to be installed, typically in the form of DIMM modules containing DRAM chips.

- A chipset which forms an interface between the CPU's front-side bus, main memory, and peripheral buses.

- Non-volatile memory chips (usually Flash ROM in modern motherboards) containing the system's firmware or BIOS.

- A clock generator which produces the system clock signal to synchronize the various components.

- Slots for expansion cards (the interface to the system via the buses supported by the chipset).

- Power connectors, which receive electrical power from the computer power supply and distribute it to the CPU, chipset, main memory, and expansion cards. As of 2007, some graphics cards (e.g. GeForce 8 and Radeon R600) require more power than the motherboard can provide, and thus dedicated connectors have been introduced to attach them directly to the power supply.

- Connectors for hard drives, typically SATA only. Disk drives also connect to the power supply.

Additionally, nearly all motherboards include logic and connectors to support commonly used input devices, such as USB for mouse devices and keyboards. Early personal computers such as the Apple II or IBM PC included only this minimal peripheral support on the motherboard. Occasionally video interface hardware was also integrated into the motherboard; for example, on the Apple II and rarely on IBM-compatible computers such as the IBM PC Jr. Additional peripherals such as disk controllers and serial ports were provided as expansion cards.

Given the high thermal design power of high-speed computer CPUs and components, modern motherboards nearly always include heat sinks and mounting points for fans to dissipate excess heat.

Form Factor

Motherboards are produced in a variety of sizes and shape called computer form factor, some of which are specific to individual computer manufacturers. However, the motherboards used in IBM-compatible systems are designed to fit various case sizes. As of 2007, most desktop computer motherboards use the ATX standard form factor — even those found in Macintosh and Sun computers, which have not been built from commodity components. A case's motherboard and power supply unit (PSU) form factor must all match, though some smaller form factor motherboards of the same family will fit larger cases. For example, an ATX case will usually accommodate a microATX motherboard. Computers generally use highly integrated, miniaturized and customized motherboards. This is one of the reasons that laptop computers are difficult to upgrade and expensive to repair. Often the failure of one laptop component requires the replacement of the entire motherboard, which is usually more expensive than a desktop motherboard.

CPU Sockets

A CPU socket (central processing unit) or slot is an electrical component that attaches to a Printed Circuit Board (PCB) and is designed to house a CPU (also called a microprocessor). It is a special type of integrated circuit socket designed for very high pin counts. A CPU socket provides many functions, including a physical structure to support the CPU, support for a heat sink, facilitating replacement (as well as reducing cost), and most importantly, forming an electrical interface both with the CPU and the PCB. CPU sockets on the motherboard can most often be found in most desktop and server computers (laptops typically use surface mount CPUs), particularly those based on the Intel x86 architecture. A CPU socket type and motherboard chipset must support the CPU series and speed.

Integrated Peripherals

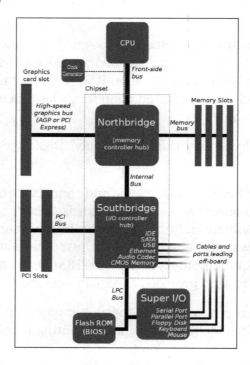

Block diagram of a modern motherboard, which supports many on-board peripheral functions as well as several expansion slots.

With the steadily declining costs and size of integrated circuits, it is now possible to include support for many peripherals on the motherboard. By combining many functions on one PCB, the physical size and total cost of the system may be reduced; highly integrated motherboards are thus especially popular in small form factor and budget computers.

- Disk controllers for a floppy disk drive, up to 2 PATA drives, and up to 6 SATA drives (including RAID 0/1 support).

- Integrated graphics controller supporting 2D and 3D graphics, with VGA and TV output.

- Integrated sound card supporting 8-channel (7.1) audio and S/PDIF output.

- Ethernet network controller for connection to a LAN and to receive Internet.

- UsB controller supporting up to 12 USB ports.

- IrDA controller for infrared data communication (e.g. with an IrDA-enabled cellular phone or printer).

- Temperature, voltage, and fan-speed sensors that allow software to monitor the health of computer components.

Peripheral Card Slots

A typical motherboard will have a different number of connections depending on its standard and form factor.

A standard, modern ATX motherboard will typically have two or three PCI-Express 16x connection for a graphics card, one or two legacy PCI slots for various expansion cards, and one or two PCI-E 1x (which has superseded PCI). A standard EATX motherboard will have two to four PCI-E 16x connection for graphics cards, and a varying number of PCI and PCI-E 1x slots. It can sometimes also have a PCI-E 4x slot (will vary between brands and models).

Some motherboards have two or more PCI-E 16x slots, to allow more than 2 monitors without special hardware, or use a special graphics technology called SLI (for Nvidia) and Crossfire (for AMD). These allow 2 to 4 graphics cards to be linked together, to allow better performance in intensive graphical computing tasks, such as gaming, video editing, etc.

Temperature and Reliability

| A motherboard of a Vaio E series laptop. | A microATX motherboard with some faulty capacitors. |

Motherboards are generally air cooled with heat sinks often mounted on larger chips, such as the Northbridge, in modern motherboards. Insufficient or improper cooling can cause damage to the internal components of the computer, or cause it to crash. Passive cooling, or a single fan mounted on the power supply, was sufficient for many desktop computer CPU's until the late 1990s; since then, most have required CPU fans mounted on their heat sinks, due to rising clock speeds and power consumption. Most motherboards have connectors for additional computer fans and integrated temperature sensors to detect motherboard and CPU temperatures and controllable fan connectors which the BIOS or operating system can use to regulate fan speed. Alternatively computers can use a water cooling system instead of many fans.

Some small form factor computers and home theater PCs designed for quiet and energy-efficient operation boast fan-less designs. This typically requires the use of a low-power CPU, as well as a careful layout of the motherboard and other components to allow for heat sink placement.

A 2003 study found that some spurious computer crashes and general reliability issues, ranging from screen image distortions to I/O read/write errors, can be attributed not to software or peripheral hardware but to aging capacitors on PC motherboards. Ultimately this was shown to be the result of a faulty electrolyte formulation, an issue termed capacitor plague.

Standard motherboards use electrolytic capacitors to filter the DC power distributed around the board. These capacitors age at a temperature-dependent rate, as their water based electrolytes slowly evaporate. This can lead to loss of capacitance and subsequent motherboard malfunctions due to voltage instabilities. While most capacitors are rated for 2000 hours of operation at 105 °C (221 °F), their expected design life roughly doubles for every 10 °C (18 °F) below this. At 65 °C (149 °F) a lifetime of 3 to 4 years can be expected. However, many manufacturers deliver substandard capacitors, which significantly reduce life expectancy. Inadequate case cooling and elevated temperatures around the CPU socket exacerbate this problem. With top blowers, the motherboard components can be kept under 95 °C (203 °F), effectively doubling the motherboard lifetime.

Mid-range and high-end motherboards, on the other hand, use solid capacitors exclusively. For every 10 °C less, their average lifespan is multiplied approximately by three, resulting in a 6-times higher lifetime expectancy at 65 °C (149 °F). These capacitors may be rated for 5000, 10000 or 12000 hours of operation at 105 °C (221 °F), extending the projected lifetime in comparison with standard solid capacitors.

Bootstrapping using the Basic Input/Output System

Motherboards contain some non-volatile memory to initialize the system and load some start-up software, usually an operating system, from some external peripheral device. Microcomputers such as the Apple II and IBM PC used ROM chips mounted in sockets on the motherboard. At power-up, the central processor would load its program counter with the address of the boot ROM and start executing instructions from the ROM. These instructions initialized and tested the system hardware displayed system information on the screen, performed RAM checks, and then loaded an initial program from a peripheral device. If none was available, then the computer would perform tasks from other memory stores or display an error message, depending on the model and design of the computer and the ROM version. For example, both the Apple II and the original IBM PC had Microsoft Cassette BASIC in ROM and would start that if no program could be loaded from disk.

Most modern motherboard designs use a BIOS, stored in an EEPROM chip soldered to or socketed on the motherboard, to boot an operating system. Non-operating system boot programs are still supported on modern IBM PC-descended machines, but nowadays it is assumed that the boot program will be a complex operating system such as Microsoft Windows or Linux. When power is first supplied to the motherboard, the BIOS firmware tests and configures memory, circuitry, and peripherals. This Power-On Self Test (POST) may include testing some of the following things:

- Video adapter.

- Cards inserted into slots, such as conventional PCI.

- Floppy drive.

- Temperatures, voltages, and fan speeds for hardware monitoring.

- CMOS memory used to store BIOS setup configuration.

- Keyboard and Mouse.

- Network controller.

- Optical drives: CD-ROM or DVD-ROM.

- SCSI hard drive.

- IDE, EIDE, or Serial ATA Hard disk drive.

- Security devices, such as a fingerprint reader or the state of a latching switch to detect intrusion.

- USB devices, such as a memory storage device.

Input Devices

In computing, an input device is a piece of computer hardware equipment used to provide data and control signals to an information processing system such as a computer or information appliance. Examples of input devices include keyboards, mouse, scanners, digital cameras, joysticks, and microphones.

Input devices can be categorized based on:

- Modality of input (e.g. mechanical motion, audio, visual, etc.).

- Whether the input is discrete (e.g. pressing of key) or continuous (e.g. a mouse's position, though digitized into a discrete quantity, is fast enough to be considered continuous).

- The number of degrees of freedom involved (e.g. two-dimensional traditional mice, or three-dimensional navigators designed for CAD applications).

Keyboard

'Keyboards' are a human interface device which is represented as a layout of buttons. Each button, or key, can be used to either input a linguistic character to a computer, or to call upon a particular function of the computer. They act as the main text entry interface for most users. Traditional keyboards use spring-based buttons, though newer variations employ virtual keys, or even projected keyboards. It is typewriter like device composed of a matrix of switches. There also happens to be another keyboard that is like an input device for musical instrument which helps to produce sound.

Examples of types of keyboards include:

- Keyer,

- Keyboard,

- Lighted Program Function Keyboard (LPFK),

- Thumb Keyboard.

Mouse

A computer mouse.

Pointing devices are the most commonly used input devices today. A pointing device is any human interface device that allows a user to input spatial data to a computer. In the case of mouse and touchpads, this is usually achieved by detecting movement across a physical surface. Analog devices, such as 3D mice, joysticks, or pointing sticks, function by reporting their angle of deflection. Movements of the pointing device are echoed on the screen by movements of the pointer, creating a simple, intuitive way to navigate a computer's graphical user interface (GUI).

Pointing devices, which are input devices used to specify a position in space, can further be classified according to:

- Whether the input is direct or indirect. With direct input, the input space coincides with the display space, i.e. pointing is done in the space where visual feedback or the pointer appears. Touchscreens and light pens involve direct input. Examples involving indirect input include the mouse and trackball.

- Whether the positional information is absolute (e.g. on a touch screen) or relative (e.g. with a mouse that can be lifted and repositioned).

For pointing devices, direct input is almost necessarily absolute, but indirect input may be either absolute or relative. For example, digitizing graphics tablets that do not have an embedded screen involve indirect input and sense absolute positions and are often run in an absolute input mode, but they may also be set up to simulate a relative input mode like that of a touchpad, where the stylus or puck can be lifted and repositioned. Embeded LCD tablets which are also referred to as graphics tablet monitor is the extension of digitizing graphics tablets. It enables users to see the real-time positions via the screen while using.

Examples of types of pointing devices include:

- Mouse,

- Touchpad,

- Pointing Stick,
- Touchscreen,
- Trackball.

High-degree of Freedom Input Devices

Some devices allow many continuous degrees of freedom as input. These can be used as pointing devices, but are generally used in ways that don't involve pointing to a location in space, such as the control of a camera angle while in 3D applications. These kinds of devices are typically used in virtual reality systems (CAVEs), where input that registers six degrees of freedom is required.

Composite Devices

Wii Remote with attached strap.

Input devices, such as buttons and joysticks, can be combined on a single physical device that could be thought of as a composite device. Many gaming devices have controllers like this. Technically mice are composite devices, as they both track movement and provide buttons for clicking, but composite devices are generally considered to have more than two different forms of input.

Examples of types of composite devices include:

- Joystick controller,
- Gamepad (or joypad),
- Paddle (game controller),
- Jog dial/shuttle (or knob),
- Wii Remote.

Video Input Devices

Microsoft Kinect sensor, works by detecting human motion visually.

Video input devices are used to digitize images or video from the outside world into the computer. The information can be stored in a multitude of formats depending on the user's requirement.

Examples of types of a video input devices include:

- Digital camera,
- Digital camcorder,
- Portable media player,
- Webcam,
- Microsoft Kinect Sensor,
- Image scanner,
- Fingerprint scanner,
- Barcode reader,
- 3D scanner,
- Laser rangefinder,
- Eye gaze tracker,
- Computed tomography,
- Magnetic resonance imaging,
- Positron emission tomography,
- Medical ultrasonography,

Audio Input Devices

Audio input devices are used to capture sound. In some cases, an audio output device can be used as an input device, in order to capture produced sound. Audio input devices allow a user to send audio signals to a computer for processing, recording, or carrying out commands. Devices such as microphones allow users to speak to the computer in order to record a voice message or navigate software. Aside from recording, audio input devices are also used with speech recognition software.

Examples of types of audio input devices include:

- Microphones,
- MIDI keyboard or other digital musical instrument.

Output Devices

Computer output devices receive information from the computer, and carry data that has been processed by the computer to the user. Output devices provide data in myriad different forms, some of which include audio, visual, and hard copy media. The devices are usually used for display, projection, or for physical reproduction. Monitors and printers are two of the most commonly -known output devices used with a computer.

Computer output devices are all peripheral hardware, and are connected to a computer by cables, or by wireless networking.

Reasons for having an Output Device

A computer can still function without an output device. However, without an output device, there's no way to determine what the computer is doing. There is no indicator of errors, nor of the need for additional input. For example, if you detach your monitor from your computer, the computer will still function, but it's not going to be very helpful.

Examples of Output Devices

Monitor: This is the most common computer output device. It creates a visual display by the use of which users can view processed data. Monitors come in various sizes and resolutions.

Common Types of Monitors

- Cathode Ray Tube: this uses phosphorescent dots to generate the pixels that constitute displayed images.

- Flat Panel Screen: This makes use of liquid crystals or plasma to produce output. Light is passed through the liquid crystals in order to generate pixels.

All monitors depend on a video card, which is positioned either on the computer motherboard or in a special expansion slot. The video card sorts out the computer data into image details that the monitors can then show.

Printer: This device generates a hard copy version of processed data, like documents and photographs. The computer transmits the image data to the printer, which then physically recreates the image, typically on paper.

Types of Printers

- Ink Jet: This kind of printer sprays tiny dots of ink onto a surface to form an image.

- Laser: This type utilises toner drums that roll through magnetized pigment, and then transfers the pigment onto a surface.

- Dot Matrix: Dot matrix printers utilise a print head to set images on a surface, using an ink ribbon.

Speakers: Speakers are attached to computers to facilitate the output of sound; sound cards are required in the computer for speakers to function. The different kinds of speakers range from simple, two-speaker output devices right the way up to surround-sound multi-channel units.

Headset: This is a combination of speakers and microphone. It is mostly used by gamers, and is also a great tool for communicating with family and friends over the internet using some VOIP program or other.

Projector: This is a display device that projects a computer-created image onto another surface: usually some sort of whiteboard or wall. The computer transmits the image data to its video card, which then sends the video image to the projector. It is most often used for presentations, or for viewing videos.

Plotter: This generates a hard copy of a digitally depicted design. The design is sent to the plotter through a graphics card, and the design is formed by using a pen. It is generally used with engineering applications, and essentially draws a given image using a series of straight lines.

Input/Output Devices

Input/Output devices don't only produce output, but can also be used as storageand input devices. The computer transmits data to the drive, where it is saved and can be later accessed.

Examples of I/O devices are CD drives, DVD drives, USB drives, hard disk drives (HDDs), and floppy disk drives.

CDs and DVDs are two kinds of optical disc which save data in a digital format. Data is written onto the disc using a laser writer that embeds the data directly into the disc's coating.

A floppy disk is a magnetic storage device. A layer of magnetised material is placed within a proactive plastic casing. The computer then embeds the data into the magnetized material, by using a writing head.

Storage Devices

A storage device refers to a computing hardware used to store information permanently or temporarily. The device can be external or internal to a computer, server, and other computing systems. Storage devices are also known as storage medias or storage medium. There are two types of storage device: secondary storage device and primary storage device.

Secondary Storage Device

A secondary storage device has a larger storage capacity and can store data permanently. The device can be both external and internal to a computer and includes; compact disk, USB drive, hard disk, etc.

Primary Storage Device

A primary storage device is quite smaller in size and it's designed to capture or hold data for a temporary period. Most primary storage devices are found inside the computer, and they have the fastest access to data. Examples of Primary devices include Cache memory and RAM.

Common Problems encountered with Storage devices:

- Hardware failure: Hardware failure is one of the most problematic issues affecting most users. Appropriate handling and regular maintenance can be used to prolong the durability of storage devices.

- Data loss: Intentional and accidental file deletion can make one to lose precious data. Data recovery programs provide a solution for lost files, deleted data, corrupt documents and hidden files. In the event of a data loss scenario, a reliable data recovery software can be used to retrieve back 70% of the lost data.

Hard Drive (HDD)

A hard disk drive (HDD), hard disk, hard drive, or fixed disk is an electro-mechanical data storage device that uses magnetic storage to store and retrieve digital information using one or more rigid rapidly rotating disks (platters) coated with magnetic material. The platters are paired with magnetic heads, usually arranged on a moving actuator arm, which read and write data to the platter surfaces. Data is accessed in a random-access manner, meaning that individual blocks of data can be stored or retrieved in any order and not only sequentially. HDDs are a type of non-volatile storage, retaining stored data even when powered off.

Introduced by IBM in 1956, HDDs became the dominant secondary storage device for general-purpose computers by the early 1960s. Continuously improved, HDDs have maintained this position into the modern era of servers and personal computers. More than 224 companies have produced HDDs historically, though after extensive industry consolidation most units are manufactured by Seagate, Toshiba, and Western Digital. HDDs dominate the volume of storage produced (exabytes per year) for servers. Though production is growing slowly, sales revenues and unit shipments are declining because solid-state drives (SSDs) have higher data-transfer rates, higher areal storage density, better reliability, and much lower latency and access times.

The revenues for SSDs, most of which use NAND, slightly exceed those for HDDs. Flash storage products had more than twice the revenue of hard disk drives as of 2017. Though SSDs have nine times higher cost per bit, they are replacing HDDs in applications where speed, power consumption, small size, high capacity and durability are important. Cost per bit for SSDs is falling, and the price premium over HDDs has narrowed.

The primary characteristics of an HDD are its capacity and performance. Capacity is specified in unit prefixes corresponding to powers of 1000: a 1-terabyte (TB) drive has a capacity of 1,000 gigabytes (GB; where 1 gigabyte = 1 billion bytes). Typically, some of an HDD's capacity is unavailable to the user because it is used by the file system and the computer operating system, and possibly inbuilt redundancy for error correction and recovery. Also there is confusion regarding storage capacity, since capacities are stated in decimal Gigabytes (powers of 10) by HDD manufacturers, whereas some operating systems report capacities in binary Gibibytes, which results in a smaller number than advertised. Performance is specified by the time required to move the heads to a track or cylinder (average access time) adding the time it takes for the desired sector to move under the head (average latency, which is a function of the physical rotational speed in revolutions per minute), and finally the speed at which the data is transmitted (data rate).

The two most common form factors for modern HDDs are 3.5-inch, for desktop computers, and 2.5-inch, primarily for laptops. HDDs are connected to systems by standard interface cables such as PATA (Parallel ATA), SATA (Serial ATA), USB or SAS (Serial Attached SCSI) cables.

Hard Disk Drive

Internals of a 2.5-inch SATA hard disk drive.

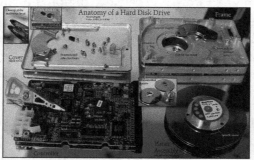

A disassembled and labeled 1997 HDD lying atop a mirror.

Technology

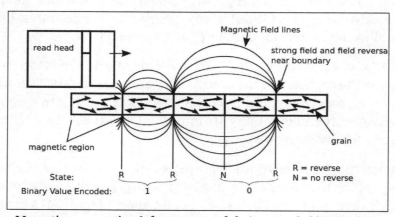

Magnetic cross section & frequency modulation encoded binary data.

Magnetic Recording

A modern HDD records data by magnetizing a thin film of ferromagnetic material[e] on both sides of a disk. Sequential changes in the direction of magnetization represent binary data bits. The data is read from the disk by detecting the transitions in magnetization. User data is encoded using an encoding scheme, such as run-length limited encoding, which determines how the data is represented by the magnetic transitions.

A typical HDD design consists of a spindle that holds flat circular disks, called platters, which hold the recorded data. The platters are made from a non-magnetic material, usually aluminum alloy, glass, or ceramic. They are coated with a shallow layer of magnetic material typically 10–20 nm in depth, with an outer layer of carbon for protection. For reference, a standard piece of copy paper is 0.07–0.18 mm (70,000–180,000 nm) thick.

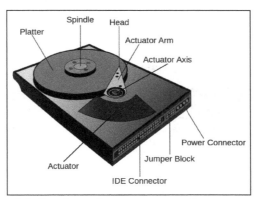

Diagram labeling the major components of a computer HDD.

The platters in contemporary HDDs are spun at speeds varying from 4,200 RPM in energy-efficient portable devices, to 15,000 rpm for high-performance servers. The first HDDs spun at 1,200 rpm and, for many years, 3,600 rpm was the norm. As of November 2019, the platters in most consumer-grade HDDs spin at 5,400 or 7,200 RPM.

Information is written to and read from a platter as it rotates past devices called read-and-write heads that are positioned to operate very close to the magnetic surface, with their flying height often in the range of tens of nanometers. The read-and-write head is used to detect and modify the magnetization of the material passing immediately under it.

In modern drives, there is one head for each magnetic platter surface on the spindle, mounted on a common arm. An actuator arm (or access arm) moves the heads on an arc (roughly radially) across the platters as they spin, allowing each head to access almost the entire surface of the platter as it spins. The arm is moved using a voice coil actuator or in some older designs a stepper motor. Early hard disk drives wrote data at some constant bits per second, resulting in all tracks having the same amount of data per track but modern drives (since the 1990s) use zone bit recording – increasing the write speed from inner to outer zone and thereby storing more data per track in the outer zones.

Destroyed hard disk, glass platter visible.

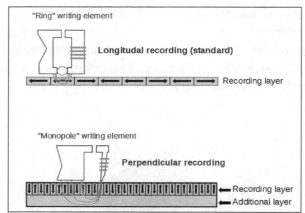

Longitudinal recording (standard) & perpendicular recording diagram.

In modern drives, the small size of the magnetic regions creates the danger that their magnetic state might be lost because of thermal effects — thermally induced magnetic instability which is commonly known as the "superparamagnetic limit". To counter this, the platters are coated with two parallel magnetic layers, separated by a three-atom layer of the non-magnetic element ruthenium, and the two layers are magnetized in opposite orientation, thus reinforcing each other. Another technology used to overcome thermal effects to allow greater recording densities is perpendicular recording, first shipped in 2005, and as of 2007 used in certain HDDs.

In 2004, a new concept was introduced to allow further increase of the data density in magnetic recording: the use of recording media consisting of coupled soft and hard magnetic layers. So-called exchange spring media magnetic storage technology, also known as exchange coupled composite media, allows good writability due to the write-assist nature of the soft layer. However, the thermal stability is determined only by the hardest layer and not influenced by the soft layer.

Components

An HDD with disks and motor hub removed, exposing copper-colored stator coils surrounding a bearing in the center of the spindle motor. The orange stripe along the side of the arm is a thin printed-circuit cable, the spindle bearing is in the center and the actuator is in the upper left.

A typical HDD has two electric motors: a spindle motor that spins the disks and an actuator (motor) that positions the read/write head assembly across the spinning disks. The disk motor has an external rotor attached to the disks; the stator windings are fixed in place. Opposite the actuator at the end of the head support arm is the read-write head; thin printed-circuit cables connect the read-write heads to amplifier electronics mounted at the pivot of the actuator. The head support arm is very light, but also stiff; in modern drives, acceleration at the head reaches 550 *g*.

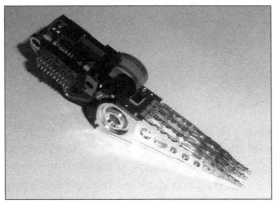

Head stack with an actuator coil on the left and read/write heads on the right.

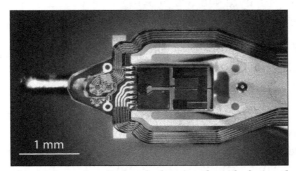

Close-up of a single read-write head, showing the side facing the platter.

The actuator is a permanent magnet and moving coil motor that swings the heads to the desired position. A metal plate supports a squat neodymium-iron-boron (NIB) high-flux magnet. Beneath this plate is the moving coil, often referred to as the voice coil by analogy to the coil in loudspeakers, which is attached to the actuator hub, and beneath that is a second NIB magnet, mounted on the bottom plate of the motor (some drives have only one magnet).

The voice coil itself is shaped rather like an arrowhead and is made of doubly coated copper magnet wire. The inner layer is insulation, and the outer is thermoplastic, which bonds the coil together after it is wound on a form, making it self-supporting. The portions of the coil along the two sides of the arrowhead (which point to the center of the actuator bearing) then interact with the magnetic field of the fixed magnet. Current flowing radially outward along one side of the arrowhead and radially inward on the other produces the tangential force. If the magnetic field were uniform, each side would generate opposing forces that would cancel each other out. Therefore, the surface of the magnet is half north pole and half south pole, with the radial dividing line in the middle, causing the two sides of the coil to see opposite magnetic fields and produce forces that add instead of canceling. Currents along the top and bottom of the coil produce radial forces that do not rotate the head.

The HDD's electronics control the movement of the actuator and the rotation of the disk and perform reads and writes on demand from the disk controller. Feedback of the drive electronics is accomplished by means of special segments of the disk dedicated to servo feedback. These are either complete concentric circles (in the case of dedicated servo technology) or segments interspersed with real data (in the case of embedded servo technology). The servo feedback optimizes the signal-to-noise ratio of the GMR sensors by adjusting the voice coil of the actuated arm. The spinning of the disk also uses a servo motor. Modern disk firmware is capable of scheduling reads and writes efficiently on the platter surfaces and remapping sectors of the media which have failed.

Error Rates and Handling

Modern drives make extensive use of error correction codes (ECCs), particularly Reed–Solomon error correction. These techniques store extra bits, determined by mathematical formulas, for each block of data; the extra bits allow many errors to be corrected invisibly. The extra bits themselves take up space on the HDD, but allow higher recording densities to be employed without causing uncorrectable errors, resulting in much larger storage capacity. For example, a typical 1 TB hard disk with 512-byte sectors provides additional capacity of about 93 GB for the ECC data.

In the newest drives, as of 2009, low-density parity-check codes (LDPC) were supplanting Reed–Solomon; LDPC codes enable performance close to the Shannon Limit and thus provide the highest storage density available.

Typical hard disk drives attempt to "remap" the data in a physical sector that is failing to a spare physical sector provided by the drive's "spare sector pool" (also called "reserve pool"), while relying on the ECC to recover stored data while the number of errors in a bad sector is still low enough. The S.M.A.R.T (Self-Monitoring, Analysis and Reporting Technology) feature counts the total number of errors in the entire HDD fixed by ECC (although not on all hard drives as the related S.M.A.R.T attributes "Hardware ECC Recovered" and "Soft ECC Correction" are not consistently supported), and the total number of performed sector remappings, as the occurrence of many such errors may predict an HDD failure.

The "No-ID Format", developed by IBM in the mid-1990s, contains information about which sectors are bad and where remapped sectors have been located.

Only a tiny fraction of the detected errors end up as not correctable. Examples of specified uncorrected bit read error rates include:

- 2013 specifications for enterprise SAS disk drives state the error rate to be one uncorrected bit read error in every 1016 bits read,

- 2018 specifications for consumer SATA hard drives state the error rate to be one uncorrected bit read error in every 1014 bits.

Within a given manufacturers model the uncorrected bit error rate is typically the same regardless of capacity of the drive.

The worst type of errors are silent data corruptions which are errors undetected by the disk firmware or the host operating system; some of these errors may be caused by hard disk drive malfunctions while others originate elsewhere in the connection between the drive and the host.

Development

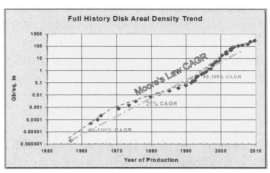

Leading-edge hard disk drive areal densities from 1956 through 2009 compared to Moore's law.

The rate of areal density advancement was similar to Moore's law (doubling every two years) through 2010: 60% per year during 1988–1996, 100% during 1996–2003 and 30% during 2003–2010. Speaking in 1997, Gordon Moore called the increase "flabbergasting", while observing later that growth cannot continue forever. Price improvement decelerated to −12% per year during 2010–2017, as the growth of areal density slowed. The rate of advancement for areal density slowed to 10% per year during 2010–2016, and there was difficulty in migrating from perpendicular recording to newer technologies.

As bit cell size decreases, more data can be put onto a single drive platter. In 2013, a production desktop 3 TB HDD (with four platters) would have had an areal density of about 500 Gbit/in2 which would have amounted to a bit cell comprising about 18 magnetic grains (11 by 1.6 grains). Since the mid-2000s areal density progress has increasingly been challenged by a superparamagnetic trilemma involving grain size, grain magnetic strength and ability of the head to write. In order to maintain acceptable signal to noise smaller grains are required; smaller grains may self-reverse (electrothermal instability) unless their magnetic strength is increased, but known write head materials are unable to generate a strong enough magnetic field sufficient to write the medium in the increasingly-smaller space taken by grains.

Several new magnetic storage technologies are being developed to address this trilemma, and compete with flash memory–based solid-state drives (SSDs). In 2013, Seagate introduced shingled magnetic recording (SMR), intended as something of a "stopgap" technology between PMR and Seagate's intended successor heat-assisted magnetic recording (HAMR), SMR utilises overlapping tracks for increased data density, at the cost of design complexity and lower data access speeds (particularly write speeds and random access 4k speeds). By contrast, Western Digital focused on developing ways to seal helium-filled drives instead of the usual filtered air. This reduces turbulence and friction, and fits more platters into the same enclosure space, though helium gas is notoriously difficult to prevent escaping.

Other new recording technologies that remain under development as of February 2019, include Seagate's heat-assisted magnetic recording (HAMR) drives, scheduled for commercial launch in the first half of 2019, HAMR's planned successor, bit-patterned recording (BPR), Western Digital's microwave-assisted magnetic recording (MAMR), two-dimensional magnetic recording (TDMR), and "current perpendicular to plane" giant magnetoresistance (CPP/GMR) heads.

The rate of areal density growth has dropped below the historical Moore's law rate of 40% per year, and the deceleration is expected to persist through at least 2020. Depending upon assumptions on feasibility and timing of these technologies, the median forecast by industry observers and analysts for 2020 and beyond for areal density growth is 20% per year with a range of 10–30%. The achievable limit for the HAMR technology in combination with BPR and SMR may be 10 Tbit/in2, which would be 20 times higher than the 500 Gbit/in2 represented by 2013 production desktop HDDs. Seagate began sampling HAMR HDDs in 2018. They require a different architecture, with redesigned media and read/write heads, new lasers, and new near-field optical transducers.

Capacity

Since June 2019, the highest-capacity desktop HDDs stored 16 TB. The capacity of a hard disk drive, as reported by an operating system to the end user, is smaller than the amount stated by the manufacturer for several reasons: the operating system using some space, use of some space for data redundancy, and space use for file system structures. Also the difference in capacity reported in SI decimal prefixed units vs. binary prefixes can lead to a false impression of missing capacity.

Calculation

Modern hard disk drives appear to their host controller as a contiguous set of logical blocks, and the gross drive capacity is calculated by multiplying the number of blocks by the block size. This information is available from the manufacturer's product specification, and from the drive itself through use of operating system functions that invoke low-level drive commands.

The gross capacity of older HDDs is calculated as the product of the number of cylinders per recording zone, the number of bytes per sector (most commonly 512), and the count of zones of the drive. Some modern SATA drives also report cylinder-head-sector (CHS) capacities, but these are not physical parameters because the reported values are constrained by historic operating system interfaces. The C/H/S scheme has been replaced by logical block addressing (LBA), a simple linear addressing scheme that locates blocks by an integer index, which starts at LBA 0 for the first block and increments thereafter. When using the C/H/S method to describe modern large drives, the number of heads is often set to 64, although a typical hard disk drive, as of 2013, has between one and four platters.

In modern HDDs, spare capacity for defect management is not included in the published capacity; however, in many early HDDs a certain number of sectors were reserved as spares, thereby reducing the capacity available to the operating system.

For RAID subsystems, data integrity and fault-tolerance requirements also reduce the realized capacity. For example, a RAID 1 array has about half the total capacity as a result of data mirroring, while a RAID 5 array with x drives loses 1/x of capacity (which equals to the capacity of a single drive) due to storing parity information. RAID subsystems are multiple drives that appear to be one drive or more drives to the user, but provide fault tolerance. Most RAID vendors use checksums to improve data integrity at the block level. Some vendors design systems using HDDs with sectors of 520 bytes to contain 512 bytes of user data and eight checksum bytes, or by using separate 512-byte sectors for the checksum data.

Some systems may use hidden partitions for system recovery, reducing the capacity available to the end user.

Formatting

Data is stored on a hard drive in a series of logical blocks. Each block is delimited by markers identifying its start and end, error detecting and correcting information, and space between blocks to allow for minor timing variations. These blocks often contained 512 bytes of usable data, but other sizes have been used. As drive density increased, an initiative known as Advanced Format extended the block size to 4096 bytes of usable data, with a resulting significant reduction in the amount of disk space used for block headers, error checking data, and spacing.

The process of initializing these logical blocks on the physical disk platters is called low-level formatting, which is usually performed at the factory and is not normally changed in the field. High-level formatting writes data structures used by the operating system to organize data files on the disk. This includes writing partition and file system structures into selected logical blocks. For example, some of the disk space will be used to hold a directory of disk file names and a list of logical blocks associated with a particular file.

Examples of partition mapping scheme include Master boot record (MBR) and GUID Partition Table (GPT). Examples of data structures stored on disk to retrieve files include the File Allocation Table (FAT) in the DOS file system and inodes in many UNIX file systems, as well as other operating system data structures (also known as metadata). As a consequence, not all the space on an HDD is available for user files, but this system overhead is usually small compared with user data.

Units

Decimal and binary unit prefixes interpretation					
Capacity advertised by manufacturers		Capacity expected by some consumers		Reported capacity	
With prefix	Bytes	Bytes	Diff.	Windows	macOS ver 10.6 +
100 GB	100,000,000,000	107,374,182,400	7.37%	93.1 GB	100 GB
1 TB	1,000,000,000,000	1,099,511,627,776	9.95%	931 GB	1,000 GB, 1,000,000 MB

The total capacity of HDDs is given by manufacturers using SI decimal prefixes such as gigabytes (1 GB = 1,000,000,000 bytes) and terabytes (1 TB = 1,000,000,000,000 bytes). This practice dates back to the early days of computing; by the 1970s, "million", "mega" and "M" were consistently used in the decimal sense for drive capacity. However, capacities of memory are quoted using a binary interpretation of the prefixes, i.e. using powers of 1024 instead of 1000.

Software reports hard disk drive or memory capacity in different forms using either decimal or binary prefixes. The Microsoft Windows family of operating systems uses the binary convention when reporting storage capacity, so an HDD offered by its manufacturer as a 1 TB drive is reported by these operating systems as a 931 GB HDD. Mac OS X 10.6 ("Snow Leopard") uses decimal convention when reporting HDD capacity. The default behavior of the df command-line utility on Linux is to report the HDD capacity as a number of 1024-byte units.

The difference between the decimal and binary prefix interpretation caused some consumer confusion and led to class action suits against HDD manufacturers. The plaintiffs argued that the use of decimal prefixes effectively misled consumers while the defendants denied any wrongdoing or liability, asserting that their marketing and advertising complied in all respects with the law and that no class member sustained any damages or injuries.

Price Evolution

HDD price per byte improved at the rate of −40% per year during 1988–1996, −51% per year during 1996–2003 and −34% per year during 2003–2010. The price improvement decelerated to −13% per year during 2011–2014, as areal density increase slowed and the 2011 Thailand floods damaged manufacturing facilities and have held at -11% per year during 2010-2017.

Form Factors

8-, 5.25-, 3.5-, 2.5-, 1.8- and 1-inch HDDs, together with a ruler to
show the length of platters and read-write heads.

A newer 2.5-inch (63.5 mm) 6,495 MB HDD compared
to an older 5.25-inch full-height 110 MB HDD.

IBM's first hard disk drive, the IBM 350, used a stack of fifty 24-inch platters, stored 3.75 MB of data (approximately the size of one modern digital picture), and was of a size comparable to two large refrigerators. In 1962, IBM introduced its model 1311 disk, which used six 14-inch (nominal size) platters in a removable pack and was roughly the size of a washing machine. This became a standard platter size for many years, used also by other manufacturers. The IBM 2314 used platters of the same size in an eleven-high pack and introduced the "drive in a drawer" layout. sometimes called the"pizza oven", although the "drawer" was not the complete drive. Into the 1970s HDDs were offered in standalone cabinets of varying dimensions containing from one to four HDDs.

Beginning in the late 1960s drives were offered that fit entirely into a chassis that would mount in a 19-inch rack. Digital's RK05 and RL01 were early examples using single 14-inch platters in removable packs, the entire drive fitting in a 10.5-inch-high rack space (six rack units). In the mid-to-late 1980s the similarly sized Fujitsu Eagle, which used (coincidentally) 10.5-inch platters, was a popular product.

With increasing sales of microcomputers having built in floppy-disk drives (FDDs), HDDs that would fit to the FDD mountings became desirable. Starting with the Shugart Associates SA1000 HDD Form factors, initially followed those of 8-inch, 5½-inch, and 3½-inch floppy disk drives. Although referred to by these nominal sizes, the actual sizes for those three drives respectively are 9.5", 5.75" and 4" wide. Because there were no smaller floppy disk drives, smaller HDD form factors developed from product offerings or industry standards. 2½-inch drives are actually 2.75" wide.

As of 2019, 2½-inch and 3½-inch hard disks are the most popular sizes. By 2009, all manufacturers had discontinued the development of new products for the 1.3-inch, 1-inch and 0.85-inch form factors due to falling prices of flash memory, which has no moving parts. While nominal sizes are in inches, actual dimensions are specified in millimeters.

Performance Characteristics

The factors that limit the time to access the data on an HDD are mostly related to the mechanical nature of the rotating disks and moving heads, including:

- Seek time is a measure of how long it takes the head assembly to travel to the track of the disk that contains data.

- Rotational latency is incurred because the desired disk sector may not be directly under the head when data transfer is requested. Average rotational latency is shown in the table, based on the statistical relation that the average latency is one-half the rotational period.

- The bit rate or data transfer rate (once the head is in the right position) creates delay which is a function of the number of blocks transferred; typically relatively small, but can be quite long with the transfer of large contiguous files.

Delay may also occur if the drive disks are stopped to save energy.

Defragmentation is a procedure used to minimize delay in retrieving data by moving related items to physically proximate areas on the disk. Some computer operating systems perform defragmentation automatically. Although automatic defragmentation is intended to reduce access delays, performance will be temporarily reduced while the procedure is in progress.

Time to access data can be improved by increasing rotational speed (thus reducing latency) or by reducing the time spent seeking. Increasing areal density increases throughput by increasing data rate and by increasing the amount of data under a set of heads, thereby potentially reducing seek activity for a given amount of data. The time to access data has not kept up with throughput increases, which themselves have not kept up with growth in bit density and storage capacity.

Latency

Rotational speed [rpm]	Average rotational latency [ms]
15,000	2
10,000	3
7,200	4.16
5,400	5.55
4,800	6.25

Data Transfer Rate

As of 2010, a typical 7,200-rpm desktop HDD has a sustained "disk-to-buffer" data transfer rate up to 1,030 Mbit/s. This rate depends on the track location; the rate is higher for data on the outer tracks (where there are more data sectors per rotation) and lower toward the inner tracks (where there are fewer data sectors per rotation); and is generally somewhat higher for 10,000-rpm drives. A current widely used standard for the "buffer-to-computer" interface is 3.0 Gbit/s SATA, which can send about 300 megabyte/s (10-bit encoding) from the buffer to the computer, and thus is still comfortably ahead of today's disk-to-buffer transfer rates. Data transfer rate (read/write) can be measured by writing a large file to disk using special file generator tools, then reading back the file. Transfer rate can be influenced by file system fragmentation and the layout of the files.

HDD data transfer rate depends upon the rotational speed of the platters and the data recording density. Because heat and vibration limit rotational speed, advancing density becomes the main method to improve sequential transfer rates. Higher speeds require a more powerful spindle motor, which creates more heat. While areal density advances by increasing both the number of tracks across the disk and the number of sectors per track, only the latter increases the data transfer rate for a given rpm. Since data transfer rate performance tracks only one of the two components of areal density, its performance improves at a lower rate.

Other Considerations

Other performance considerations include quality-adjusted price, power consumption, audible noise, and both operating and non-operating shock resistance.

The Federal Reserve Board has a quality-adjusted price index for large-scale enterprise storage systems including three or more enterprise HDDs and associated controllers, racks and cables. Prices for these large-scale storage systems improved at the rate of −30% per year during 2004–2009 and −22% per year during 2009–2014.

Access and Interfaces

Inner view of a 1998 Seagate HDD that used Parallel ATA interface.

2.5-inch SATA drive on top of 3.5-inch SATA drive,
showing close-up of (7-pin) data and (15-pin) power connectors.

Current hard drives connect to a computer over one of several bus types, including parallel ATA, Serial ATA , SCSI, Serial Attached SCSI (SAS), and Fibre Channel. Some drives, especially external portable drives, use IEEE 1394, or USB. All of these interfaces are digital; electronics on the drive process the analog signals from the read/write heads. Current drives present a consistent interface to the rest of the computer, independent of the data encoding scheme used internally, and independent of the physical number of disks and heads within the drive.

Typically a DSP in the electronics inside the drive takes the raw analog voltages from the read head and uses PRML and Reed–Solomon error correction to decode the data, then sends that data out the standard interface. That DSP also watches the error rate detected by error detection and correction, and performs bad sector remapping, data collection for Self-Monitoring, Analysis, and Reporting Technology, and other internal tasks.

Modern interfaces connect the drive to the host interface with a single data/control cable. Each drive also has an additional power cable, usually direct to the power supply unit. Older interfaces had separate cables for data signals and for drive control signals.

- Small Computer System Interface (SCSI), originally named SASI for Shugart Associates System Interface, was standard on servers, workstations, Commodore Amiga, Atari ST and Apple Macintosh computers through the mid-1990s, by which time most models had been transitioned to IDE (and later, SATA) family disks. The length limit of the data cable allows for external SCSI devices.

- Integrated Drive Electronics (IDE), later standardized under the name AT Attachment (ATA, with the alias PATA (Parallel ATA) retroactively added upon introduction of SATA) moved the HDD controller from the interface card to the disk drive. This helped to standardize the host/controller interface, reduce the programming complexity in the host device driver, and reduced system cost and complexity. The 40-pin IDE/ATA connection transfers 16 bits of data at a time on the data cable. The data cable was originally 40-conductor, but later higher speed requirements led to an "ultra DMA" (UDMA) mode using an 80-conductor cable with additional wires to reduce cross talk at high speed.

- EIDE was an unofficial update (by Western Digital) to the original IDE standard, with the key improvement being the use of direct memory access (DMA) to transfer data between the disk and the computer without the involvement of the CPU, an improvement later adopted by the official ATA standards. By directly transferring data between memory and disk, DMA eliminates the need for the CPU to copy byte per byte, therefore allowing it to process other tasks while the data transfer occurs.

- Fibre Channel (FC) is a successor to parallel SCSI interface on enterprise market. It is a serial protocol. In disk drives usually the Fibre Channel Arbitrated Loop (FC-AL) connection topology is used. FC has much broader usage than mere disk interfaces, and it is the cornerstone of storage area networks (SANs). Recently other protocols for this field, like iSCSI and ATA over Ethernet have been developed as well. Confusingly, drives usually use *copper* twisted-pair cables for Fibre Channel, not fibre optics. The latter are traditionally reserved for larger devices, such as servers or disk array controllers.

- Serial Attached SCSI (SAS). The SAS is a new generation serial communication protocol for devices designed to allow for much higher speed data transfers and is compatible with

SATA. SAS uses a mechanically identical data and power connector to standard 3.5-inch SATA1/SATA2 HDDs, and many server-oriented SAS RAID controllers are also capable of addressing SATA HDDs. SAS uses serial communication instead of the parallel method found in traditional SCSI devices but still uses SCSI commands.

- Serial ATA (SATA). The SATA data cable has one data pair for differential transmission of data to the device, and one pair for differential receiving from the device, just like EIA-422. That requires that data be transmitted serially. A similar differential signaling system is used in RS485, LocalTalk, USB, FireWire, and differential SCSI. SATA I to III are designed to be compatible with, and use, a subset of SAS commands, and compatible interfaces. Therefore, a SATA hard drive can be connected to and controlled by a SAS hard drive controller (with some minor exceptions such as drives/controllers with limited compatibility). However they cannot be connected the other way round—a SATA controller cannot be connected to a SAS drive.

Integrity and Failure

Close-up of an HDD head resting on a disk platter;
its mirror reflection is visible on the platter surface.

Due to the extremely close spacing between the heads and the disk surface, HDDs are vulnerable to being damaged by a head crash – a failure of the disk in which the head scrapes across the platter surface, often grinding away the thin magnetic film and causing data loss. Head crashes can be caused by electronic failure, a sudden power failure, physical shock, contamination of the drive's internal enclosure, wear and tear, corrosion, or poorly manufactured platters and heads.

The HDD's spindle system relies on air density inside the disk enclosure to support the heads at their proper flying height while the disk rotates. HDDs require a certain range of air densities to operate properly. The connection to the external environment and density occurs through a small hole in the enclosure (about 0.5 mm in breadth), usually with a filter on the inside (the breather filter). If the air density is too low, then there is not enough lift for the flying head, so the head gets too close to the disk, and there is a risk of head crashes and data loss. Specially manufactured sealed and pressurized disks are needed for reliable high-altitude operation, above about 3,000 m (9,800 ft). Modern disks include temperature sensors and adjust their operation to the operating environment. Breather holes can be seen on all disk drives – they usually have a sticker next to them, warning the user not to cover the holes. The air inside the operating drive is constantly moving too, being swept in motion by friction with the spinning platters. This air passes through an internal recirculation (or "recirc") filter to remove any leftover contaminants from manufacture, any particles or chemicals that may have somehow entered the enclosure, and any particles or outgassing generated internally in normal operation. Very high humidity present for extended periods of time can corrode the heads and platters.

For giant magnetoresistive (GMR) heads in particular, a minor head crash from contamination (that does not remove the magnetic surface of the disk) still results in the head temporarily over-heating, due to friction with the disk surface, and can render the data unreadable for a short period until the head temperature stabilizes (so called "thermal asperity", a problem which can partially be dealt with by proper electronic filtering of the read signal).

When the logic board of a hard disk fails, the drive can often be restored to functioning order and the data recovered by replacing the circuit board with one of an identical hard disk. In the case of read-write head faults, they can be replaced using specialized tools in a dust-free environment. If the disk platters are undamaged, they can be transferred into an identical enclosure and the data can be copied or cloned onto a new drive. In the event of disk-platter failures, disassembly and imaging of the disk platters may be required. For logical damage to file systems, a variety of tools, including fsck on UNIX-like systems and CHKDSK on Windows, can be used for data recovery. Recovery from logical damage can require file carving.

A common expectation is that hard disk drives designed and marketed for server use will fail less frequently than consumer-grade drives usually used in desktop computers. However, two independent studies by Carnegie Mellon University and Google found that the "grade" of a drive does not relate to the drive's failure rate.

A 2011 summary of research, into SSD and magnetic disk failure patterns by Tom's Hardware summarized research findings as follows:

- Mean time between failures (MTBF) does not indicate reliability; the annualized failure rate is higher and usually more relevant.

- Magnetic disks do not have a specific tendency to fail during early use, and temperature has only a minor effect; instead, failure rates steadily increase with age.

- S.M.A.R.T. warns of mechanical issues but not other issues affecting reliability, and is therefore not a reliable indicator of condition.

- Failure rates of drives sold as "enterprise" and "consumer" are "very much similar", although these drive types are customized for their different operating environments.

- In drive arrays, one drive's failure significantly increases the short-term risk of a second drive failing.

Market Segments

Desktop HDDs

They typically store between 60 GB and 8 TB and rotate at 5,400 to 10,000 rpm, and have a media transfer rate of 0.5 Gbit/s or higher (1 GB = 10^9 bytes; 1 Gbit/s = 10^9 bit/s). As of May 2019, the highest-capacity desktop HDDs stored 14 TB, with plans to release 16 TB and 18 TB drives later in 2019. As of 2016, the typical speed of a hard drive in an average desktop computer is 7200 RPM, whereas low-cost desktop computers may use 5900 RPM or 5400 RPM drives. For some time in the 2000s and early 2010s some desktop users also used 10k RPM drives such as Western Digital Raptor but such drives have become much rarer as of 2016 and are not commonly used now, having been replaced by NAND flash-based SSDs.

Mobile (Laptop) HDDs

Two enterprise-grade SATA 2.5-inch 10,000 rpm HDDs,
factory-mounted in 3.5-inch adapter frames.

Smaller than their desktop and enterprise counterparts, they tend to be slower and have lower capacity. Mobile HDDs spin at 4,200 rpm, 5,200 rpm, 5,400 rpm, or 7,200 rpm, with 5,400 rpm being typical. 7,200 rpm drives tend to be more expensive and have smaller capacities, while 4,200 rpm models usually have very high storage capacities. Because of smaller platters, mobile HDDs generally have lower capacity than their desktop counterparts.

There are also 2.5-inch drives spinning at 10,000 rpm, which belong to the enterprise segment with no intention to be used in laptops.

Enterprise HDDs

Typically used with multiple-user computers running enterprise software. Examples are: transaction processing databases, internet infrastructure (email, webserver, e-commerce), scientific computing software, and nearline storage management software. Enterprise drives commonly operate continuously ("24/7") in demanding environments while delivering the highest possible performance without sacrificing reliability. Maximum capacity is not the primary goal, and as a result the drives are often offered in capacities that are relatively low in relation to their cost.

The fastest enterprise HDDs spin at 10,000 or 15,000 rpm, and can achieve sequential media transfer speeds above 1.6 Gbit/s and a sustained transfer rate up to 1 Gbit/s. Drives running at 10,000 or 15,000 rpm use smaller platters to mitigate increased power requirements (as they have less air drag) and therefore generally have lower capacity than the highest capacity desktop drives. Enterprise HDDs are commonly connected through Serial Attached SCSI (SAS) or Fibre Channel (FC). Some support multiple ports, so they can be connected to a redundant host bus adapter.

Enterprise HDDs can have sector sizes larger than 512 bytes (often 520, 524, 528 or 536 bytes). The additional per-sector space can be used by hardware RAID controllers or applications for storing Data Integrity Field (DIF) or Data Integrity Extensions (DIX) data, resulting in higher reliability and prevention of silent data corruption.

Consumer Electronics HDDs

They include drives embedded into digital video recorders and automotive vehicles. The former are configured to provide a guaranteed streaming capacity, even in the face of read and write errors, while the latter are built to resist larger amounts of shock. They usually spin at a speed of 5400 RPM.

Manufacturers and Sales

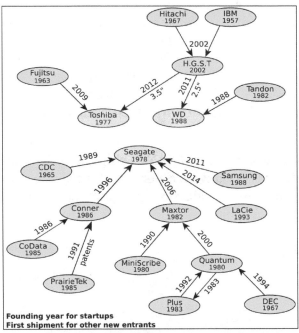

Diagram of HDD manufacturer consolidation.

More than 200 companies have manufactured HDDs over time, but consolidations have concentrated production to just three manufacturers today: Western Digital, Seagate, and Toshiba. Production is mainly in the Pacific rim.

Worldwide revenue for disk storage declined 4% per year, from a peak of $38 billion in 2012 to $27 billion in 2016. Production of HDDs grew 16% per year, from 335 exabytes in 2011 to 693 exabytes in 2016. Shipments declined 7% per year during this time period, from 620 million units to 425 million. In 2018, Seagate has 40% of unit shipments, Western Digital has 37% of unit shipments, while Toshiba has 23% of unit shipments. The average sales price for the two largest manufacturers was $60 per unit in 2015.

Competition from Solid-state Drives

HDDs are being superseded by SSDs in markets where their higher speed (up to 3500 megabytes per second for m.2 SSDs or 2500 megabytes per second for PCIe drives), ruggedness and lower power are more important than price since SSDs are still twice as expensive than an HDD of the same capacity. They also have a relatively short lifespan (Enterprise HDDs can be rated for up to 550TB of read and/or write endurance per year of warranty where as SSDs are usually not) and their performance drops over time, because NAND flash memory, on which most SSDs are based, degrades with every write operation. The lifespan or write endurance of SSDs is measured by either Terabytes Written (TBW) or Drive Writes Per Day (DWPD). In the case of the latter, if a 1 TB drive is rated for 1 DWPD, and the drive has a 1-year warranty, the Terabytes Written will be equal to 365. Some SSDs offer larger capacities (up to 100 TB) than the largest HDD and/or higher storage densities (100 TB and 30 TB SSDs are housed in 2.5 inch HDD cases but with the same height as a 3.5-inch HDD), although their cost remains prohibitive.

The maximum areal storage density for flash memory used in solid state drives (SSDs) is 2.8 Tbit/in² in laboratory demonstrations as of 2016, and the maximum for HDDs is 1.5 Tbit/in². The areal density of flash memory is doubling every two years, similar to Moore's law (40% per year) and faster than the 10–20% per year for HDDs. As of 2018, the maximum possible capacity was 16 terabytes for an HDD, and 100 terabytes for an SSD. HDDs were used in 70% of the desktop and notebook computers produced in 2016, and SSDs were used in 30%. The usage share of HDDs is declining and could drop below 50% in 2018–2019 according to one forecast, because SSDs are replacing smaller-capacity (less than one-terabyte) HDDs in desktop and notebook computers and MP3 players.

The market for silicon-based flash memory (NAND) chips, used in SSDs and other applications, is growing rapidly. Worldwide revenue grew 12% per year during 2011–2016. It rose from $22 billion in 2011 to $39 billion in 2016, while production grew 46% per year from 19 exabytes to 120 exabytes.

External Hard Disk Drives

External USB 2.0 hard disk drive.

External hard disk drives typically connect via USB; variants using USB 2.0 interface generally have slower data transfer rates when compared to internally mounted hard drives connected through SATA. Plug and play drive functionality offers system compatibility and features large storage options and portable design. As of March 2015, available capacities for external hard disk drives ranged from 500 GB to 10 TB.

External hard disk drives are usually available as assembled integrated products but may be also assembled by combining an external enclosure (with USB or other interface) with a separately purchased drive. They are available in 2.5-inch and 3.5-inch sizes; 2.5-inch variants are typically called portable external drives, while 3.5-inch variants are referred to as desktop external drives. "Portable" drives are packaged in smaller and lighter enclosures than the "desktop" drives; additionally, "portable" drives use power provided by the USB connection, while "desktop" drives require external power bricks.

Features such as encryption, biometric security or multiple interfaces (for example, FireWire) are available at a higher cost. There are pre-assembled external hard disk drives that, when taken out from their enclosures, cannot be used internally in a laptop or desktop computer due to embedded USB interface on their printed circuit boards, and lack of SATA (or Parallel ATA) interfaces.

In GUIs, hard disk drives are commonly symbolized with a drive icon.

Solid-state Drive (SSD)

A solid-state drive (SSD) is a solid-state storage device that uses integrated circuit assemblies to store data persistently, typically using flash memory, and functioning as secondary storage in the hierarchy of computer storage. It is also sometimes called a solid-state device or a solid-state disk, although SSDs lack the physical spinning disks and movable read-write heads used hard drives ("HDD") or floppy disks.

Compared with the electromechanical drives, SSDs are typically more resistant to physical shock, run silently, and have quicker access time and lower latency. SSDs store data in semiconductor cells. As of 2019, cells can contain between 1 and 4 bits of data. SSD storage devices vary in their properties according to the number of bits stored in each cell, with single bit cells ("SLC") being generally the most reliable, durable, fast, and expensive type, compared with 2 and 3 bit cells ("MLC" and "TLC"), and finally quad bit cells ("QLC") being used for consumer devices that do not require such extreme properties and are the cheapest of the four. In addition, 3D XPoint memory (sold by Intel under the Optane brand), stores data by changing the electrical resistance of cells instead of storing electrical charges in cells, and SSDs made from RAM can be used for high speed, when data persistence after power loss is not required, or may use battery power to retain data when its usual power source is unavailable. Hybrid drives or solid-state hybrid drives (SSHDs), such as Apple's Fusion Drive, combine features of SSDs and HDDs in the same unit using both flash memory and a HDD in order to improve the performance of frequently-accessed data.

While the price of SSDs has continued to decline over time, SSDs are still more expensive per unit of storage than HDDs and are expected to remain so into the next decade.

SSDs based on NAND Flash will slowly leak charge over time if left for long periods without power. This causes worn-out drives (that have exceeded their endurance rating) to start losing data typically after one year (if stored at 30 °C) to two years (at 25 °C) in storage; for new drives it takes longer. Therefore, SSDs are not suitable for archival storage. 3D XPoint is a possible exception to this rule, however it is a relatively new technology with unknown data-retention characteristics.

SSDs can use traditional hard disk drive (HDD) interfaces and form factors, or newer interfaces and form factors that exploit specific advantages of the flash memory in SSDs. Traditional interfaces (e.g., SATA and SAS) and standard HDD form factors allow such SSDs to be used as drop-in replacements for HDDs in computers and other devices. Newer form factors such as mSATA, M.2, U.2, and EDSFF (formerly known as Ruler SSD) and higher speed interfaces such as NVMe over PCI Express can increase performance over HDD performance.

A PCI-attached IO Accelerator SSD.

An mSATA SSD with an external enclosure.

512GB Samsung 960 PRO NVMe M.2 SSD.

Architecture and Function

The key components of an SSD are the controller and the memory to store the data. The primary memory component in an SSD was traditionally DRAM volatile memory, but since 2009 it is more commonly NAND flash non-volatile memory.

Controller

Every SSD includes a controller that incorporates the electronics that bridge the NAND memory components to the host computer. The controller is an embedded processor that executes firmware-level code and is one of the most important factors of SSD performance. Some of the functions performed by the controller include:

- Bad block mapping.
- Read and write caching.
- Encryption.

- Crypto-shredding.

- Error detection and correction via error-correcting code (ECC).

- Garbage collection.

- Read scrubbing and read disturb management.

- Wear leveling.

The performance of an SSD can scale with the number of parallel NAND flash chips used in the device. A single NAND chip is relatively slow, due to the narrow (8/16 bit) asynchronous I/O interface, and additional high latency of basic I/O operations (typical for SLC NAND, ~25 µs to fetch a 4 KB page from the array to the I/O buffer on a read, ~250 µs to commit a 4 KB page from the IO buffer to the array on a write, ~2 ms to erase a 256 KB block). When multiple NAND devices operate in parallel inside an SSD, the bandwidth scales, and the high latencies can be hidden, as long as enough outstanding operations are pending and the load is evenly distributed between devices.

Micron and Intel initially made faster SSDs by implementing data striping (similar to RAID 0) and interleaving in their architecture. This enabled the creation of ultra-fast SSDs with 250 MB/s effective read/write speeds with the SATA 3 Gbit/s interface in 2009. Two years later, SandForce continued to leverage this parallel flash connectivity, releasing consumer-grade SATA 6 Gbit/s SSD controllers which supported 500 MB/s read/write speeds. SandForce controllers compress the data before sending it to the flash memory. This process may result in less writing and higher logical throughput, depending on the compressibility of the data.

Wear Leveling

If a particular block is programmed and erased repeatedly without writing to any other blocks, that block will wear out before all the other blocks — thereby prematurely ending the life of the SSD. For this reason, SSD controllers use a technique called wear leveling to distribute writes as evenly as possible across all the flash blocks in the SSD.

In a perfect scenario, this would enable every block to be written to its maximum life so they all fail at the same time. Unfortunately, the process to evenly distribute writes requires data previously written and not changing (cold data) to be moved, so that data which are changing more frequently (hot data) can be written into those blocks. Each time data are relocated without being changed by the host system, this increases the write amplification and thus reduces the life of the flash memory. The key is to find an optimum algorithm which maximizes them both.

Memory

Flash-memory-based

Comparison of architectures		
Comparison characteristics	MLC : SLC	NAND : NOR
Persistence ratio	1 : 10	1 : 10
Sequential write ratio	1 : 3	1 : 4

Sequential read ratio	1 : 1	1 : 5
Price ratio	1 : 1.3	1 : 0.7

Most SSD manufacturers use non-volatile NAND flash memory in the construction of their SSDs because of the lower cost compared with DRAM and the ability to retain the data without a constant power supply, ensuring data persistence through sudden power outages. Flash memory SSDs were initially slower than DRAM solutions, and some early designs were even slower than HDDs after continued use. This problem was resolved by controllers that came out in 2009 and later.

Flash-based SSDs store data in metal-oxide-semiconductor (MOS) integrated circuit chips which contain non-volatile floating-gate memory cells. Flash memory-based solutions are typically packaged in standard disk drive form factors (1.8-, 2.5-, and 3.5-inch), but also in smaller more compact form factors, such as the M.2 form factor, made possible by the small size of flash memory.

Lower-priced drives usually use triple-level cell (TLC) or multi-level cell (MLC) flash memory, which is slower and less reliable than single-level cell (SLC) flash memory. This can be mitigated or even reversed by the internal design structure of the SSD, such as interleaving, changes to writing algorithms, and higher over-provisioning (more excess capacity) with which the wear-leveling algorithms can work.

DRAM-based

SSDs based on volatile memory such as DRAM are characterized by very fast data access, generally less than 10 microseconds, and are used primarily to accelerate applications that would otherwise be held back by the latency of flash SSDs or traditional HDDs.

DRAM-based SSDs usually incorporate either an internal battery or an external AC/DC adapter and backup storage systems to ensure data persistence while no power is being supplied to the drive from external sources. If power is lost, the battery provides power while all information is copied from random access memory (RAM) to back-up storage. When the power is restored, the information is copied back to the RAM from the back-up storage, and the SSD resumes normal operation (similar to the hibernate function used in modern operating systems).

SSDs of this type are usually fitted with DRAM modules of the same type used in regular PCs and servers, which can be swapped out and replaced by larger modules. Such as i-RAM, Hyper-Os HyperDrive, DDRdrive X1, etc. Some manufacturers of DRAM SSDs solder the DRAM chips directly to the drive, and do not intend the chips to be swapped out—such as ZeusRAM, Aeon Drive, etc.

A remote, indirect memory-access disk (RIndMA Disk) uses a secondary computer with a fast network or (direct) Infiniband connection to act like a RAM-based SSD, but the new, faster, flash-memory based, SSDs already available in 2009 are making this option not as cost effective.

While the price of DRAM continues to fall, the price of Flash memory falls even faster. The "Flash becomes cheaper than DRAM" crossover point occurred approximately 2004.

3D XPoint-based

In 2015, Intel and Micron announced 3D XPoint as a new non-volatile memory technology. Intel released the first 3D XPoint-based drive (branded as Intel Optane SSD) in March 2017 starting with data center product - Intel Optane SSD DC P4800X Series, and following with the client version - Intel Optane SSD 900P Series in October 2017. Both products operate faster and with higher endurance than NAND-based SSDs, while the areal density is comparable at 128 gigabits per chip. For the price per bit, 3D XPoint is more expensive than NAND, but cheaper than DRAM.

Other

Some SSDs, called NVDIMM or Hyper DIMM devices, use both DRAM and flash memory. When the power goes down, the SSD copies all the data from its DRAM to flash; when the power comes back up, the SSD copies all the data from its flash to its DRAM. In a somewhat similar way, some SSDs use form factors and buses actually designed for DIMM modules, while using only flash memory and making it appear as if it were DRAM. Such SSDs are usually known as ULLtraDIMM devices.

Drives known as hybrid drives or solid-state hybrid drives (SSHDs) use a hybrid of spinning disks and flash memory. Some SSDs use magnetoresistive random-access memory (MRAM) for storing data.

Cache or Buffer

A flash-based SSD typically uses a small amount of DRAM as a volatile cache, similar to the buffers in hard disk drives. A directory of block placement and wear leveling data is also kept in the cache while the drive is operating. One SSD controller manufacturer, SandForce, does not use an external DRAM cache on their designs but still achieves high performance. Such an elimination of the external DRAM reduces the power consumption and enables further size reduction of SSDs.

Battery or Supercapacitor

Another component in higher-performing SSDs is a capacitor or some form of battery, which are necessary to maintain data integrity so the data in the cache can be flushed to the drive when power is lost; some may even hold power long enough to maintain data in the cache until power is resumed. In the case of MLC flash memory, a problem called lower page corruption can occur when MLC flash memory loses power while programming an upper page. The result is that data written previously and presumed safe can be corrupted if the memory is not supported by a supercapacitor in the event of a sudden power loss. This problem does not exist with SLC flash memory.

Most consumer-class SSDs do not have built-in batteries or capacitors; among the exceptions are the Crucial M500 and MX100 series, the Intel 320 series, and the more expensive Intel 710 and 730 series. Enterprise-class SSDs, such as the Intel DC S3700 series, usually have built-in batteries or capacitors.

Host Interface

An SSD with 1.2 TB of MLC NAND, using PCI Express as the host interface.

The host interface is physically a connector with the signalling managed by the SSD's controller. It is most often one of the interfaces found in HDDs. They include:

- Serial attached SCSI (SAS-3, 12.0 Gbit/s) – generally found on servers.

- Serial ATA and mSATA variant (SATA 3.0, 6.0 Gbit/s).

- PCI Express (PCIe 3.0 ×4, 31.5 Gbit/s).

- M.2 (6.0 Gbit/s for SATA 3.0 logical device interface, 31.5 Gbit/s for PCIe 3.0 ×4).

- U.2 (PCIe 3.0 ×4).

- Fibre Channel (128 Gbit/s) – almost exclusively found on servers.

- USB (10 Gbit/s).

- Parallel ATA (UDMA, 1064 Mbit/s) – mostly replaced by SATA.

- (Parallel) SCSI (40 Mbit/s- 2560 Mbit/s) – generally found on servers, mostly replaced by SAS; last SCSI-based SSD was introduced in 2004.

SSDs support various logical device interfaces, such as the original ATAPI, Advanced Host Controller Interface (AHCI), NVM Express (NVMe), and other proprietary interfaces. Logical device interfaces define the command sets used by operating systems to communicate with SSDs and host bus adapters (HBAs).

Configurations

The size and shape of any device is largely driven by the size and shape of the components used to make that device. Traditional HDDs and optical drives are designed around the rotating platter(s) or optical disc along with the spindle motor inside. If an SSD is made up of various interconnected integrated circuits (ICs) and an interface connector, then its shape is no longer limited to the shape of rotating media drives. Some solid state storage solutions come in a larger chassis that may even be a rack-mount form factor with numerous SSDs inside. They would all connect to a common bus inside the chassis and connect outside the box with a single connector.

For general computer use, the 2.5-inch form factor (typically found in laptops) is the most popular. For desktop computers with 3.5-inch hard disk drive slots, a simple adapter plate can be used to make such a drive fit. Other types of form factors are more common in enterprise applications. An SSD can also be completely integrated in the other circuitry of the device, as in the Apple MacBook Air (starting with the fall 2010 model). As of 2014, mSATA and M.2 form factors also gained popularity, primarily in laptops.

Standard HDD form Factors

An SSD with HDD form factor, opened to show solid state electronics.

The benefit of using a current HDD form factor would be to take advantage of the extensive infrastructure already in place to mount and connect the drives to the host system. These traditional form factors are known by the size of the rotating media, e.g., 5.25-inch, 3.5-inch, 2.5-inch, 1.8-inch, not by the dimensions of the drive casing.

Standard Card form Factors

For applications where space is at premium, like for ultrabooks or tablet computers, a few compact form factors were standardized for flash-based SSDs.

There is the mSATA form factor, which uses the PCI Express Mini Card physical layout. It remains electrically compatible with the PCI Express Mini Card interface specification, while requiring an additional connection to the SATA host controller through the same connector.

M.2 form factor, formerly known as the Next Generation Form Factor (NGFF), is a natural transition from the mSATA and physical layout it used, to a more usable and more advanced form factor. While mSATA took advantage of an existing form factor and connector, M.2 has been designed to maximize usage of the card space, while minimizing the footprint. The M.2 standard allows both SATA and PCI Express SSDs to be fitted onto M.2 modules.

Disk-on-a-module form Factors

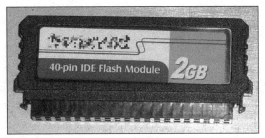

A 2 GB disk-on-a-module with PATA interface.

A disk-on-a-module (DOM) is a flash drive with either 40/44-pin Parallel ATA (PATA) or SATA interface, intended to be plugged directly into the motherboard and used as a computer hard disk drive (HDD). DOM devices emulate a traditional hard disk drive, resulting in no need for special drivers or other specific operating system support. DOMs are usually used in embedded systems, which are often deployed in harsh environments where mechanical HDDs would simply fail, or in thin clients because of small size, low power consumption and silent operation.

As of 2016, storage capacities range from 4 MB to 128 GB with different variations in physical layouts, including vertical or horizontal orientation.

Box form Factors

Many of the DRAM-based solutions use a box that is often designed to fit in a rack-mount system. The number of DRAM components required to get sufficient capacity to store the data along with the backup power supplies requires a larger space than traditional HDD form factors.

Bare-board form Factors

Viking Technology SATA Cube and AMP SATA Bridge multi-layer SSDs.

Viking Technology SATADIMM based SSD.

MO-297 SATA disk-on-a-module (DOM) SSD form factor.

A custom-connector SATA SSD.

Form factors which were more common to memory modules are now being used by SSDs to take advantage of their flexibility in laying out the components. Some of these include PCIe, mini PCIe, mini-DIMM, MO-297, and many more. The SATADIMM from Viking Technology uses an empty DDR3 DIMM slot on the motherboard to provide power to the SSD with a separate SATA connector to provide the data connection back to the computer. The result is an easy-to-install SSD with a capacity equal to drives that typically take a full 2.5-inch drive bay. At least one manufacturer, Innodisk, has produced a drive that sits directly on the SATA connector (SATADOM) on the motherboard without any need for a power cable. Some SSDs are based on the PCIe form factor and connect both the data interface and power through the PCIe connector to the host. These drives can use either direct PCIe flash controllers or a PCIe-to-SATA bridge device which then connects to SATA flash controllers.

Ball Grid Array form Factors

In the early 2000s, a few companies introduced SSDs in Ball Grid Array (BGA) form factors, such as M-Systems' (now SanDisk) DiskOnChip and Silicon Storage Technology's NANDrive (now produced by Greenliant Systems), and Memoright's M1000 for use in embedded systems. The main benefits of BGA SSDs are their low power consumption, small chip package size to fit into compact subsystems, and that they can be soldered directly onto a system motherboard to reduce adverse effects from vibration and shock.

Such embedded drives often adhere to the eMMC and eUFS standards.

Comparison with other Technologies

Hard Disk Drives

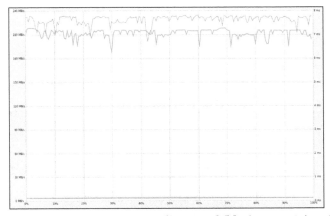

SSD benchmark, showing about 230 MB/s reading speed (blue), 210 MB/s writing speed (red) and about 0.1 ms seek time (green), all independent from the accessed disk location.

Making a comparison between SSDs and ordinary (spinning) HDDs is difficult. Traditional HDD benchmarks tend to focus on the performance characteristics that are poor with HDDs, such as rotational latency and seek time. As SSDs do not need to spin or seek to locate data, they may prove vastly superior to HDDs in such tests. However, SSDs have challenges with mixed reads and writes, and their performance may degrade over time. SSD testing must start from the (in use) full drive, as the new and empty (fresh, out-of-the-box) drive may have much better write performance than it would show after only weeks of use.

Most of the advantages of solid-state drives over traditional hard drives are due to their ability to access data completely electronically instead of electromechanically, resulting in superior transfer speeds and mechanical ruggedness. On the other hand, hard disk drives offer significantly higher capacity for their price.

Some field failure rates indicate that SSDs are significantly more reliable than HDDs but others do not. However, SSDs are uniquely sensitive to sudden power interruption, resulting in aborted writes or even cases of the complete loss of the drive. The reliability of both HDDs and SSDs varies greatly among models.

As with HDDs, there is a tradeoff between cost and performance of different SSDs. Single-level cell (SLC) SSDs, while significantly more expensive than multi-level (MLC) SSDs, offer a significant speed advantage. At the same time, DRAM-based solid-state storage is currently considered the fastest and most costly, with average response times of 10 microseconds instead of the average 100 microseconds of other SSDs. Enterprise flash devices (EFDs) are designed to handle the demands of tier-1 application with performance and response times similar to less-expensive SSDs.

In traditional HDDs, a re-written file will generally occupy the same location on the disk surface as the original file, whereas in SSDs the new copy will often be written to different NAND cells for the purpose of wear leveling. The wear-leveling algorithms are complex and difficult to test exhaustively; as a result, one major cause of data loss in SSDs is firmware bugs.

Comparison of NAND-based SSD and HDD

Price Per Capacity

Solid-state drive:

- SSDs generally are more expensive than HDDs and expected to remain so into the next decade.

- SSD price as of first quarter 2018 around 30 cents (US) per gigabyte based on 4 TB models.

- Prices have generally declined annually and as of 2018 are expected to continue to do so.

Hard disk drive:

- HDD price as of first quarter 2018 around 2 to 3 cents (US) per gigabyte based on 1 TB models.

- Prices have generally declined annually and as of 2018 are expected to continue to do so.

Storage Capacity

Solid-state drive:

- In 2018, SSDs were available in sizes up to 100 TB, but less costly, 120 to 512 GB models were more common.

Hard disk drive:

- In 2018, HDDs of up to 16 TB were available.

Reliability on Storage Retention

Solid-state drive:

- If left without power, worn out SSDs typically start to lose data after about one to two years in storage, depending on temperature. New drives are supposed to retain data for about ten years. MLC and TLC based devices tend to lose data earlier than SLC-based devices. SSDs are not suited for archival use.

Hard disk drive:

- If kept in a dry environment at low temperature, HDDs can retain their data for a very long period of time even without power. However, the mechanical parts tend to become clotted over time and the drive fails to spin up after a few years in storage.

Reliability and Lifetime

Solid-state Drive:

- SSDs have no moving parts to fail mechanically so in theory should be more reliable than HDDs. However, in practice this is unclear.

- Each block of a flash-based SSD can only be erased (and therefore written) a limited number of times before it fails. The controllers manage this limitation so that drives can last for many years under normal use. SSDs based on DRAM do not have a limited number of writes. However the failure of a controller can make a SSD unusable. Reliability varies significantly across different SSD manufacturers and models with return rates reaching 40% for specific drives. Many SSDs critically fail on power outages; a December 2013 survey of many SSDs found that only some of them are able to survive multiple power outages. Owever, SSDs have undergone many revisions that have made them more reliable and long lasting. New SSDs in the market today have power loss protection circuits and wear leveling techniques implemented to ensure longevity.

Hard Disk Drive:

- HDDs have moving parts, and are subject to potential mechanical failures from the resulting wear and tear so in theory should be less reliable than SSDs. However, in practice this is unclear.

- The storage medium itself (magnetic platter) does not essentially degrade from read and write operations.

- When stored offline (unpowered in shelf) in long term, the magnetic medium of HDD retains data significantly longer than flash memory used in SSDs.

Start-up Time

Solid-state drive:

- Almost instantaneous; no mechanical components to prepare. May need a few milliseconds to come out of an automatic power-saving mode.

Hard disk drive:

- Drive spin-up may take several seconds. A system with many drives may need to stagger spin-up to limit peak power drawn, which is briefly high when an HDD is first started.

Sequential Access Performance

Solid-state drive:

- In consumer products the maximum transfer rate typically ranges from about 200 MB/s to 3500 MB/s, depending on the drive. Enterprise SSDs can have multi-gigabyte per second throughput.

Hard disk drive:

- Once the head is positioned, when reading or writing a continuous track, a modern HDD can transfer data at about 200 MB/s. Data transfer rate depends also upon rotational speed, which can range from 3,600 to 15,000 rpm and also upon the track (reading from the outer tracks is faster). Data transfer speed can be up to 480 MB/s(-experimental).

Random Access Performance

Solid-state drive:

- Random access time typically under 0.1 ms. As data can be retrieved directly from various locations of the flash memory, access time is usually not a big performance bottleneck. Read performance does not change based on where data is stored. In applications, where hard disk drive seeks are the limiting factor, this results in faster boot and application launch times.

- SSD technology can deliver rather consistent read/write speed, but when lots of individual smaller blocks are accessed, performance is reduced. SSDs suffer from a write performance degradation phenomenon called write amplification, where the NAND cells show a measurable drop in performance, and will continue degrading throughout the life of the SSD. A technique called wear leveling is implemented to mitigate this effect, but due to the nature of the NAND chips, the drive will inevitably degrade at a noticeable rate.

Hard disk drive:

- Read latency time is much higher than SSDs. Random access time ranges from 2.9 (high end server drive) to 12 ms (laptop HDD) due to the need to move the heads and wait for the data to rotate under the magnetic head. Read time is different for every different seek, since the location of the data and the location of the head are likely different. If data from different areas of the platter must be accessed, as with fragmented files, response times will be increased by the need to seek each fragment.

Impacts of File System Fragmentation

Solid-state drive:

- There is limited benefit to reading data sequentially (beyond typical FS block sizes, say 4 KB), making fragmentation negligible for SSDs. Defragmentation would cause wear by making additional writes of the NAND flash cells, which have a limited cycle life. However, even on SSDs there is a practical limit on how much fragmentation certain file systems can sustain; once that limit is reached, subsequent file allocations fail. Consequently, defragmentation may still be necessary, although to a lesser degree.

Hard disk drive:

- Some file systems, like NTFS, become fragmented over time if frequently written; periodic defragmentation is required to maintain optimum performance.
- This is usually not an issue in modern file systems.

Noise (Acoustic)

Solid-state drive:

- SSDs have no moving parts and therefore are silent, although, on some SSDs, high pitch noise from the high voltage generator (for erasing blocks) may occur.

Hard disk drive:

- HDDs have moving parts (heads, actuator, and spindle motor) and make characteristic sounds of whirring and clicking; noise levels vary depending on the RPM, but can be significant (while often much lower than the sound from the cooling fans). Laptop hard drives are relatively quiet.

Temperature Control

Solid-state drive:

- A study conducted by Facebook found a consistent failure rate at temperatures between 30 and 40 °C. Failure rate rises when operating at temperatures higher than 40 °C, further increase of temperature may trigger thermal throttling around 70 °C, resulting in reduced runtime performance. Reliability of early SSDs without thermal throttling are more affected by temperature than newer ones with thermal throttling. In practice, SSDs usually do not require any special cooling and can tolerate higher temperatures than HDDs. High-end enterprise models installed as add-on cards or 2.5-inch bay devices may ship with heat sinks to dissipate generated heat, requiring certain volumes of airflow to operate.

Hard disk drive:

- Ambient temperatures above 35 °C (95 °F) can shorten the life of a hard disk, and reliability will be compromised at drive temperatures above 55 °C (131 °F). Fan cooling may be required if temperatures would otherwise exceed these values. In practice, modern HDDs may be used with no special arrangements for cooling.

Lowest Operating Temperature

Solid-state drive:

- SSDs can operate at −55 °C (−67 °F).

Hard disk drive:

- Most modern HDDs can operate at 0 °C (32 °F).

Highest Altitude when Operating

Solid-state drive:

- SSDs have no issues on this.

Hard disk drive:

- HDDs can operate safely at an altitude of at most 3,000 meters (10,000 ft). HDDs will fail to operate at altitudes above 12,000 meters (40,000 ft). With the introduction of helium-filled (sealed) HDDs, this is expected to be less of an issue.

Moving from a Cold Environment to a Warmer Environment

Solid-state drive:

- SSDs have no issues on this.

Hard disk drive:

- A certain amount of acclimation time is needed when moving HDDs from a cold environment to a warmer environment before operating it; otherwise, internal condensation will occur and operating it immediately will result in damage to its internal components.

Breather Hole

Solid-state drive:

- SSDs do not require a breather hole.

Hard disk drive:

- Most modern HDDs require a breather hole in order to function properly. Helium-filled devices are sealed and do not have a hole.

Susceptibility to Environmental Factors

Solid-state drive:

- No moving parts, very resistant to shock, vibration, movement, and contamination.

Hard disk drive:

- Heads flying above rapidly rotating platters are susceptible to shock, vibration, movement, and contamination which could damage the medium.

Installation and Mounting

Solid-state drive:

- Not sensitive to orientation, vibration, or shock. Usually no exposed circuitry. Circuitry may be exposed in a card form device and it must not be short-circuited by conductive materials.

Hard disk drive:

- Circuitry may be exposed, and it must not be short-circuited by conductive materials (such as the metal chassis of a computer). Should be mounted to protect against vibration and shock. Some HDDs should not be installed in a tilted position.

Susceptibility to Magnetic Fields

Solid-state drive:

- Low impact on flash memory, but an electromagnetic pulse will damage any electrical system, especially integrated circuits.

Hard disk drive:

- In general, magnets or magnetic surges may result in data corruption or mechanical damage to the drive internals. Drive's metal case provides a low level of shielding to the magnetic platters.

Weight and Size

Solid-state drive:

- SSDs, essentially semiconductor memory devices mounted on a circuit board, are small and lightweight. They often follow the same form factors as HDDs (2.5-inch or 1.8-inch), but the enclosures are made mostly of plastic.

Hard disk drive:

- HDDs are generally heavier than SSDs, as the enclosures are made mostly of metal, and they contain heavy objects such as motors and large magnets. 3.5-inch drives typically weigh around 700 grams (about 1.5 pounds).

Secure Writing Limitations

Solid-state drive:

- NAND flash memory cannot be overwritten, but has to be rewritten to previously erased blocks. If a software encryption program encrypts data already on the SSD, the overwritten data is still unsecured, unencrypted, and accessible (drive-based hardware encryption does not have this problem). Also data cannot be securely erased by overwriting the original file without special "Secure Erase" procedures built into the drive.

Hard disk drive:

- HDDs can overwrite data directly on the drive in any particular sector. However, the drive's firmware may exchange damaged blocks with spare areas, so bits and pieces may still be present. Some manufacturers' HDDs fill the entire drive with zeroes, including relocated sectors, on ATA Secure Erase Enhanced Erase command.

Read/Write Performance Symmetry

Solid-state drive:

- Less expensive SSDs typically have write speeds significantly lower than their read speeds. Higher performing SSDs have similar read and write speeds.

Hard disk drive:

- HDDs generally have slightly longer (worse) seek times for writing than for reading.

Free Block Availability and TRIM

Solid-state drive:

- SSD write performance is significantly impacted by the availability of free, programmable blocks. Previously written data blocks no longer in use can be reclaimed by TRIM; however, even with TRIM, fewer free blocks cause slower performance.

Hard disk drive:

- HDDs are not affected by free blocks and do not benefit from TRIM.

Power Consumption

Solid-state drive:

- High performance flash-based SSDs generally require half to a third of the power of HDDs. High-performance DRAM SSDs generally require as much power as HDDs, and must be connected to power even when the rest of the system is shut down. Emerging technologies like DevSlp can minimize power requirements of idle drives.

Hard disk drive:

The lowest-power HDDs (1.8-inch size) can use as little as 0.35 watts when idle. 2.5-inch drives typically use 2 to 5 watts. The highest-performance 3.5-inch drives can use up to about 20 watts.

Maximum Areal Storage Density (Terabits Per Square Inch)

Solid-state drive:

2.8

Hard disk drive:

1.2.

Memory Cards

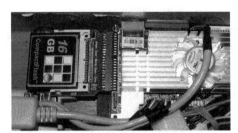

CompactFlash card used as an SSD.

While both memory cards and most SSDs use flash memory, they serve very different markets and purposes. Each has a number of different attributes which are optimized and adjusted to best meet the needs of particular users. Some of these characteristics include power consumption, performance, size, and reliability.

SSDs were originally designed for use in a computer system. The first units were intended to replace or augment hard disk drives, so the operating system recognized them as a hard drive. Originally, solid state drives were even shaped and mounted in the computer like hard drives. Later SSDs became smaller and more compact, eventually developing their own unique form factors such as the M.2 form factor. The SSD was designed to be installed permanently inside a computer.

In contrast, memory cards (such as Secure Digital (SD), CompactFlash (CF), and many others) were originally designed for digital cameras and later found their way into cell phones, gaming devices, GPS units, etc. Most memory cards are physically smaller than SSDs, and designed to be inserted and removed repeatedly. There are adapters which enable some memory cards to interface to a computer, allowing use as an SSD, but they are not intended to be the primary storage device in the computer. The typical CompactFlash card interface is three to four times slower than an SSD. As memory cards are not designed to tolerate the amount of reading and writing which occurs during typical computer use, their data may get damaged unless special procedures are taken to reduce the wear on the card to a minimum.

SSD Failure

SSDs have very different failure modes than traditional magnetic hard drives. Because of their design, some kinds of failure are inapplicable (motors or magnetic heads cannot fail, because they are not needed in an SSD). Instead, other kinds of failure are possible (for example, incomplete or failed writes due to sudden power failure can be more of a problem than with HDDs, and if a chip fails then all the data on it is lost, a scenario not applicable to magnetic drives). However, on the whole statistics show that SSDs are generally highly reliable, and often continue working far beyond the expected lifetime as stated by their manufacturer.

SSD Reliability and Failure Modes

An early test by Techreport.com which ran for 18 months during 2013 - 2015 had previously tested a number of SSDs to destruction to identify how and at what point they failed; the test found that "All of the drives surpassed their official endurance specifications by writing hundreds of terabytes without issue", described as being far beyond any usual size for a "typical consumer". The first SSD to fail was a TLC based drive - a type of design expected to be less durable than either SLC or MLC - and the SSD concerned managed to write over 800,000 GB (800 TB or 0.8 petabytes) before failing; three SSDs in the test managed to write almost three times that amount (almost 2.5 PB) before they also failed. So the capability of even consumer SSDs to be remarkably reliable was already established.

A 2016 study of "millions of drive days" in production use by SSDs over a six-year period, reported that "4-10%" of their SSDs were replaced in a 4 year period and concluded based upon annual failure rates of HDDs published in 2007 that SSDs fail at a "significantly lower" rate than HDDs; however a 2016 study of 71,940 HDDs (26 million drive days) reported annual failure rates comparable to the reported SSD rates, that is, the HDDs on the average had a calculated four year failure rate of 7.5% and with a lowest rate of 1.6%. The 2016 SDD study concluded SSD localized data loss due to unreadable blocks to be more of a problem than with HDDs. It also contained a number of "unexpected conclusions".

- In the real world, MLC based designs - believed less reliable than SLC designs - are often as reliable as SLC. (The findings state that "SLC is not generally more reliable than MLC").

- Device age, measured by days in use, is the main factor in SSD reliability, and not amount of data read or written, which are measured by TBW or DWPD. Because this finding persists after controlling for early failure and other factors, it is likely that factors such as "silicon aging" is a cause of this trend. The correlation is significant (around 0.2 - 0.4).

- Raw bit error rates (RBER) grows much slower than usually believed and is not exponential as often assumed, nor is it a good predictor of other errors or SSD failure.

- The uncorrectable bit error rate (UBER) is widely used but is not a good predictor of failure either. However SSD UBER rates are higher than those for HDDs, so although they do not predict failure, they can lead to data loss due to unreadable blocks being more common on SSDs than HDDs. The conclusion states that although more reliable overall, the rate of uncorrectable errors able to impact a user is larger.

- "Bad blocks in new SSDs are common, and drives with a large number of bad blocks are much more likely to lose hundreds of other blocks, most likely due to die or chip failure. 30-80 percent of SSDs develop at least one bad block and 2-7 percent develop at least one bad chip in the first four years of deployment."

- There is no sharp increase in errors after the expected lifetime is reached.

- Most SSDs develop no more than a few bad blocks, perhaps 2 - 4. SSDs that develop many bad blocks often go on to develop far more (perhaps hundreds), and may be prone to failure.

However most drives (99%+) are shipped with bad blocks from manufacture. The finding overall was that bad blocks are common and 30-80% of drives will develop at least one in use, but even a few bad blocks (2 - 4) is a predictor of up to hundreds of bad blocks at a later time. The bad block count at manufacture correlates with later development of further bad blocks. The report conclusion added that SSDs tended to either have "less than a handful" of bad blocks or "a large number", and suggested that this might be a basis for predicting eventual failure.

- Around 2-7% of SSDs will develop bad chips in their first 4 years of use. Over 2/3 of these chips will have breached their manufacturers' tolerances and specifications, which typically guarantee that no more than 2% of blocks on a chip will fail within its expected write lifetime.

- 96% of those SSDs that need repair (warranty servicing), need repair only once in their life. Days between repair vary from "a couple of thousand days" to "nearly 15,000 days" depending on the model.

Data Recovery and Secure Deletion

Solid state drives have set new challenges for data recovery companies, as the way of storing data is non-linear and much more complex than that of hard disk drives. The strategy the drive operates by internally can largely vary between manufacturers, and the TRIM command zeroes the whole range of a deleted file. Wear leveling also means that the physical address of the data and the address exposed to the operating system are different.

As for secure deletion of data, ATA Secure Erase command could be used. A program such as hdparm can be used for this purpose.

Applications

Due to their generally prohibitive cost versus HDD's at the time, until 2009, SSDs were mainly used in those aspects of mission critical applications where the speed of the storage system needed to be as high as possible. Since flash memory has become a common component of SSDs, the falling prices and increased densities have made it more cost-effective for many other applications. For instance, in the distributed computing environment, SSDs can be used as the building block for a distributed cache layer that temporarily absorbs the large volume of user requests to the slower HDD based backend storage system. This layer provides much higher bandwidth and lower latency than the storage system, and can be managed in a number of forms, such as distributed key-value database and distributed file system. On the supercomputers, this layer is typically referred to as burst buffer. With this fast layer, users often experience shorter system response time. Organizations that can benefit from faster access of system data include equity trading companies, telecommunication corporations, and streaming media and video editing firms. The list of applications which could benefit from faster storage is vast.

Flash-based solid-state drives can be used to create network appliances from general-purpose personal computer hardware. A write protected flash drive containing the operating system and application software can substitute for larger, less reliable disk drives or CD-ROMs. Appliances built this way can provide an inexpensive alternative to expensive router and firewall hardware.

SSDs based on an SD card with a live SD operating system are easily write-locked. Combined with a cloud computing environment or other writable medium, to maintain persistence, an OS booted from a write-locked SD card is robust, rugged, reliable, and impervious to permanent corruption. If the running OS degrades, simply turning the machine off and then on returns it back to its initial un-corrupted state and thus is particularly solid. The SD card installed OS does not require removal of corrupted components since it was write-locked though any written media may need to be restored.

File System Support for SSDs

Typically the same file systems used on hard disk drives can also be used on solid state drives. It is usually expected for the file system to support the TRIM command which helps the SSD to recycle discarded data (support for TRIM arrived some years after SSDs themselves but is now nearly universal). This means that file system does not need to manage wear leveling or other flash memory characteristics, as they are handled internally by the SSD. Some flash file systems using log-based designs (F2FS, JFFS2) help to reduce write amplification on SSDs, especially in situations where only very small amounts of data are changed, such as when updating file system metadata.

While not a file system feature, operating systems should also aim to align partitions correctly, which avoids excessive read-modify-write cycles. A typical practice for personal computers is to have each partition aligned to start at a 1 MB (= 1,048,576 bytes) mark, which covers all common SSD page and block size scenarios, as it is divisible by all commonly used sizes - 1 MB, 512 KB, 128 KB, 4 KB, and 512 bytes. Modern operating system installation software and disk tools handle this automatically.

Linux

The ext4, Btrfs, XFS, JFS, and F2FS file systems include support for the discard (TRIM or UN-MAP) function. As of November 2013, ext4 can be recommended as a safe choice. F2FS is a modern file system optimized for flash-based storage, and from a technical perspective is a very good choice, but is still in experimental stage.

Kernel support for the TRIM operation was introduced in version 2.6.33 of the Linux kernel mainline, released on 24 February 2010. To make use of it, a filesystem must be mounted using the discard parameter. Linux swap partitions are by default performing discard operations when the underlying drive supports TRIM, with the possibility to turn them off, or to select between one-time or continuous discard operations. Support for queued TRIM, which is a SATA 3.1 feature that results in TRIM commands not disrupting the command queues, was introduced in Linux kernel 3.12, released on November 2, 2013.

An alternative to the kernel-level TRIM operation is to use a user-space utility called fstrim that goes through all of the unused blocks in a filesystem and dispatches TRIM commands for those areas. fstrim utility is usually run by cron as a scheduled task. As of November 2013, it is used by the Ubuntu Linux distribution, in which it is enabled only for Intel and Samsung solid-state drives for reliability reasons; vendor check can be disabled by editing file /etc/cron.weekly/fstrim using instructions contained within the file itself.

Since 2010, standard Linux drive utilities have taken care of appropriate partition alignment by default.

Linux Performance Considerations

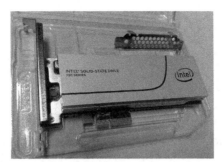

An SSD that uses NVM Express as the logical device interface,
in form of a PCI Express 3.0 ×4 expansion card.

During installation, Linux distributions usually do not configure the installed system to use TRIM and thus the /etc/fstab file requires manual modifications. This is because of the notion that the current Linux TRIM command implementation might not be optimal. It has been proven to cause a performance degradation instead of a performance increase under certain circumstances. As of January 2014, Linux sends an individual TRIM command to each sector, instead of a vectorized list defining a TRIM range as recommended by the TRIM specification. This deficiency has existed for years and there are no known plans to eliminate it.

For performance reasons, it is recommended to switch the I/O scheduler from the default CFQ (Completely Fair Queuing) to NOOP or Deadline. CFQ was designed for traditional magnetic media and seek optimizations, thus many of those I/O scheduling efforts are wasted when used with SSDs. As part of their designs, SSDs offer much bigger levels of parallelism for I/O operations, so it is preferable to leave scheduling decisions to their internal logic – especially for high-end SSDs.

A scalable block layer for high-performance SSD storage, known as blk-multiqueue or blk-mq and developed primarily by Fusion-io engineers, was merged into the Linux kernel mainline in kernel version 3.13, released on 19 January 2014. This leverages the performance offered by SSDs and NVM Express, by allowing much higher I/O submission rates. With this new design of the Linux kernel block layer, internal queues are split into two levels (per-CPU and hardware-submission queues), thus removing bottlenecks and allowing much higher levels of I/O parallelization. As of version 4.0 of the Linux kernel, released on 12 April 2015, VirtIO block driver, the SCSI layer (which is used by Serial ATA drivers), device mapper framework, loop device driver, unsorted block images (UBI) driver (which implements erase block management layer for flash memory devices) and RBD driver (which exports Ceph RADOS objects as block devices) have been modified to actually use this new interface; other drivers will be ported in the following releases.

MacOS

Versions since Mac OS X 10.6.8 (Snow Leopard) support TRIM but only when used with an Apple-purchased SSD. TRIM is not automatically enabled for third-party drives, although it can be enabled by using third-party utilities such as Trim Enabler. The status of TRIM can be checked in the System Information application or in the system_profiler command-line tool.

Versions since OS X 10.10.4 (Yosemite) include sudo trimforce enable as a Terminal command that enables TRIM on non-Apple SSDs. There is also a technique to enable TRIM in versions earlier than Mac OS X 10.6.8, although it remains uncertain whether TRIM is actually utilized properly in those cases.

Microsoft Windows

Versions of Microsoft Windows before 7 do not take any special measures to support solid state drives. Starting from Windows 7, the standard NTFS file system provides TRIM support (other file systems on Windows do not support TRIM).

By default, Windows 7 and newer versions execute TRIM commands automatically if the device is detected to be a solid-state drive. To change this behavior, in the Registry key HKEY_LOCAL_MACHINE\SYSTEM\CurrentControlSet\Control\FileSystem the value DisableDeleteNotification can be set to 1 to prevent the mass storage driver from issuing the TRIM command. This can be useful in situations where data recovery is preferred over wear leveling (in most cases, TRIM irreversibly resets all freed space).

Windows implements TRIM command for more than just file delete operations. The TRIM operation is fully integrated with partition- and volume-level commands like format and delete, with file system commands relating to truncate and compression, and with the System Restore (also known as Volume Snapshot) feature.

Windows 7

Windows 7 and later versions have native support for SSDs. The operating system detects the presence of an SSD and optimizes operation accordingly. For SSD devices Windows disables SuperFetch and ReadyBoost, boot-time and application prefetching operations. Despite the initial statement by Steven Sinofsky before the release of Windows 7, however, defragmentation is not disabled, even though its behavior on SSDs differs. One reason is the low performance of Volume Shadow Copy Service on fragmented SSDs. The second reason is to avoid reaching the practical maximum number of file fragments that a volume can handle. If this maximum is reached, subsequent attempts to write to the drive will fail with an error message.

Windows 7 also includes support for the TRIM command to reduce garbage collection for data which the operating system has already determined is no longer valid. Without support for TRIM, the SSD would be unaware of this data being invalid and would unnecessarily continue to rewrite it during garbage collection causing further wear on the SSD. It is beneficial to make some changes that prevent SSDs from being treated more like HDDs, for example cancelling defragmentation, not filling them to more than about 75% of capacity, not storing frequently written-to files such as log and temporary files on them if a hard drive is available, and enabling the TRIM process.

Windows 8.1

Windows 8.1 and later Windows systems like Windows 10 also support automatic TRIM for PCI Express SSDs based on NVMe. For Windows 7, the KB2990941 update is required for this functionality and needs to be integrated into Windows Setup using DISM if Windows 7 has to be installed on the NVMe SSD. Windows 8/8.1 also support the SCSI unmap command for USB-attached SSDs or SATA-to-USB enclosures. SCSI Unmap is a full analog of the SATA TRIM command. It is also supported over USB Attached SCSI Protocol (UASP).

The graphical Windows Disk Defagmenter in Windows 8.1 also recognizes SSDs distinctly from hard disk drives in a separate Media Type column. While Windows 7 supported automatic TRIM for internal SATA SSDs, Windows 8.1 and Windows 10 support manual TRIM (via an "Optimize" function in Disk Defragmenter) as well as automatic TRIM for SATA, NVMe and USB-attached SSDs.

Windows Vista

Windows Vista generally expects hard disk drives rather than SSDs. Windows Vista includes ReadyBoost to exploit characteristics of USB-connected flash devices, but for SSDs it only improves the default partition alignment to prevent read-modify-write operations that reduce the speed of SSDs. Most SSDs are typically split into 4 kB sectors, while most systems are based on 512 byte sectors with their default partition setups unaligned to the 4 KB boundaries. The proper alignment does not help the SSD's endurance over the life of the drive; however, some Vista operations, if not disabled, can shorten the life of the SSD.

Drive defragmentation should be disabled because the location of the file components on an SSD doesn't significantly impact its performance, but moving the files to make them contiguous using the Windows Defrag routine will cause unnecessary write wear on the limited number of P/E cycles on the SSD. The Superfetch feature will not materially improve the performance of the system and causes additional overhead in the system and SSD, although it does not cause wear. Windows Vista does not send the TRIM command to solid state drives, but some third part utilities such as SSD Doctor will periodically scan the drive and TRIM the appropriate entries.

ZFS

Solaris as of version 10 Update 6 (released in October 2008), and recent[when?] versions of Open-Solaris, Solaris Express Community Edition, Illumos, Linux with ZFS on Linux, and FreeBSD all can use SSDs as a performance booster for ZFS. A low-latency SSD can be used for the ZFS Intent Log (ZIL), where it is named the SLOG. This is used every time a synchronous write to the drive occurs. An SSD (not necessarily with a low-latency) may also be used for the level 2 Adaptive Replacement Cache (L2ARC), which is used to cache data for reading. When used either alone or in combination, large increases in performance are generally seen.

FreeBSD

ZFS for FreeBSD introduced support for TRIM on September 23, 2012. The code builds a map of regions of data that were freed; on every write the code consults the map and eventually removes ranges that were freed before, but are now overwritten. There is a low-priority thread that TRIMs ranges when the time comes.

Also the Unix File System (UFS) supports the TRIM command.

Swap Partitions

- According to Microsoft's former Windows division president Steven Sinofsky, "there are few files better than the pagefile to place on an SSD". According to collected telemetry data, Microsoft had found the pagefile.sys to be an ideal match for SSD storage.

- Linux swap partitions are by default performing TRIM operations when the underlying block device supports TRIM, with the possibility to turn them off, or to select between one-time or continuous TRIM operations.

- If an operating system does not support using TRIM on discrete swap partitions, it might be possible to use swap files inside an ordinary file system instead. For example, OS X does not support swap partitions; it only swaps to files within a file system, so it can use TRIM when, for example, swap files are deleted.

- DragonFly BSD allows SSD-configured swap to also be used as file system cache. This can be used to boost performance on both desktop and server workloads. The bcache, dm-cache, and Flashcache projects provide a similar concept for the Linux kernel.

Optical Drive

A CD/DVD-ROM computer drive.

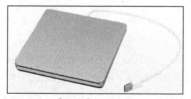

An external Apple USB SuperDrive.

A removable internal Lenovo disc drive.

In computing, an optical disc drive (ODD) is a disc drive that uses laser light or electromagnetic waves within or near the visible light spectrum as part of the process of reading or writing data to or from optical discs. Some drives can only read from certain discs, but recent drives can both read and record, also called burners or writers. Compact discs, DVDs, and Blu-ray discs are common types of optical media which can be read and recorded by such drives. Optical disc drives that are no longer in production include CD-ROM drive, CD writer drive, combo (CD-RW/DVD-ROM) drive, and DVD writer drive supporting certain recordable and rewritable DVD formats (such as DVD-R(W) only, DVD+R(W) only, DVD-RAM only, and all DVD formats except DVD-R DL). As of 2015, DVD writer drive supporting all existing recordable and rewritable DVD formats is the most common for desktop PCs and laptops. There are also the DVD-ROM drive, BD-ROM drive, Blu-ray Disc combo (BD-ROM/DVD±RW/CD-RW) drive, and Blu-ray Disc writer drive.

Optical disc drives are an integral part of standalone appliances such as CD players, DVD players, Blu-ray disc players, DVD recorders, certain desktop video game consoles, such as Sony PlayStation 4, Microsoft Xbox One, Nintendo Wii U, and Sony PlayStation 3, and certain portable video game consoles, such as Sony PlayStation Portable. They are also very commonly used in computers to read software and consumer media distributed on disc and to record discs for archival and data exchange purposes. Floppy disk drives, with capacity of 1.44 MB, have been made obsolete: optical media are cheap and have vastly higher capacity to handle the large files used since the days of floppy discs, and the vast majority of computers and much consumer entertainment hardware have optical writers. USB flash drives, high-capacity, small, and inexpensive, are suitable where read/write capability is required.

Disc recording is restricted to storing files playable on consumer appliances (films, music, etc.), relatively small volumes of data (e.g. a standard DVD holds 4.7 gigabytes) for local use, and data for distribution, but only on a small scale; mass-producing large numbers of identical discs is cheaper and faster than individual recording.

Optical discs are used to back up relatively small volumes of data, but backing up of entire hard drives, which as of 2015 typically contain many hundreds of gigabytes or even multiple terabytes, is less practical. Large backups are often instead made on external hard drives, as their price has dropped to a level making this viable; in professional environments magnetic tape drives are also used.

The CD/DVD drive lens on an Acer laptop.

Lenses from a Blu-ray writer in a Sony Vaio E series laptop.

Key Components

Laser and Optics

The most important part of an optical disc drive is an optical path, placed in a pickup head (PUH), usually consisting of a semiconductor laser diode, a lens for focusing the laser beam, and photodiodes for detecting the light reflected from the disc's surface.

Initially, CD-type lasers with a wavelength of 780 nm (within the infrared) were used. For DVDs, the wavelength was reduced to 650 nm (red color), and for Blu-ray Disc this was reduced even further to 405 nm (violet color).

Two main servomechanisms are used, the first to maintain the proper distance between lens and disc, to ensure the laser beam is focused as a small laser spot on the disc. The second servo moves the pickup head along the disc's radius, keeping the beam on the track, a continuous spiral data path. Optical disc media are 'read' beginning at the inner radius to the outer edge.

The optical sensor out of a CD/DVD drive. The two larger rectangles are the photodiodes for pits, the inner one for land. This one also includes amplification and minor processing.

On read only media (ROM), during the manufacturing process the tracks are formed by pressing a thermoplastic resin into a glass 'master' with raised 'bumps' on a flat surface, creating pits and lands in the plastic disk. Because the depth of the pits is approximately one-quarter to one-sixth of the laser's wavelength, the reflected beam's phase is shifted in relation to the incoming beam, causing mutual destructive interference and reducing the reflected beam's intensity. This is detected by photodiodes that create corresponding electrical signals.

An optical disk recorder encodes (also known as burning) data onto a recordable CD-R, DVD-R, DVD+R, or BD-R disc (called a blank) by selectively heating parts of an organic dye layer with a laser. This changes the reflectivity of the dye, thereby creating marks that can be read like the pits and lands on pressed discs. For recordable discs, the process is permanent and the media can be written to only once. While the reading laser is usually not stronger than 5 mW, the writing laser is considerably more powerful. The higher the writing speed, the less time a laser has to heat a point on the media, thus its power has to increase proportionally. DVD burners' lasers often peak at about 200 mW, either in continuous wave and pulses, although some have been driven up to 400 mW before the diode fails.

For rewritable CD-RW, DVD-RW, DVD+RW, DVD-RAM, or BD-RE media, the laser is used to melt a crystalline metal alloy in the recording layer of the disc. Depending on the amount of power applied, the substance may be allowed to melt back (change the phase back) into crystalline form or left in an amorphous form, enabling marks of varying reflectivity to be created.

Double-sided media may be used, but they are not easily accessed with a standard drive, as they must be physically turned over to access the data on the other side.

Double layer (DL) media have two independent data layers separated by a semi-reflective layer. Both layers are accessible from the same side, but require the optics to change the laser's focus. Traditional single layer (SL) writable media are produced with a spiral groove molded in the protective polycarbonate layer (not in the data recording layer), to lead and synchronize the speed of recording head. Double-layered writable media have: a first polycarbonate layer with a (shallow) groove, a first data layer, a semi-reflective layer, a second (spacer) polycarbonate layer with another (deep) groove, and a second data layer. The first groove spiral usually starts on the inner edge and extends outwards, while the second groove starts on the outer edge and extends inwards.

Some drives support Hewlett-Packard's LightScribe photothermal printing technology for labeling specially coated discs.

Rotational Mechanism

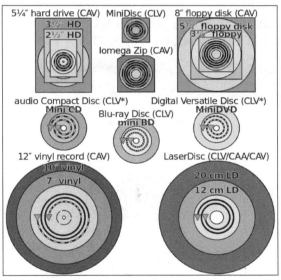

Comparison of several forms of disk storage showing tracks (not-to-scale); green denotes start and red denotes end.
* Some CD-R(W) and DVD-R(W)/DVD+R(W) recorders operate in ZCLV, CAA or CAV modes.

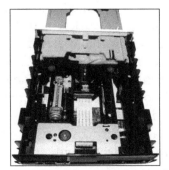

A CD-ROM drive (without case).

The rotational mechanism in an optical drive differs considerably from that of a hard disk drive's, in that the latter keeps a constant angular velocity (CAV), in other words a constant number of revolutions per minute (RPM). With CAV, a higher throughput is generally achievable at the outer disc compared to the inner.

On the other hand, optical drives were developed with an assumption of achieving a constant throughput, in CD drives initially equal to 150 KiB/s. It was a feature important for streaming audio data that always tend to require a constant bit rate. But to ensure no disc capacity was wasted, a head had to transfer data at a maximum linear rate at all times too, without slowing on the outer rim of disc. This led to optical drives—until recently—operating with a constant linear velocity (CLV). The spiral *groove* of the disc passed under its head at a constant speed. The implication of CLV, as opposed to CAV, is that disc angular velocity is no longer constant, and the spindle motor needed to be designed to vary its speed from between 200 RPM on the outer rim and 500 RPM on the inner.

Later CD drives kept the CLV paradigm, but evolved to achieve higher rotational speeds, popularly described in multiples of a base speed. As a result, a 4× drive, for instance, would rotate at 800-2000 RPM, while transferring data steadily at 600 KiB/s, which is equal to 4 × 150 KiB/s.

For DVDs, base or 1× speed is 1.385 MB/s, equal to 1.32 MiB/s, approximately nine times faster than the CD base speed. For Blu-ray drives, base speed is 6.74 MB/s, equal to 6.43 MiB/s.

The Z-CLV recording pattern is easily visible after burning a DVD-R.

Because keeping a constant transfer rate for the whole disc is not so important in most contemporary CD uses, a pure CLV approach had to be abandoned to keep the rotational speed of the disc safely low while maximizing data rate. Some drives work in a partial CLV (PCLV) scheme, by switching from CLV to CAV only when a rotational limit is reached. But switching to CAV requires considerable changes in hardware design, so instead most drives use the zoned constant linear velocity (Z-CLV) scheme. This divides the disc into several zones, each having its own constant linear velocity. A Z-CLV recorder rated at "52×", for example, would write at 20× on the innermost zone and then progressively increase the speed in several discrete steps up to 52× at the outer rim. Without higher rotational speeds, increased read performance may be attainable by simultaneously reading more than one point of a data groove, but drives with such mechanisms are more expensive, less compatible, and very uncommon.

Limit

An exploded disc.

Both DVDs and CDs have been known to explode when damaged or spun at excessive speed. This imposes a constraint on the maximum speed (56× for CDs or around 18× in the case of DVDs) at which drives can operate.

Loading Mechanisms

Current optical drives use either a tray-loading mechanism, where the disc is loaded onto a motorized or manually operated tray, or a slot-loading mechanism, where the disc is slid into a slot and drawn in by motorized rollers. With both types of mechanisms, if a CD or DVD is left in the drive after the computer is turned off, the disc cannot be ejected using the normal eject mechanism of the drive. However, tray-loading drives account for this situation by providing a small hole where one can insert a straightened paperclip to manually open the drive tray to retrieve the disc. Slot-loading optical disc drives have the disadvantages that they cannot usually accept the smaller 80 mm discs (unless 80 mm optical disc adapter is used) or any non-standard sizes, usually have no emergency eject hole or eject button, and therefore have to be disassembled if the optical disc cannot be ejected normally. However, the Nintendo Wii, because of backward compatibility with Nintendo GameCube games, and PlayStation 3 video game consoles are able to load standard size DVDs and 80 mm discs in the same slot-loading drive.

A small number of drive models, mostly compact portable units, have a top-loading mechanism where the drive lid is opened upwards and the disc is placed directly onto the spindle (for example, all PlayStation One consoles, most portable CD players, and some standalone CD recorders feature top-loading drives). These sometimes have the advantage of using spring-loaded ball bearings to hold the disc in place, minimizing damage to the disc if the drive is moved while it is spun up.

Some early CD-ROM drives used a mechanism where CDs had to be inserted into special cartridges or caddies, somewhat similar in appearance to a 3.5" floppy diskette. This was intended to protect the disc from accidental damage by enclosing it in a tougher plastic casing, but did not gain wide acceptance due to the additional cost and compatibility concerns—such drives would also inconveniently require "bare" discs to be manually inserted into an openable caddy before use. Ultra Density Optical and Universal Media Disc use optical disc cartridges.

There were also some early CD-ROM drives for desktop PCs in which its tray-loading mechanism will eject slightly and user has to pull out the tray manually to load CD, similar to the tray ejecting method used in internal optical disc drives of modern laptops and modern external slim portable optical disc drives. Like the top-loading mechanism, they have spring-loaded ball bearings on the spindle.

Computer Interfaces

Digital audio output, analog audio output, and parallel ATA interface.

Most internal drives for personal computers, servers, and workstations are designed to fit in a standard 5.25" drive bay and connect to their host via an ATA or SATA interface. Additionally, there may be digital and analog outputs for audio. The outputs may be connected via a header cable to the sound card or the motherboard. At one time, computer software resembling CD players controlled playback of the CD. Today the information is extracted from the disc as data, to be played back or converted to other file formats.

External drives usually have USB or FireWire interfaces. Some portable versions for laptops power themselves from batteries or directly from their interface bus.

Drives with SCSI interface were made, but they are less common and tend to be more expensive, because of the cost of their interface chipsets, more complex SCSI connectors, and small volume of sales.

When the optical disc drive was first developed, it was not easy to add to computer systems. Some computers such as the IBM PS/2 were standardizing on the 3.5" floppy and 3.5" hard disk and did not include a place for a large internal device. Also IBM PCs and clones at first only included a single (parallel) ATA drive interface, which by the time the CDROM was introduced, was already being used to support two hard drives. Early laptops simply had no built-in high-speed interface for supporting an external storage device.

HP C4381A CD-Writer Plus 7200 Series, showing parallel ports
to connect between a printer and the computer.

This was solved through several techniques:

- Early sound cards could include a CD-ROM drive interface. Initially, such interfaces were proprietary to each CD-ROM manufacturer. A sound card could often have two or three different interfaces which are able to communicate with cdrom drive.

- A parallel port external drive was developed that connected a printer and the computer. This was slow but an option for laptops.

- A PCMCIA optical drive interface was also developed for laptops.

- A SCSI card could be installed in desktop PCs for an external SCSI drive enclosure, though SCSI was typically much more expensive than other options.

Internal Mechanism of a Drive

Internal mechanism of a DVD-ROM Drive.

The optical drives in the photos are shown right side up; the disc would sit on top of them. The laser and optical system scans the underside of the disc.

With reference to the top photo, just to the right of image center is the disc motor, a metal cylinder, with a gray centering hub and black rubber drive ring on top. There is a disc-shaped round clamp, loosely held inside the cover and free to rotate; it's not in the photo. After the disc tray stops moving inward, as the motor and its attached parts rise, a magnet near the top of the rotating assembly contacts and strongly attracts the clamp to hold and center the disc. This motor is an "outrunner"-style brushless DC motor which has an external rotor – every visible part of it spins.

Two parallel guide rods that run between upper left and lower right in the photo carry the "sled", the moving optical read-write head. As shown, this "sled" is close to, or at the position where it reads or writes at the edge of the disc. To move the "sled" during continuous read or write operations, a stepper motor rotates a leadscrew to move the "sled" throughout its total travel range. The motor, itself, is the short gray cylinder just to the left of the most-distant shock mount; its shaft is parallel to the support rods. The leadscrew is the rod with evenly-spaced darker details; these are the helical grooves that engage a pin on the "sled".

In contrast, the mechanism shown in the second photo, which comes from a cheaply made DVD player, uses less accurate and less efficient brushed DC motors to both move the sled and spin the disc. Some older drives use a DC motor to move the sled, but also have a magnetic rotary encoder to keep track of the position. Most drives in computers use stepper motors.

The gray metal chassis is shock-mounted at its four corners to reduce sensitivity to external shocks, and to reduce drive noise from residual imbalance when running fast. The soft shock mount grommets are just below the brass-colored screws at the four corners (the left one is obscured).

In the third photo, the components under the cover of the lens mechanism are visible. The two permanent magnets on either side of the lens holder as well as the coils that move the lens can be seen. This allows the lens to be moved up, down, forwards, and backwards to stabilize the focus of the beam.

In the fourth photo, the inside of the optics package can be seen. Note that since this is a CD-ROM drive, there is only one laser, which is the black component mounted to the bottom left of the assembly. Just above the laser are the first focusing lens and prism that direct the beam at the disc. The tall, thin object in the center is a half-silvered mirror that splits the laser beam in multiple directions. To the bottom right of the mirror is the main photodiode that senses the beam reflected off the disc. Above the main photodiode is a second photodiode that is used to sense and regulate the power of the laser.

The irregular orange material is flexible etched copper foil supported by thin sheet plastic; these are "flexible printed circuits" that connect everything to the electronics (which is not shown).

Recording Performance

During the times of CD writer drives, they are often marked with three different speed ratings. In these cases, the first speed is for write-once (R) operations, the second speed for re-write (RW) operations, and the last speed for read-only (ROM) operations. For example, a 40×/16×/48× CD writer drive is capable of writing to CD-R media at speed of 40× (6,000 kbit/s), writing to CD-RW media at speed of 16× (2,400 kbit/s), and reading from a CD-ROM media at speed of 48× (7,200 kbit/s).

During the times of combo (CD-RW/DVD-ROM) drives, an additional speed rating (e.g. the 16× in 52×/32×/52×/16×) is designated for DVD-ROM media reading operations.

For DVD writer drives, Blu-ray disc combo drives, and Blu-ray disc writer drives, the writing and reading speed of their respective optical media are specified in its retail box, user's manual, or bundled brochures or pamphlets.

In the late 1990s, buffer underruns became a very common problem as high-speed CD recorders began to appear in home and office computers, which—for a variety of reasons—often could not muster the I/O performance to keep the data stream to the recorder steadily fed. The recorder, should it run short, would be forced to halt the recording process, leaving a truncated track that usually renders the disc useless.

In response, manufacturers of CD recorders began shipping drives with "buffer underrun protection" (under various trade names, such as Sanyo's "BURN-Proof", Ricoh's "JustLink" and Yamaha's "Lossless Link"). These can suspend and resume the recording process in such a way that the gap the stoppage produces can be dealt with by the error-correcting logic built into CD players and CD-ROM drives. The first of these drives were rated at 12× and 16×.

While drives are burning DVD+R, DVD+RW and all Blu-ray formats, they do not require any such error correcting recovery as the recorder is able to place the new data exactly on the end of the suspended write effectively producing a continuous track (this is what the DVD+ technology achieved). Although later interfaces were able to stream data at the required speed, many drives now write in a 'zoned constant linear velocity'. This means that the drive has to temporarily suspend the write operation while it changes speed and then recommence it once the new speed is attained. This is handled in the same manner as a buffer underrun.

The internal buffer of optical disc writer drives is: 8 MiB or 4 MiB when recording BD-R, BD-R DL, BD-RE, or BD-RE DL media; 2 MiB when recording DVD-R, DVD-RW, DVD-R DL, DVD+R, DVD+RW, DVD+RW DL, DVD-RAM, CD-R, or CD-RW media.

Recording Schemes

CD recording on personal computers was originally a batch-oriented task in that it required specialised authoring software to create an "image" of the data to record and to record it to disc in the one session. This was acceptable for archival purposes, but limited the general convenience of CD-R and CD-RW discs as a removable storage medium.

Packet writing is a scheme in which the recorder writes incrementally to disc in short bursts, or packets. Sequential packet writing fills the disc with packets from bottom up. To make it readable in CD-ROM and DVD-ROM drives, the disc can be *closed* at any time by writing a final table-of-contents to the start of the disc; thereafter, the disc cannot be packet-written any further. Packet writing, together with support from the operating system and a file system like UDF, can be used to mimic random write-access as in media like flash memory and magnetic disks.

Fixed-length packet writing (on CD-RW and DVD-RW media) divides up the disc into padded, fixed-size packets. The padding reduces the capacity of the disc, but allows the recorder to start and stop recording on an individual packet without affecting its neighbours. These resemble the block-writable access offered by magnetic media closely enough that many conventional file systems will work as-is. Such discs, however, are not readable in most CD-ROM and DVD-ROM drives or on most operating systems without additional third-party drivers. The division into packets is not as reliable as it may seem as CD-R(W) and DVD-R(W) drives can only locate data to within a data block. Although generous gaps (the padding referred to above) are left between blocks, the drive nevertheless can occasionally miss and either destroy some existing data or even render the disc unreadable.

The DVD+RW disc format eliminates this unreliability by embedding more accurate timing hints in the data groove of the disc and allowing individual data blocks (or even bytes) to be replaced without affecting backward compatibility (a feature dubbed "lossless linking"). The format itself was designed to deal with discontinuous recording because it was expected to be widely used in digital video recorders. Many such DVRs use variable-rate video compression schemes which require them to record in short bursts; some allow simultaneous playback and recording by alternating quickly between recording to the tail of the disc whilst reading from elsewhere. The Blu-ray disc system also encompasses this technology.

Mount Rainier aims to make packet-written CD-RW and DVD+RW discs as convenient to use as that of removable magnetic media by having the firmware format new discs in the background and manage media defects (by automatically mapping parts of the disc which have been worn out by erase cycles to reserve space elsewhere on the disc). As of February 2007, support for Mount Rainier is natively supported in Windows Vista. All previous versions of Windows require a third-party solution, as does Mac OS X.

Recorder Unique Identifier

Owing to pressure from the music industry, as represented by the IFPI and RIAA, Philips developed the Recorder Identification Code (RID) to allow media to be uniquely associated with the recorder that has written it. This standard is contained in the Rainbow Books. The RID-Code consists of a supplier code (e.g. "PHI" for Philips), a model number and the unique ID of the recorder. Quoting Philips, the RID "enables a trace for each disc back to the exact machine on which it was made using coded information in the recording itself. The use of the RID code is mandatory."

Although the RID was introduced for music and video industry purposes, the RID is included on every disc written by every drive, including data and backup discs. The value of the RID is questionable as it is (currently) impossible to locate any individual recorder due to there being no database.

Source Identification Code

The Source Identification Code (SID) is an eight character supplier code that is placed on optical discs by the manufacturer. The SID identifies not only manufacturer, but also the individual factory and machine that produced the disc.

According to Phillips, the administrator of the SID codes, the SID code provides an optical disc production facility with the means to identify all discs mastered or replicated in its plant, including the specific Laser Beam Recorder (LBR) signal processor or mould that produced a particular stamper or disc.

Use of RID and SID Together in Forensics

The standard use of RID and SID mean that each disc written contains a record of the machine that produced a disc (the SID), and which drive wrote it (the RID). This combined knowledge may be very useful to law enforcement, to investigative agencies, and to private or corporate investigators.

Hardware Upgrade

With computer hardware, an upgrade is a term that describes adding new hardware in a computer that improves its performance. For example, with a hardware upgrade, you could replace your hard drive with an SSD and get a huge boost in performance or upgrade the RAM, so the computer runs more smoothly.

Benefits of a Hardware Upgrade

- Performance increase, which makes the overall computer run faster and more smoothly.

- Capacity increase. For example, adding a larger hard drive allows the computer to store more information. Adding more memory increases the computers ability to run more programs efficiently.

- It may be necessary to upgrade the computer to meet a program or games system requirements.

Disadvantages of a Hardware Upgrade

Although the benefits are always going to outweigh the disadvantages of a hardware upgrade, it is still worth noting what disadvantages there may be when upgrading hardware.

- Damage during install. It is possible, if not done correctly (e.g., not taking ESD precautions) or using to much force, you may damage the new hardware during the upgrade.

- When upgrading major computer components, such as a hard drive or motherboard, you may need to reinstall all your software that can be a significant time investment.

References

- Hardware, definition: techtarget.com, Retrieved 18 April, 2019

- Gigabyte --geeks column of the week - all solid capacitor. Www.gigabyte.com. Archived from the original on 2017-03-27. Retrieved 2017-05-06

- What-is-computer-hardware: crucial.com, Retrieved 11 January, 2019

- Cpu socket types explained: from socket 5 to bga [makeuseof explains]". 2013-01-25. Archived from the original on 2015-04-07. Retrieved 2015-04-12

- What-is-storage-device, howto: cleverfiles.com, Retrieved 14 July, 2019

- P. Pal chaudhuri, p. Pal (april 15, 2008). Computer organization and design (3rd edition). Phi learning pvt. Ltd. P. 568. Isbn 978-81-203-3511-0

- Output-devices: teachcomputerscience.com, Retrieved 29 June, 2019

- Upgrade, jargon: computerhope.com, Retrieved 30 April, 2019

Computer Software 4

Computer software is a set of programs and data that are designed to perform certain functions in a computer system. Software programming, programming paradigms, application software, etc. fall under its domain. This chapter closely examines about these computer hardware to provide an extensive understanding of the subject.

Computer software is a general term that describes computer programs. Related terms such as software programs, applications, scripts, and instruction sets all fall under the category of computer software. Therefore, installing new programs or applications on your computer is synonymous with installing new software on your computer.

Software can be difficult to describe because it is "virtual," or not physical like computer hardware. Instead, software consists of lines of code written by computer programmers that have been compiled into a computer program. Software programs are stored as binary data that is copied to a computer's hard drive, when it is installed. Since software is virtual and does not take up any physical space, it is much easier (and often cheaper) to upgrade than computer hardware. While at its most basic level, software consists of binary data, CD-ROMs, DVDs, and other types of media that are used to distribute software can also be called software. Therefore, when you buy a software program, it often comes on a disc, which is a physical means of storing the software.

System Software

System Software can be designed as the software in such a way so that it can control and work with computer hardware. It acts as an interface between the device and the end user.

It also provides the platform for the running of other software.

Example: Operating systems, antivirus software etc.

Features of the System Software

- It is difficult to design.

- It is written in the low-level language, or you can say that it is written in machine language which is only understood by the machine.

- It is difficult to manipulate.

- System software is very close to the system.

- The speed of the system software is fast.

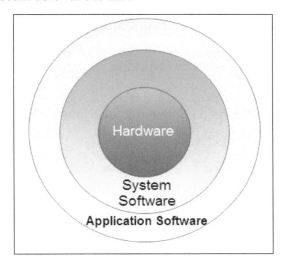

Components of System Software

System software consists of the following elements:

- Device Driver: It is a computer program. Computer hardware can interact with the higher level computer programs with the help of device drivers. These device drivers act as a translator between the application of the user and the hardware device. Due to this, it simplifies programming.

- Operating System: The operating system is the system which manages the hardware of the computer. The operating system consists of program and data. An operating system also provides us with services so that we can execute the application software.

    Example: Linux, Unix, Microsoft Windows etc.

- Server: It is a program which works like a socket listener in a computer networking system. A server computer is a series of computers which link other computers with itself. The server can provide some essential services to both private users and public users via the internet across a network.

- Utility Software: It performs small tasks which are used to manage computer hardware and application software.

    Example: System utilities, virus scanners etc.

- Windowing System: It supports the implementation of window managers. Windowing system provides essential support to graphics hardware and pointing devices like keyboard and mice. The windowing system is a component of the graphical user interface.

Types of System Software

There are five types of system software which are as follows:

Operating System

The operating system is the central part of the computer system, or you can say that it is the lifeline of the computer. We will install the OS on a computer so that it can function smoothly. Suppose all the devices like keyboard, mouse, CPU, monitor are connected and now you think as we switch on the power supply, the computer will start working. No, this is not possible until we install the operating system on it.

It is necessary to install as it performs the following functions:

- It will allocate resources to each task.
- It will keep the all hardware parts of the system in a ready state so that it can follow the instructions given by the user.
- It enables the user to access and use application software.
- It schedules the multiple tasks by priority.
- It controls the improper use of the computer.
- It sets the coordination between the different devices.
- It prevents the error during the use of the software.
- It enables the computer to access network.
- It manages different computer resources such as software, hardware etc.
- It controls the input and output devices of the computer.
- It detects, installs and troubleshoot the devices.

Example: The earlier OS was MS-DOS which make use of Command Line Interface(CLI). After then, windows was developed by Microsoft which make use of Graphical User Interface(GUI). So, they keep on evolving.

Programming Language Translators

Programming Language Translators are those who convert the high-level language and middle-level language into machine language as machine understands only its language. The high-level language is the language through which the user interacts with the computer. Java, C, C++, PHP, Python all are the examples of high-level language. Machine language is the code which is understood by the processor only. The average human being cannot be able to understand it.

Some famous translators are Compiler, Interpreter and assembler. They are designed by the manufacturers of the computer. Translators can completely translate the code into machine code at once, or they can do it line by line.

Translators also help in various tasks like:

- When the code rules are not followed, they provide the diagnostic reports.

- It will make a list of both source code and program details.

- Translators identify syntax errors when the system is translated. So, we can make the required changes.

- It allocates the storage of the data.

Device Drivers

Driver software is a type of system software so that we can use our devices smoothly without any troubleshooting problem. This type of software enables the components to perform their tasks as directed by the OS.

There are some examples of devices which require drivers:

- Mouse.

- Keyboard.

- Touch pad.

- Printer.

- Display card.

- Network card.

- Sound.

- Function keys.

Some tools are there, whose drivers are already installed on the computer by default for ex-mouse, keyboard and touchpad.

If the device is new for the operating system like the printer, then we have to install the drivers so that it gets familiar with the OS. We can install them from the websites of the manufacturers or some other alternative source like from the internet.

Firmware Software

It is the operational software which is already embedded in flash, ROM, EPROM, EEPROM memory chips so that the OS can identify them quickly. The task of the firmware is to directly manage and control all the activities of any single hardware.

Traditionally, firmware was installed on the non-volatile chips. We can upgrade them by changing with the new programmed chips.

However, nowadays, firmware was installed on the flash chips. So, now we can upgrade them without swapping the chips.

There are two types of chips: BIOS(Basic Input/Output System) chip and UEFI(Unified Extended Firmware Interface) chip. The manufacturer installs the firmware on the motherboard, and it can be accessed through these two types of chips. It is the configuration interface. When the computer is powered on and is going through POST (Power on Self Test), then it is first loaded.

The motherboard firmware wakes all the hardware when it starts. It ensures that all the components of a computer are operational. If all the ingredients are properly working, then it will run the bootloader, which will further load the operating system. If there is a fault in RAM of the system, then the BIOS will not allow the computer to boot.

The main difference between the firmware and the driver is that firmware will reside within the devices whereas the drivers will install in the operating system.

Utility Software

Utility software is a kind of system software which acts as an interface between system software and application software. These are those programs which are specifically designed for some particular purpose like maintenance of the computer or diagnose any error in the computer.

Generally, these are third-party tools which come along with the operating system.

The features of the utility software are as follows:

- To protect us against external threats, the inclusion of a firewall is there.

  Example: windows firewall.

- It can scan hardware diagnostic services like performance monitor, hard disk sentinel.

- It can also compress files so that the disk space can be optimized. E.g., WinRAR, WinZip.

- Utility can do disk partition services like Windows Disk Management.

- Utility can help us in recovering in our lost data. E.g., iCare Data Recovery, Ease Us Data Recovery Wizard etc.

- Utility can back up our data to increase the security of our systems like Cobian and Clonezilla.

- Utility can do defragmentation of a disk so that the scattered file can be organized on the drive. E.g., Disk Defragmenter, Little Snitch etc.

- Utility can perform antivirus and security software so that the security of the files and the applications can be maintained. E.g., AVG, Microsoft Security Essentials etc.

Difference between System Software and Application Software

System Software	Application Software
We make use of system software for operating hardware of the computer.	The user makes use of application software to perform some specific task.

When the operating system is installed on the computer, then the system software is also mounted on the machine.	We install the application software according to the requirement of the user.
System software works in the background. So the user is not able to interact with it.	Generally, the user interacts with the application software.
It can run independently as it provides the platform for the running application software.	It can't run independently because it is not able to run without the presence of system software.
Example: compiler, assembler, interpreter etc.	Example: word processor, web browser, media player etc.

Operating System

An operating system (OS) is system software that manages computer hardware, software resources, and provides common services for computer programs.

Time-sharing operating systems schedule tasks for efficient use of the system and may also include accounting software for cost allocation of processor time, mass storage, printing, and other resources.

For hardware functions such as input and output and memory allocation, the operating system acts as an intermediary between programs and the computer hardware, although the application code is usually executed directly by the hardware and frequently makes system calls to an OS function or is interrupted by it. Operating systems are found on many devices that contain a computer – from cellular phones and video game consoles to web servers and supercomputers.

The dominant desktop operating system is Microsoft Windows with a market share of around 82.74%. macOS by Apple Inc. is in second place (13.23%), and the varieties of Linux are collectively in third place (1.57%). In the mobile (including smartphones and tablets) sector, Google Android's share is up to 70% in the year 2017. According to third quarter 2016 data, Android's share on smartphones is dominant with 87.5 percent with also a growth rate of 10.3 percent per year, followed by Apple's iOS with 12.1 percent with per year decrease in market share of 5.2 percent, while other operating systems amount to just 0.3 percent. Linux distributions are dominant in the server and supercomputing sectors. Other specialized classes of operating systems, such as embedded and real-time systems, exist for many applications.

Types of Operating Systems

Single-tasking and Multi-tasking

A single-tasking system can only run one program at a time, while a multi-tasking operating system allows more than one program to be running in concurrency. This is achieved by time-sharing, where the available processor time is divided between multiple processes. These processes are each interrupted repeatedly in time slices by a task-scheduling subsystem of the operating system. Multi-tasking may be characterized in preemptive and co-operative types. In preemptive multi-tasking, the operating system slices the CPU time and dedicates a slot to each of the programs. Unix-like operating systems, such as Solaris and Linux—as well as non-Unix-like, such as

AmigaOS—support preemptive multitasking. Cooperative multitasking is achieved by relying on each process to provide time to the other processes in a defined manner. 16-bit versions of Microsoft Windows used cooperative multi-tasking. 32-bit versions of both Windows NT and Win9x used preemptive multi-tasking.

Single- and Multi-user

Single-user operating systems have no facilities to distinguish users, but may allow multiple programs to run in tandem. A multi-user operating system extends the basic concept of multi-tasking with facilities that identify processes and resources, such as disk space, belonging to multiple users, and the system permits multiple users to interact with the system at the same time. Time-sharing operating systems schedule tasks for efficient use of the system and may also include accounting software for cost allocation of processor time, mass storage, printing, and other resources to multiple users.

Distributed

A distributed operating system manages a group of distinct computers and makes them appear to be a single computer. The development of networked computers that could be linked and communicate with each other gave rise to distributed computing. Distributed computations are carried out on more than one machine. When computers in a group work in cooperation, they form a distributed system.

Templated

In an OS, distributed and cloud computing context, templating refers to creating a single virtual machine image as a guest operating system, then saving it as a tool for multiple running virtual machines. The technique is used both in virtualization and cloud computing management, and is common in large server warehouses.

Embedded

Embedded operating systems are designed to be used in embedded computer systems. They are designed to operate on small machines like PDAs with less autonomy. They are able to operate with a limited number of resources. They are very compact and extremely efficient by design. Windows CE and Minix 3 are some examples of embedded operating systems.

Real-time

A real-time operating system is an operating system that guarantees to process events or data by a specific moment in time. A real-time operating system may be single- or multi-tasking, but when multitasking, it uses specialized scheduling algorithms so that a deterministic nature of behavior is achieved. An event-driven system switches between tasks based on their priorities or external events while time-sharing operating systems switch tasks based on clock interrupts.

Library

A library operating system is one in which the services that a typical operating system provides, such as networking, are provided in the form of libraries and composed with the application and configuration code to construct a unikernel: a specialized, single address space, machine image that can be deployed to cloud or embedded environments.

Unix and Unix-like Operating Systems

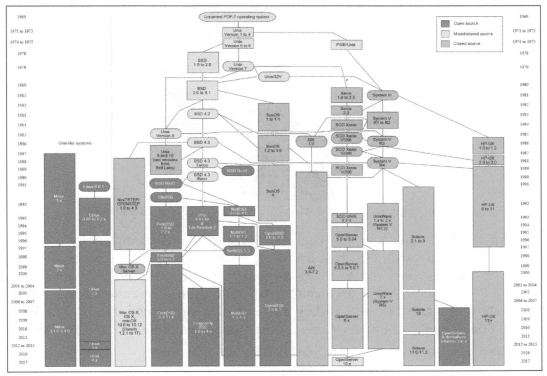

Evolution of Unix systems.

Unix was originally written in assembly language. Ken Thompson wrote B, mainly based on BCPL, based on his experience in the MULTICS project. B was replaced by C, and Unix, rewritten in C, developed into a large, complex family of inter-related operating systems which have been influential in every modern operating system.

The Unix-like family is a diverse group of operating systems, with several major sub-categories including System V, BSD, and Linux. The name "UNIX" is a trademark of The Open Group which licenses it for use with any operating system that has been shown to conform to their definitions. "UNIX-like" is commonly used to refer to the large set of operating systems which resemble the original UNIX.

Unix-like systems run on a wide variety of computer architectures. They are used heavily for servers in business, as well as workstations in academic and engineering environments. Free UNIX variants, such as Linux and BSD, are popular in these areas.

Four operating systems are certified by The Open Group (holder of the Unix trademark) as Unix. HP's HP-UX and IBM's AIX are both descendants of the original System V Unix and are designed to run only on their respective vendor's hardware. In contrast, Sun Microsystems's Solaris can run on multiple types of hardware, including x86 and Sparc servers, and PCs. Apple's macOS, a replacement for Apple's earlier (non-Unix) Mac OS, is a hybrid kernel-based BSD variant derived from NeXTSTEP, Mach, and FreeBSD.

Unix interoperability was sought by establishing the POSIX standard. The POSIX standard can be applied to any operating system, although it was originally created for various Unix variants.

BSD and its Descendants

The first server for the World Wide Web ran on NeXTSTEP, based on BSD.

A subgroup of the Unix family is the Berkeley Software Distribution family, which includes FreeBSD, NetBSD, and OpenBSD. These operating systems are most commonly found on web-servers, although they can also function as a personal computer OS. The Internet owes much of its existence to BSD, as many of the protocols now commonly used by computers to connect, send and receive data over a network were widely implemented and refined in BSD. The World Wide Web was also first demonstrated on a number of computers running an OS based on BSD called NeXTSTEP.

In 1974, University of California, Berkeley installed its first Unix system. Over time, students and staff in the computer science department there began adding new programs to make things easier, such as text editors. When Berkeley received new VAX computers in 1978 with Unix installed, the school's undergraduates modified Unix even more in order to take advantage of the computer's hardware possibilities. The Defense Advanced Research Projects Agency of the US Department of Defense took interest, and decided to fund the project. Many schools, corporations, and government organizations took notice and started to use Berkeley's version of Unix instead of the official one distributed by AT&T.

Steve Jobs, upon leaving Apple Inc. in 1985, formed NeXT Inc., a company that manufactured high-end computers running on a variation of BSD called NeXTSTEP. One of these computers was used by Tim Berners-Lee as the first webserver to create the World Wide Web.

Developers like Keith Bostic encouraged the project to replace any non-free code that originated with Bell Labs. Once this was done, however, AT&T sued. After two years of legal disputes, the BSD project spawned a number of free derivatives, such as NetBSD and FreeBSD (both in 1993), and OpenBSD (from NetBSD in 1995).

MacOS

MacOS (formerly "Mac OS X" and later "OS X") is a line of open core graphical operating systems developed, marketed, and sold by Apple Inc., the latest of which is pre-loaded on all currently shipping Macintosh computers. macOS is the successor to the original classic Mac OS, which had been Apple's primary operating system since 1984. Unlike its predecessor, macOS is a UNIX operating system built on technology that had been developed at NeXT through the second half of the 1980s and up until Apple purchased the company in early 1997. The operating system was first released in 1999 as Mac OS X Server 1.0, followed in March 2001 by a client version (Mac OS X v10.0 "Cheetah"). Since then, six more distinct "client" and "server" editions of macOS have been released, until the two were merged in OS X 10.7 "Lion".

Prior to its merging with macOS, the server edition – macOS Server – was architecturally identical to its desktop counterpart and usually ran on Apple's line of Macintosh server hardware. macOS Server included work group management and administration software tools that provide simplified access to key network services, including a mail transfer agent, a Samba server, an LDAP server, a domain name server, and others. With Mac OS X v10.7 Lion, all server aspects of Mac OS X Server have been integrated into the client version and the product re-branded as "OS X" (dropping "Mac" from the name). The server tools are now offered as an application.

Linux

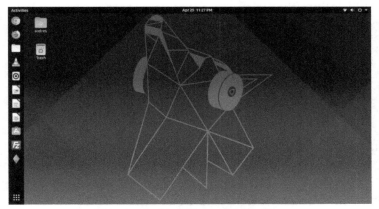

Ubuntu, desktop Linux distribution.

The Linux kernel originated in 1991, as a project of Linus Torvalds, while a university student in Finland. He posted information about his project on a newsgroup for computer students and programmers, and received support and assistance from volunteers who succeeded in creating a complete and functional kernel.

Linux is Unix-like, but was developed without any Unix code, unlike BSD and its variants. Because of its open license model, the Linux kernel code is available for study and modification, which resulted in its use on a wide range of computing machinery from supercomputers to smart-watches. Although estimates suggest that Linux is used on only 1.82% of all "desktop" (or laptop) PCs, it has been widely adopted for use in servers and embedded systems such as cell phones. Linux has superseded Unix on many platforms and is used on most supercomputers including the top 385. Many of the same computers are also on Green500 (but in different order), and Linux runs on the top 10. Linux is also commonly used on other small energy-efficient computers, such as smartphones and smartwatches. The Linux kernel is used in some popular distributions, such as Red Hat, Debian, Ubuntu, Linux Mint and Google's Android, Chrome OS, and Chromium OS.

Microsoft Windows

Microsoft Windows is a family of proprietary operating systems designed by Microsoft Corporation and primarily targeted to Intel architecture based computers, with an estimated 88.9 percent total usage share on Web connected computers. The latest version is Windows 10.

In 2011, Windows 7 overtook Windows XP as most common version in use.

Microsoft Windows was first released in 1985, as an operating environment running on top of MS-DOS, which was the standard operating system shipped on most Intel architecture personal computers at the time. In 1995, Windows 95 was released which only used MS-DOS as a boot-strap. For backwards compatibility, Win9x could run real-mode MS-DOS and 16-bit Windows 3.x drivers. Windows ME, released in 2000, was the last version in the Win9x family. Later versions have all been based on the Windows NT kernel. Current client versions of Windows run on IA-32, x86-64 and 32-bit ARM microprocessors. In addition Itanium is still supported in older server version Windows Server 2008 R2. In the past, Windows NT supported additional architectures.

Server editions of Windows are widely used. In recent years, Microsoft has expended significant capital in an effort to promote the use of Windows as a server operating system. However, Windows' usage on servers is not as widespread as on personal computers as Windows competes against Linux and BSD for server market share.

ReactOS is a Windows-alternative operating system, which is being developed on the principles of Windows – without using any of Microsoft's code.

Other

There have been many operating systems that were significant in their day but are no longer so, such as AmigaOS; OS/2 from IBM and Microsoft; classic Mac OS, the non-Unix precursor to Apple's macOS; BeOS; XTS-300; RISC OS; MorphOS; Haiku; BareMetal and FreeMint. Some are still used in niche markets and continue to be developed as minority platforms for enthusiast communities and specialist applications. OpenVMS, formerly from DEC, is still under active development by Hewlett-Packard. Yet other operating systems are used almost exclusively in academia, for operating systems education or to do research on operating system concepts. A typical example of a system that fulfills both roles is MINIX, while for example Singularity is used purely for research. Another example is the Oberon System designed at ETH Zürich by Niklaus Wirth, Jürg Gutknecht and a group of students at the former Computer Systems Institute in the 1980s. It was used mainly for research, teaching, and daily work in Wirth's group.

Other operating systems have failed to win significant market share, but have introduced innovations that have influenced mainstream operating systems, not least Bell Labs' Plan 9.

Components

The components of an operating system all exist in order to make the different parts of a computer work together. All user software needs to go through the operating system in order to use any of the hardware, whether it be as simple as a mouse or keyboard or as complex as an Internet component.

Kernel

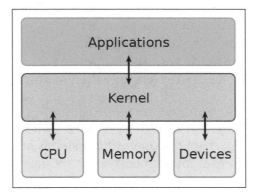

A kernel connects the application software to the hardware of a computer. With the aid of the firmware and device drivers, the kernel provides the most basic level of control over all of the computer's hardware devices. It manages memory access for programs in the RAM, it determines which programs get access to which hardware resources, it sets up or resets the CPU's operating states for optimal operation at all times, and it organizes the data for long-term non-volatile storage with file systems on such media as disks, tapes, flash memory, etc.

Program Execution

The operating system provides an interface between an application program and the computer hardware, so that an application program can interact with the hardware only by obeying rules and procedures programmed into the operating system. The operating system is also a set of services which simplify development and execution of application programs. Executing an application program involves the creation of a process by the operating system kernel which assigns memory space and other resources, establishes a priority for the process in multi-tasking systems, loads program binary code into memory, and initiates execution of the application program which then interacts with the user and with hardware devices.

Interrupts

Interrupts are central to operating systems, as they provide an efficient way for the operating system to interact with and react to its environment. The alternative – having the operating system "watch" the various sources of input for events (polling) that require action – can be found in older systems with very small stacks (50 or 60 bytes) but is unusual in modern systems with large stacks. Interrupt-based programming is directly supported by most modern CPUs. Interrupts provide a computer with a way of automatically saving local register contexts, and running specific code in response to events. Even very basic computers support hardware interrupts, and allow the programmer to specify code which may be run when that event takes place.

When an interrupt is received, the computer's hardware automatically suspends whatever program is currently running, saves its status, and runs computer code previously associated with the interrupt; this is analogous to placing a bookmark in a book in response to a phone call. In modern operating systems, interrupts are handled by the operating system's kernel. Interrupts may come from either the computer's hardware or the running program.

When a hardware device triggers an interrupt, the operating system's kernel decides how to deal with this event, generally by running some processing code. The amount of code being run depends on the priority of the interrupt (for example: a person usually responds to a smoke detector alarm before answering the phone). The processing of hardware interrupts is a task that is usually delegated to software called a device driver, which may be part of the operating system's kernel, part of another program, or both. Device drivers may then relay information to a running program by various means.

A program may also trigger an interrupt to the operating system. If a program wishes to access hardware, for example, it may interrupt the operating system's kernel, which causes control to be passed back to the kernel. The kernel then processes the request. If a program wishes additional resources (or wishes to shed resources) such as memory, it triggers an interrupt to get the kernel's attention.

Modes

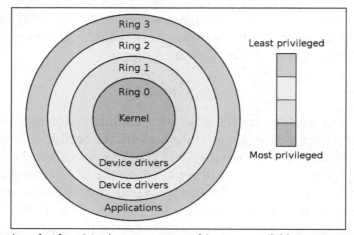

Privilege rings for the x86 microprocessor architecture available in protected mode.
Operating systems determine which processes run in each mode.

Modern microprocessors (CPU or MPU) support multiple modes of operation. CPUs with this capability offer at least two modes: user mode and supervisor mode. In general terms, supervisor mode operation allows unrestricted access to all machine resources, including all MPU instructions. User mode operation sets limits on instruction use and typically disallows direct access to machine resources. CPUs might have other modes similar to user mode as well, such as the virtual modes in order to emulate older processor types, such as 16-bit processors on a 32-bit one, or 32-bit processors on a 64-bit one.

At power-on or reset, the system begins in supervisor mode. Once an operating system kernel has been loaded and started, the boundary between user mode and supervisor mode (also known as kernel mode) can be established.

Supervisor mode is used by the kernel for low level tasks that need unrestricted access to hardware, such as controlling how memory is accessed, and communicating with devices such as disk drives and video display devices. User mode, in contrast, is used for almost everything else. Application programs, such as word processors and database managers, operate within user mode, and can only access machine resources by turning control over to the kernel, a process which causes a switch to supervisor mode. Typically, the transfer of control to the kernel is achieved by executing a software interrupt instruction, such as the Motorola 68000 TRAP instruction. The software interrupt causes the microprocessor to switch from user mode to supervisor mode and begin executing code that allows the kernel to take control.

In user mode, programs usually have access to a restricted set of microprocessor instructions, and generally cannot execute any instructions that could potentially cause disruption to the system's operation. In supervisor mode, instruction execution restrictions are typically removed, allowing the kernel unrestricted access to all machine resources.

The term "user mode resource" generally refers to one or more CPU registers, which contain information that the running program isn't allowed to alter. Attempts to alter these resources generally causes a switch to supervisor mode, where the operating system can deal with the illegal operation the program was attempting, for example, by forcibly terminating ("killing") the program).

Memory Management

Among other things, a multiprogramming operating system kernel must be responsible for managing all system memory which is currently in use by programs. This ensures that a program does not interfere with memory already in use by another program. Since programs time share, each program must have independent access to memory.

Cooperative memory management, used by many early operating systems, assumes that all programs make voluntary use of the kernel's memory manager, and do not exceed their allocated memory. This system of memory management is almost never seen any more, since programs often contain bugs which can cause them to exceed their allocated memory. If a program fails, it may cause memory used by one or more other programs to be affected or overwritten. Malicious programs or viruses may purposefully alter another program's memory, or may affect the operation of the operating system itself. With cooperative memory management, it takes only one misbehaved program to crash the system.

Memory protection enables the kernel to limit a process' access to the computer's memory. Various methods of memory protection exist, including memory segmentation and paging. All methods require some level of hardware support (such as the 80286 MMU), which doesn't exist in all computers.

In both segmentation and paging, certain protected mode registers specify to the CPU what memory address it should allow a running program to access. Attempts to access other addresses trigger an interrupt which cause the CPU to re-enter supervisor mode, placing the kernel in charge. This is called a segmentation violation or Seg-V for short, and since it is both difficult to assign a meaningful result to such an operation, and because it is usually a sign of a misbehaving program, the kernel generally resorts to terminating the offending program, and reports the error.

Windows versions 3.1 through ME had some level of memory protection, but programs could easily circumvent the need to use it. A general protection fault would be produced, indicating a segmentation violation had occurred; however, the system would often crash anyway.

Virtual Memory

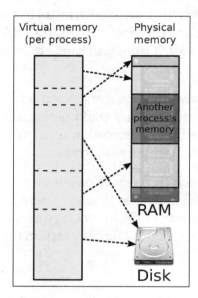

Many operating systems can "trick" programs into using memory scattered around the hard disk and RAM as if it is one continuous chunk of memory, called virtual memory.

The use of virtual memory addressing (such as paging or segmentation) means that the kernel can choose what memory each program may use at any given time, allowing the operating system to use the same memory locations for multiple tasks.

If a program tries to access memory that isn't in its current range of accessible memory, but nonetheless has been allocated to it, the kernel is interrupted in the same way as it would if the program were to exceed its allocated memory. Under UNIX this kind of interrupt is referred to as a page fault.

When the kernel detects a page fault it generally adjusts the virtual memory range of the program which triggered it, granting it access to the memory requested. This gives the kernel discretionary power over where a particular application's memory is stored, or even whether or not it has actually been allocated yet.

In modern operating systems, memory which is accessed less frequently can be temporarily stored on disk or other media to make that space available for use by other programs. This is called swapping, as an area of memory can be used by multiple programs, and what that memory area contains can be swapped or exchanged on demand.

"Virtual memory" provides the programmer or the user with the perception that there is a much larger amount of RAM in the computer than is really there.

Multitasking

Multitasking refers to the running of multiple independent computer programs on the same computer; giving the appearance that it is performing the tasks at the same time. Since most computers can do at most one or two things at one time, this is generally done via time-sharing, which means that each program uses a share of the computer's time to execute.

An operating system kernel contains a scheduling program which determines how much time each process spends executing, and in which order execution control should be passed to programs. Control is passed to a process by the kernel, which allows the program access to the CPU and memory. Later, control is returned to the kernel through some mechanism, so that another program may be allowed to use the CPU. This so-called passing of control between the kernel and applications is called a context switch.

An early model which governed the allocation of time to programs was called cooperative multitasking. In this model, when control is passed to a program by the kernel, it may execute for as long as it wants before explicitly returning control to the kernel. This means that a malicious or malfunctioning program may not only prevent any other programs from using the CPU, but it can hang the entire system if it enters an infinite loop.

Modern operating systems extend the concepts of application preemption to device drivers and kernel code, so that the operating system has preemptive control over internal run-times as well.

The philosophy governing preemptive multitasking is that of ensuring that all programs are given regular time on the CPU. This implies that all programs must be limited in how much time they are allowed to spend on the CPU without being interrupted. To accomplish this, modern operating system kernels make use of a timed interrupt. A protected mode timer is set by the kernel which triggers a return to supervisor mode after the specified time has elapsed.

On many single user operating systems cooperative multitasking is perfectly adequate, as home computers generally run a small number of well tested programs. The AmigaOS is an exception, having preemptive multitasking from its very first version. Windows NT was the first version of Microsoft Windows which enforced preemptive multitasking, but it didn't reach the home user market until Windows XP (since Windows NT was targeted at professionals).

Disk Access and File Systems

File systems allow users and programs to organize and sort files on
a computer, often through the use of directories (or "folders").

Access to data stored on disks is a central feature of all operating systems. Computers store data on disks using files, which are structured in specific ways in order to allow for faster access, higher reliability, and to make better use of the drive's available space. The specific way in which files are stored on a disk is called a file system, and enables files to have names and attributes. It also allows them to be stored in a hierarchy of directories or folders arranged in a directory tree.

Early operating systems generally supported a single type of disk drive and only one kind of file system. Early file systems were limited in their capacity, speed, and in the kinds of file names and directory structures they could use. These limitations often reflected limitations in the operating systems they were designed for, making it very difficult for an operating system to support more than one file system.

While many simpler operating systems support a limited range of options for accessing storage systems, operating systems like UNIX and Linux support a technology known as a virtual file system or VFS. An operating system such as UNIX supports a wide array of storage devices, regardless of their design or file systems, allowing them to be accessed through a common application programming interface (API). This makes it unnecessary for programs to have any knowledge about the device they are accessing. A VFS allows the operating system to provide programs with access to an unlimited number of devices with an infinite variety of file systems installed on them, through the use of specific device drivers and file system drivers.

A connected storage device, such as a hard drive, is accessed through a device driver. The device driver understands the specific language of the drive and is able to translate that language into a standard language used by the operating system to access all disk drives. On UNIX, this is the language of block devices.

When the kernel has an appropriate device driver in place, it can then access the contents of the disk drive in raw format, which may contain one or more file systems. A file system driver is used to translate the commands used to access each specific file system into a standard set of commands that the operating system can use to talk to all file systems. Programs can then deal with these file systems on the basis of filenames, and directories/folders, contained within a hierarchical structure. They can create, delete, open, and close files, as well as gather various information about them, including access permissions, size, free space, and creation and modification dates.

Various differences between file systems make supporting all file systems difficult. Allowed characters in file names, case sensitivity, and the presence of various kinds of file attributes makes the implementation of a single interface for every file system a daunting task. Operating systems tend to recommend using (and so support natively) file systems specifically designed for them; for example, NTFS in Windows and ext3 and ReiserFS in Linux. However, in practice, third party drivers are usually available to give support for the most widely used file systems in most general-purpose operating systems (for example, NTFS is available in Linux through NTFS-3g, and ext2/3 and ReiserFS are available in Windows through third-party software).

Support for file systems is highly varied among modern operating systems, although there are several common file systems which almost all operating systems include support and drivers for. Operating systems vary on file system support and on the disk formats they may be installed on. Under Windows, each file system is usually limited in application to certain media; for example, CDs must use ISO 9660 or UDF, and as of Windows Vista, NTFS is the only file system which the operating system can be installed on. It is possible to install Linux onto many types of file systems. Unlike other operating systems, Linux and UNIX allow any file system to be used regardless of the media it is stored in, whether it is a hard drive, a disc (CD, DVD), a USB flash drive, or even contained within a file located on another file system.

Device Drivers

A device driver is a specific type of computer software developed to allow interaction with hardware devices. Typically this constitutes an interface for communicating with the device, through the specific computer bus or communications subsystem that the hardware is connected to, providing commands to and/or receiving data from the device, and on the other end, the requisite interfaces to the operating system and software applications. It is a specialized hardware-dependent computer program which is also operating system specific that enables another program, typically an operating system or applications software package or computer program running under the operating system kernel, to interact transparently with a hardware device, and usually provides the requisite interrupt handling necessary for any necessary asynchronous time-dependent hardware interfacing needs.

The key design goal of device drivers is abstraction. Every model of hardware (even within the same class of device) is different. Newer models also are released by manufacturers that provide more reliable or better performance and these newer models are often controlled differently. Computers and their operating systems cannot be expected to know how to control every device, both now and in the future. To solve this problem, operating systems essentially dictate how every type of device should be controlled. The function of the device driver is then to translate these operating system mandated function calls into device specific calls. In theory a new device, which is controlled in a new manner, should function correctly if a suitable driver is available. This new driver ensures that the device appears to operate as usual from the operating system's point of view.

Under versions of Windows before Vista and versions of Linux before 2.6, all driver execution was co-operative, meaning that if a driver entered an infinite loop it would freeze the system. More recent revisions of these operating systems incorporate kernel preemption, where the kernel interrupts the driver to give it tasks, and then separates itself from the process until it receives a response from the device driver, or gives it more tasks to do.

Networking

Currently most operating systems support a variety of networking protocols, hardware, and applications for using them. This means that computers running dissimilar operating systems can participate in a common network for sharing resources such as computing, files, printers, and scanners using either wired or wireless connections. Networks can essentially allow a computer's operating system to access the resources of a remote computer to support the same functions as it could if those resources were connected directly to the local computer. This includes everything from simple communication, to using networked file systems or even sharing another computer's graphics or sound hardware. Some network services allow the resources of a computer to be accessed transparently, such as SSH which allows networked users direct access to a computer's command line interface.

Client/server networking allows a program on a computer, called a client, to connect via a network to another computer, called a server. Servers offer (or host) various services to other network computers and users. These services are usually provided through ports or numbered access points beyond the server's IP address. Each port number is usually associated with a maximum of one running program, which is responsible for handling requests to that port. A daemon, being a user program, can in turn access the local hardware resources of that computer by passing requests to the operating system kernel.

Many operating systems support one or more vendor-specific or open networking protocols as well, for example, SNA on IBM systems, DECnet on systems from Digital Equipment Corporation, and Microsoft-specific protocols (SMB) on Windows. Specific protocols for specific tasks may also be supported such as NFS for file access. Protocols like ESound, or esd can be easily extended over the network to provide sound from local applications, on a remote system's sound hardware.

Security

A computer being secure depends on a number of technologies working properly. A modern operating system provides access to a number of resources, which are available to software running on the system, and to external devices like networks via the kernel.

The operating system must be capable of distinguishing between requests which should be allowed to be processed, and others which should not be processed. While some systems may simply distinguish between "privileged" and "non-privileged", systems commonly have a form of requester identity, such as a user name. To establish identity there may be a process of authentication. Often a username must be quoted, and each username may have a password. Other methods of authentication, such as magnetic cards or biometric data, might be used instead. In some cases, especially connections from the network, resources may be accessed with no authentication at all (such as reading files over a network share). Also covered by the concept of requester identity is authorization; the particular services and resources accessible by the requester once logged into a system are tied to either the requester's user account or to the variously configured groups of users to which the requester belongs.

In addition to the allow or disallow model of security, a system with a high level of security also offers auditing options. These would allow tracking of requests for access to resources (such as, "who has been reading this file?"). Internal security, or security from an already running program is only possible if all possibly harmful requests must be carried out through interrupts to the operating system kernel. If programs can directly access hardware and resources, they cannot be secured.

External security involves a request from outside the computer, such as a login at a connected console or some kind of network connection. External requests are often passed through device drivers to the operating system's kernel, where they can be passed onto applications, or carried out directly. Security of operating systems has long been a concern because of highly sensitive data held on computers, both of a commercial and military nature. The United States Government Department of Defense (DoD) created the Trusted Computer System Evaluation Criteria (TCSEC) which is a standard that sets basic requirements for assessing the effectiveness of security. This became of vital importance to operating system makers, because the TCSEC was used to evaluate, classify and select trusted operating systems being considered for the processing, storage and retrieval of sensitive or classified information.

Network services include offerings such as file sharing, print services, email, web sites, and file transfer protocols (FTP), most of which can have compromised security. At the front line of security are hardware devices known as firewalls or intrusion detection/prevention systems. At the operating system level, there are a number of software firewalls available, as well as intrusion detection/prevention systems. Most modern operating systems include a software firewall, which is enabled by default. A software firewall can be configured to allow or deny network traffic to or from a service or application running on the operating system. Therefore, one can install and be running an insecure service, such as Telnet or FTP, and not have to be threatened by a security breach because the firewall would deny all traffic trying to connect to the service on that port.

An alternative strategy, and the only sandbox strategy available in systems that do not meet the Popek and Goldberg virtualization requirements, is where the operating system is not running user programs as native code, but instead either emulates a processor or provides a host for a p-code based system such as Java.

Internal security is especially relevant for multi-user systems; it allows each user of the system to have private files that the other users cannot tamper with or read. Internal security is also vital if auditing is to be of any use, since a program can potentially bypass the operating system, inclusive of bypassing auditing.

User Interface

```
root ~ # ping google.com
PING google.com (74.125.95.103) 56(84) bytes of data.
64 bytes from iw-in-f103.1e100.net (74.125.95.103): icmp_seq=1 ttl=47 time=15.3
ms
^C
--- google.com ping statistics ---
1 packets transmitted, 1 received, 0% packet loss, time 0ms
rtt min/avg/max/mdev = 15.453/15.453/15.453/0.000 ms
root ~ # ls
Desktop  README
root ~ # cd /
root / # ls
bin   dev  home  lost+found  mnt  proc  sbin     srv  tmp  var
boot  etc  lib   media       opt  root  [        ]  sys  usr
root / # pacman -Ss pidgin
extra/libpurple 2.6.6-1
    IM library extracted from Pidgin
extra/pidgin 2.6.6-1
    Multi-protocol instant messaging client
extra/pidgin-encryption 3.0-3
    A Pidgin plugin providing transparent RSA encryption using NSS
extra/purple-plugin-pack 2.6.3-1
    Plugin pack for Pidgin
extra/telepathy-haze 0.3.4-1 (telepathy)
    A telepathy-backend to use libpurple (Pidgin) protocols.
community/guifications 2.16-1
    A set of GUI popup notifications for pidgin
community/pidgin-fonomobutton 0.1.6-1
    Adds a video-chat button to the the conversation window
community/pidgin-libnotify 0.14-3
    pidgin plugin that enables popups when someone logs in or messages you.
community/pidgin-musictracker 0.4.21-2
    A plugin for Pidgin which displays the music track currently playing.
community/pidgin-otr 3.2.0-1
    Off-the-Record Messaging plugin for Pidgin
root / #
```

A screenshot of the Bash command line. Each command is typed out after the 'prompt', and then its output appears below, working its way down the screen. The current command prompt is at the bottom.

Every computer that is to be operated by an individual requires a user interface. The user interface is usually referred to as a shell and is essential if human interaction is to be supported. The user interface views the directory structure and requests services from the operating system that will acquire data from input hardware devices, such as a keyboard, mouse or credit card reader, and requests operating system services to display prompts, status messages and such on output hardware devices, such as a video monitor or printer. The two most common forms of a user interface have historically been the command-line interface, where computer commands are typed out line-by-line, and the graphical user interface, where a visual environment (most commonly a WIMP) is present.

Graphical User Interfaces

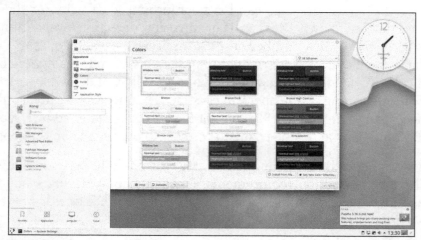

A screenshot of the KDE Plasma 5 graphical user interface. Programs take the form of images on the screen, and the files, folders (directories), and applications take the form of icons and symbols. A mouse is used to navigate the computer.

Most of the modern computer systems support graphical user interfaces (GUI), and often include them. In some computer systems, such as the original implementation of the classic Mac OS, the GUI is integrated into the kernel.

While technically a graphical user interface is not an operating system service, incorporating support for one into the operating system kernel can allow the GUI to be more responsive by reducing the number of context switches required for the GUI to perform its output functions. Other operating systems are modular, separating the graphics subsystem from the kernel and the Operating System. In the 1980s UNIX, VMS and many others had operating systems that were built this way. Linux and macOS are also built this way. Modern releases of Microsoft Windows such as Windows Vista implement a graphics subsystem that is mostly in user-space; however the graphics drawing routines of versions between Windows NT 4.0 and Windows Server 2003 exist mostly in kernel space. Windows 9x had very little distinction between the interface and the kernel.

Many computer operating systems allow the user to install or create any user interface they desire. The X Window System in conjunction with GNOME or KDE Plasma 5 is a commonly found setup on most Unix and Unix-like (BSD, Linux, Solaris) systems. A number of Windows shell replacements have been released for Microsoft Windows, which offer alternatives to the included Windows shell, but the shell itself cannot be separated from Windows.

Numerous Unix-based GUIs have existed over time, most derived from X11. Competition among the various vendors of Unix (HP, IBM, Sun) led to much fragmentation, though an effort to standardize in the 1990s to COSE and CDE failed for various reasons, and were eventually eclipsed by the widespread adoption of GNOME and K Desktop Environment. Prior to free software-based toolkits and desktop environments, Motif was the prevalent toolkit/desktop combination (and was the basis upon which CDE was developed).

Graphical user interfaces evolve over time. For example, Windows has modified its user interface almost every time a new major version of Windows is released, and the Mac OS GUI changed dramatically with the introduction of Mac OS X in 1999.

Real-time Operating Systems

A real-time operating system (RTOS) is an operating system intended for applications with fixed deadlines (real-time computing). Such applications include some small embedded systems, automobile engine controllers, industrial robots, spacecraft, industrial control, and some large-scale computing systems.

An early example of a large-scale real-time operating system was Transaction Processing Facility developed by American Airlines and IBM for the Sabre Airline Reservations System.

Embedded systems that have fixed deadlines use a real-time operating system such as VxWorks, PikeOS, eCos, QNX, MontaVista Linux and RTLinux. Windows CE is a real-time operating system that shares similar APIs to desktop Windows but shares none of desktop Windows' codebase. Symbian OS also has an RTOS kernel (EKA2) starting with version 8.0b.

Some embedded systems use operating systems such as Palm OS, BSD, and Linux, although such operating systems do not support real-time computing.

Operating System Development as a Hobby

Operating system development is one of the most complicated activities in which a computing hobbyist may engage.A hobby operating system may be classified as one whose code has not been directly derived from an existing operating system, and has few users and active developers.

In some cases, hobby development is in support of a "homebrew" computing device, for example, a simple single-board computer powered by a 6502 microprocessor. Or, development may be for an architecture already in widespread use. Operating system development may come from entirely new concepts, or may commence by modeling an existing operating system. In either case, the hobbyist is his/her own developer, or may interact with a small and sometimes unstructured group of individuals who have like interests.

Examples of a hobby operating system include Syllable and TempleOS.

Diversity of Operating Systems and Portability

Application software is generally written for use on a specific operating system, and sometimes even for specific hardware.When porting the application to run on another OS, the functionality required by that application may be implemented differently by that OS (the names of functions, meaning of arguments, etc.) requiring the application to be adapted, changed, or otherwise maintained.

Unix was the first operating system not written in assembly language, making it very portable to systems different from its native PDP-11.

This cost in supporting operating systems diversity can be avoided by instead writing applications against software platforms such as Java or Qt. These abstractions have already borne the cost of adaptation to specific operating systems and their system libraries.

Another approach is for operating system vendors to adopt standards. For example, POSIX and OS abstraction layers provide commonalities that reduce porting costs.

Utilities Software

Utility software is system software designed to help to analyze, configure, optimize or maintain a computer. It is used to support the computer infrastructure - in contrast to application software, which is aimed at directly performing tasks that benefit ordinary users. However, utilities often form part of application systems. For example a batch job may run user-written code to update a database and may then include a step that runs a utility to back up the database, or a job may run a utility to compress a disk before copying files.

Although a basic set of utility programs is usually distributed with an operating system (OS), and utility software is considered part of the operating system, users often install replacements or additional utilities. Those utilities may provide additional facilities to carry out tasks that are beyond the capabilities of the operating system.

Many utilities that might affect the entire computer system require the user to have elevated privileges, while others that operate only on the user's data do not.

System Utilities

- Anti-virus utilities scan for computer viruses and block or remove them.

- Clipboard managers expand the clipboard functionality of an operating system.

- Computer access control software grants or denies requests for access to system resources.

- Debuggers typically permit the examination and modification of data and program instructions in memory and on disk.

- Diagnostic programs determine and report the operational status of computer hardware and software. Memory testers are one example.

- Network utilities analyze the computer's network connectivity, configure network settings, check data transfer or log events.

- Package managers are used to configure, install or keep up to date other software on a computer.

- Registry cleaners clean and optimize the Windows Registry by removing old registry keys that are no longer in use.

- System monitors monitor resources and performance in a computer system.

- System profiles provide detailed information about installed software and hardware.

Storage Device Management Utilities

- Backup software makes copies of all information stored on a disk and either restores the entire disk (aka Disk cloning) in an event of disk failure or selected files that are accidentally deleted or corrupted. Undeletion utilities are sometimes more convenient.

- Disk checkers scan an operating hard drive and check for logical (filesystem) or physical errors.

- Disk compression utilities transparently compress/uncompress the contents of a disk, increasing the capacity of the disk.

- Disk defragmenters detect computer files whose contents are scattered across several locations on the hard disk and collect the fragments into one contiguous area.

- Disk formatters prepare a data storage device such as a hard disk, solid-state drive, floppy disk or USB flash drive for initial use. These are often used to permanently erase an entire device.

- Disk partition editors divide an individual drive into multiple logical drives, each with its own file system which can be mounted by the operating system and treated as an individual drive.

- Disk space analyzers provide a visualization of disk space usage by getting the size for each folder (including sub folders) and files in folder or drive showing the distribution of the used space.

- Tape initializers write a label to a magnetic tape or other magnetic medium. Initializers for DECtape formatted the tape into blocks.

File Management Utilities

Archivers output a stream or a single file when provided with a directory or a set of files. Archive suites may include compression and encryption capabilities. Some archive utilities have a separate un-archive utility for the reverse operation. One nearly universal type of archive file format is the zip file.

- Cryptographic utilities encrypt and decrypt streams and files.

- Data compression utilities output a shorter stream or a smaller file when provided with a stream or file.

- Data conversion utilities transform data from a source file to some other format, such as from a text file to a PDF document.

- Data recovery utilities are used to rescue good data from corrupted files.

- Data synchronization utilities establish consistency among data from a source to a target data storage and vice versa. There are several branches of this type of utility:

  ◦ File synchronization utilities maintain consistency between two sources. They may be used to create redundancy or backup copies but are also used to help users carry their digital music, photos and video in their mobile devices.

  ◦ Revision control utilities can recreate a coherent structure where multiple users simultaneously modify the same file.

- Disk cleaners find files that are unnecessary to computer operation, or take up considerable amounts of space. Disk cleaner helps the user to decide what to delete when their hard disk is full.

- File comparison utilities provide a standalone capability to detect differences between files.

- File managers provide a convenient method of performing routine data management, email recovery and management tasks, such as deleting, renaming, cataloging, uncataloging, moving, copying, merging, setting write protection status, setting file access permissions, generating and modifying folders and data sets.

Miscellaneous Utilities

- Data generators (e.g. IEBDG) create a file of test data according to specified patterns.

- Hex editors directly modify the text or data of a file without regard to file format. These files can be data or programs.

- HTML checkers validate HTML code and check links.

- Installation or setup utilities are used to initialize or configure programs, usually applications programs, for use in a specific computer environment. There are also Uninstallers.

- Patching utilities perform alterations of files, especially object programs when program source is unavailable.

- Screensavers prevent phosphor burn-in on CRT and plasma computer monitors.

- Sort/Merge programs arrange records (lines) of a file into a specified sequence.

- Standalone macro recorders permit use of keyboard macros in programs that do not natively support such a feature.

- Text editors are used to create and modify script and batch files.

Software Programming

Software programming involves using a computer language to develop programs. Software programmers design these programs to carry out specific functions.

Programming Languages

The information understood by computers is in machine code, which consists of binary strings of zeros and ones. This type of programming is used in software engineering to tell computers what functions to perform. The programs must be written for a specific operating system or for cross-platform use. There are two kinds of languages used in programming, which are known as high- and low-level languages.

Median Salary (2018)	$105,590 (*for all software developers*)*
Job Outlook (2016-2026)	24% growth (*for all software developers*)*
Required Education	Bachelor's degree
Similar occupations	Computer hardware engineers, computer and information systems managers, computer network architects, computer programmers

High-Level Languages

High-level languages use a format which helps to make coding more user-friendly by allowing a description of a solution in terms more closely understood by humans. Commonly used high-level languages are C, FORTRAN, Pascal and BASIC. High-level programming works independent of the machine language of the computer. High-level programming also allows the creation of large scale programs quickly.

Low-Level Languages

Programming languages that are more difficult to understand are called low-level languages. Included in this type of languages are machine and assembly languages. These languages offer predictability and performance in programming. Assembly language is designed for a specific processor. Machine language is binary code and is the only language a computer understands. All processes that a computer performs are converted into binary code. Programs written in low-level languages are more precise and efficient for the computer, though they may take more time to create.

Programming Paradigms

Programming paradigms are a way to classify programming languages based on their features. Languages can be classified into multiple paradigms.

Some paradigms are concerned mainly with implications for the execution model of the language, such as allowing side effects, or whether the sequence of operations is defined by the execution model. Other paradigms are concerned mainly with the way that code is organized, such as grouping a code into units along with the state that is modified by the code. Yet others are concerned mainly with the style of syntax and grammar.

Common programming paradigms include:

- Imperative in which the programmer instructs the machine how to change its state.
  - Procedural which groups instructions into procedures.
  - Object-oriented which groups instructions together with the part of the state they operate on.
- Declarative in which the programmer merely declares properties of the desired result, but not how to compute it.
  - Functional in which the desired result is declared as the value of a series of function applications.
  - Logic in which the desired result is declared as the answer to a question about a system of facts and rules.
  - Mathematical in which the desired result is declared as the solution of an optimization problem.

Symbolic techniques such as reflection, which allow the program to refer to itself, might also be considered as a programming paradigm. However, this is compatible with the major paradigms and thus is not a real paradigm in its own right.

For example, languages that fall into the imperative paradigm have two main features: they state the order in which operations occur, with constructs that explicitly control that order, and they allow side effects, in which state can be modified at one point in time, within one unit of code, and then later read at a different point in time inside a different unit of code. The communication between the units of code is not explicit. Meanwhile, in object-oriented programming, code is organized into objects that contain state that is only modified by the code that is part of the object. Most object-oriented languages are also imperative languages. In contrast, languages that fit the declarative paradigm do not state the order in which to execute operations. Instead, they supply a number of operations that are available in the system, along with the conditions under which each is allowed to execute. The implementation of the language's execution model tracks which operations are free to execute and chooses the order on its own. More at Comparison of multi-paradigm programming languages.

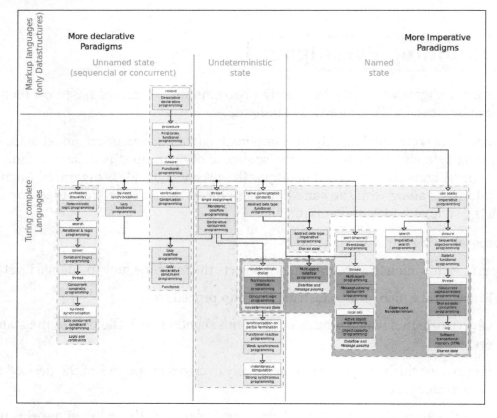

Overview of the various programming paradigms according to Peter Van Roy:

Just as software engineering (as a process) is defined by differing methodologies, so the programming languages (as models of computation) are defined by differing paradigms. Some languages are designed to support one paradigm (Smalltalk supports object-oriented programming, Haskell supports functional programming), while other programming languages support multiple paradigms (such as Object Pascal, C++, Java, JavaScript, C#, Scala, Visual Basic, Common Lisp,

Scheme, Perl, PHP, Python, Ruby, Wolfram Language, Oz, and F#). For example, programs written in C++, Object Pascal or PHP can be purely procedural, purely object-oriented, or can contain elements of both or other paradigms. Software designers and programmers decide how to use those paradigm elements.

In object-oriented programming, programs are treated as a set of interacting objects. In functional programming, programs are treated as a sequence of stateless function evaluations. When programming computers or systems with many processors, in process-oriented programming, programs are treated as sets of concurrent processes that act on a logical shared data structures.

Many programming paradigms are as well known for the techniques they forbid as for those they enable. For instance, pure functional programming disallows use of side-effects, while structured programming disallows use of the goto statement. Partly for this reason, new paradigms are often regarded as doctrinaire or overly rigid by those accustomed to earlier styles. Yet, avoiding certain techniques can make it easier to understand program behavior, and to prove theorems about program correctness.

Programming paradigms can also be compared with programming models which allow invoking an execution model by using only an API. Programming models can also be classified into paradigms, based on features of the execution model.

For parallel computing, using a programming model instead of a language is common. The reason is that details of the parallel hardware leak into the abstractions used to program the hardware. This causes the programmer to have to map patterns in the algorithm onto patterns in the execution model (which have been inserted due to leakage of hardware into the abstraction). As a consequence, no one parallel programming language maps well to all computation problems. It is thus more convenient to use a base sequential language and insert API calls to parallel execution models, via a programming model. Such parallel programming models can be classified according to abstractions that reflect the hardware, such as shared memory, distributed memory with message passing, notions of *place* visible in the code, and so forth. These can be considered flavors of programming paradigm that apply to only parallel languages and programming models.

Machine Code

The lowest-level programming paradigms are machine code, which directly represents the instructions (the contents of program memory) as a sequence of numbers, and assembly language where the machine instructions are represented by mnemonics and memory addresses can be given symbolic labels. These are sometimes called first- and second-generation languages.

In the 1960s, assembly languages were developed to support library COPY and quite sophisticated conditional macro generation and preprocessing abilities, CALL to (subroutines), external variables and common sections (globals), enabling significant code re-use and isolation from hardware specifics via use of logical operators such as READ/WRITE/GET/PUT. Assembly was, and still is, used for time critical systems and often in embedded systems as it gives the most direct control of what the machine does.

Procedural Languages

The next advance was the development of procedural languages. These third-generation languages (the first described as high-level languages) use vocabulary related to the problem being solved. For example,

- COmmon Business Oriented Language (COBOL): Uses terms like file, move and copy.

- FORmula TRANslation (FORTRAN): Using mathematical language terminology, it was developed mainly for scientific and engineering problems.

- ALGOrithmic Language (ALGOL): Focused on being an appropriate language to define algorithms, while using mathematical language terminology, targeting scientific and engineering problems, just like FORTRAN.

- Programming Language One (PL/I): A hybrid commercial-scientific general purpose language supporting pointers.

- Beginners All purpose Symbolic Instruction Code (BASIC): It was developed to enable more people to write programs.

- C: A general-purpose programming language, initially developed by Dennis Ritchie between 1969 and 1973 at AT&T Bell Labs.

All these languages follow the procedural paradigm. That is, they describe, step by step, exactly the procedure that should, according to the particular programmer at least, be followed to solve a specific problem. The efficacy and efficiency of any such solution are both therefore entirely subjective and highly dependent on that programmer's experience, inventiveness, and ability.

Object-oriented Programming

Following the widespread use of procedural languages, object-oriented programming (OOP) languages were created, such as Simula, Smalltalk, C++, C#, Eiffel, PHP, and Java. In these languages, data and methods to manipulate it are kept as one unit called an object. With perfect encapsulation, one of the distinguishing features of OOP, the only way that another object or user would be able to access the data is via the object's methods. Thus, the inner workings of an object may be changed without affecting any code that uses the object. There is still some controversy raised by Alexander Stepanov, Richard Stallman and other programmers, concerning the efficacy of the OOP paradigm versus the procedural paradigm. The need for every object to have associative methods leads some skeptics to associate OOP with software bloat; an attempt to resolve this dilemma came through polymorphism.

Because object-oriented programming is considered a paradigm, not a language, it is possible to create even an object-oriented assembler language. High Level Assembly (HLA) is an example of this that fully supports advanced data types and object-oriented assembly language programming – despite its early origins. Thus, differing programming paradigms can be seen rather like motivational memes of their advocates, rather than necessarily representing progress from one level to the next. Precise comparisons of the efficacy of competing paradigms are frequently made more difficult because of new and differing terminology applied to similar entities and processes together with numerous implementation distinctions across languages.

Further Paradigms

Literate programming, as a form of imperative programming, structures programs as a human-centered web, as in a hypertext essay: documentation is integral to the program, and the program is structured following the logic of prose exposition, rather than compiler convenience.

Independent of the imperative branch, declarative programming paradigms were developed. In these languages, the computer is told what the problem is, not how to solve the problem – the program is structured as a set of properties to find in the expected result, not as a procedure to follow. Given a database or a set of rules, the computer tries to find a solution matching all the desired properties. An archetype of a declarative language is the fourth generation language SQL, and the family of functional languages and logic programming.

Functional programming is a subset of declarative programming. Programs written using this paradigm use functions, blocks of code intended to behave like mathematical functions. Functional languages discourage changes in the value of variables through assignment, making a great deal of use of recursion instead.

The logic programming paradigm views computation as automated reasoning over a body of knowledge. Facts about the problem domain are expressed as logic formulas, and programs are executed by applying inference rules over them until an answer to the problem is found, or the set of formulas is proved inconsistent.

Symbolic programming is a paradigm that describes programs able to manipulate formulas and program components as data. Programs can thus effectively modify themselves, and appear to "learn", making them suited for applications such as artificial intelligence, expert systems, natural-language processing and computer games. Languages that support this paradigm include Lisp and Prolog.

Differentiable programming structures programs so that they can be differentiated throughout, usually via automatic differentiation.

Object Oriented Programming (OOP)

Object-oriented programming (OOP) is a programming paradigm based on the concept of "objects", which can contain data, in the form of fields (often known as attributes or properties), and code, in the form of procedures (often known as methods). A feature of objects is an object's procedures that can access and often modify the data fields of the object with which they are associated (objects have a notion of "this" or "self"). In OOP, computer programs are designed by making them out of objects that interact with one another. OOP languages are diverse, but the most popular ones are class-based, meaning that objects are instances of classes, which also determine their types.

Many of the most widely used programming languages (such as C++, Java, Python, etc.) are multi-paradigm and they support object-oriented programming to a greater or lesser degree, typically in combination with imperative, procedural programming. Significant object-oriented languages include Java, C++, C#, Python, PHP, JavaScript, Ruby, Perl, Object Pascal, Objective-C, Dart, Swift, Scala, Common Lisp, MATLAB, and Smalltalk.

Features

Object-oriented programming uses objects, but not all of the associated techniques and structures are supported directly in languages that claim to support OOP. The features listed below are common among languages considered to be strongly class- and object-oriented (or multi-paradigm with OOP support), with notable exceptions mentioned.

Shared with Non-OOP Predecessor Languages

Variables that can store information formatted in a small number of built-in data types like integers and alphanumeric characters. This may include data structures like strings, lists, and hash tables that are either built-in or result from combining variables using memory pointers.

Procedures – also known as functions, methods, routines, or subroutines – that take input, generate output, and manipulate data. Modern languages include structured programming constructs like loops and conditionals.

Modular programming support provides the ability to group procedures into files and modules for organizational purposes. Modules are namespaced so identifiers in one module will not conflict with a procedure or variable sharing the same name in another file or module.

Objects and Classes

Languages that support object-oriented programming(OOP) typically use inheritance for code reuse and extensibility in the form of either classes or prototypes. Those that use classes support two main concepts:

- Classes: The definitions for the data format and available procedures for a given type or class of object; may also contain data and procedures (known as class methods) themselves, i.e. classes contain the data members and member functions.

- Objects: Instances of classes.

Objects sometimes correspond to things found in the real world. For example, a graphics program may have objects such as "circle", "square", "menu". An online shopping system might have objects such as "shopping cart", "customer", and "product". Sometimes objects represent more abstract entities, like an object that represents an open file, or an object that provides the service of translating measurements from U.S. customary to metric.

Each object is said to be an instance of a particular class (for example, an object with its name field set to "Mary" might be an instance of class Employee). Procedures in object-oriented programming are known as methods; variables are also known as fields, members, attributes, or properties. This leads to the following terms:

- Class variables: Belong to the *class as a whole*; there is only one copy of each one.

- Instance variables or attributes: Data that belongs to individual *objects*; every object has its own copy of each one.

- Member variables: Refers to both the class and instance variables that are defined by a particular class.

- Class methods: Belong to the class as a whole and have access only to class variables and inputs from the procedure call.

- Instance methods: Belong to individual objects, and have access to instance variables for the specific object they are called on, inputs, and class variables.

Objects are accessed somewhat like variables with complex internal structure, and in many languages are effectively pointers, serving as actual references to a single instance of said object in memory within a heap or stack. They provide a layer of abstraction which can be used to separate internal from external code. External code can use an object by calling a specific instance method with a certain set of input parameters, read an instance variable, or write to an instance variable. Objects are created by calling a special type of method in the class known as a constructor. A program may create many instances of the same class as it runs, which operate independently. This is an easy way for the same procedures to be used on different sets of data.

Object-oriented programming that uses classes is sometimes called class-based programming, while prototype-based programming does not typically use classes. As a result, a significantly different yet analogous terminology is used to define the concepts of object and instance.

In some languages classes and objects can be composed using other concepts like traits and mixins.

Class-based vs. Prototype-based

In class-based languages the *classes* are defined beforehand and the *objects* are instantiated based on the classes. If two objects apple and orange are instantiated from the class Fruit, they are inherently fruits and it is guaranteed that you may handle them in the same way; e.g. a programmer can expect the existence of the same attributes such as color or sugar_content or is_ripe.

In prototype-based languages the objects are the primary entities. No classes even exist. The prototype of an object is just another object to which the object is linked. Every object has one prototype link (and only one). New objects can be created based on already existing objects chosen as their prototype. You may call two different objects apple and orange a fruit, if the object fruit exists, and both apple and orange have fruit as their prototype. The idea of the fruit class doesn't exist explicitly, but as the equivalence class of the objects sharing the same prototype. The attributes and methods of the prototype are delegated to all the objects of the equivalence class defined by this prototype. The attributes and methods owned individually by the object may not be shared by other objects of the same equivalence class; e.g. the attribute sugar_content may be unexpectedly not present in apple. Only single inheritance can be implemented through the prototype.

Dynamic Dispatch/Message Passing

It is the responsibility of the object, not any external code, to select the procedural code to execute in response to a method call, typically by looking up the method at run time in a table associated with the object. This feature is known as dynamic dispatch, and distinguishes an object from an abstract data type (or module), which has a fixed (static) implementation of the operations for all instances. If the call variability relies on more than the single type of the object on which it is called (i.e. at least one other parameter object is involved in the method choice), one speaks of multiple dispatch.

A method call is also known as message passing. It is conceptualized as a message (the name of the method and its input parameters) being passed to the object for dispatch.

Encapsulation

Encapsulation is an object-oriented programming concept that binds together the data and functions that manipulate the data, and that keeps both safe from outside interference and misuse. Data encapsulation led to the important OOP concept of data hiding.

If a class does not allow calling code to access internal object data and permits access through methods only, this is a strong form of abstraction or information hiding known as encapsulation. Some languages (Java, for example) let classes enforce access restrictions explicitly, for example denoting internal data with the private keyword and designating methods intended for use by code outside the class with the public keyword. Methods may also be designed public, private, or intermediate levels such as protected (which allows access from the same class and its subclasses, but not objects of a different class). In other languages (like Python) this is enforced only by convention (for example, private methods may have names that start with an underscore). Encapsulation prevents external code from being concerned with the internal workings of an object. This facilitates code refactoring, for example allowing the author of the class to change how objects of that class represent their data internally without changing any external code (as long as "public" method calls work the same way). It also encourages programmers to put all the code that is concerned with a certain set of data in the same class, which organizes it for easy comprehension by other programmers. Encapsulation is a technique that encourages decoupling.

Composition, Inheritance and Delegation

Objects can contain other objects in their instance variables; this is known as object composition. For example, an object in the Employee class might contain (either directly or through a pointer) an object in the Address class, in addition to its own instance variables like "first_name" and "position". Object composition is used to represent "has-a" relationships: every employee has an address, so every Employee object has access to a place to store an Address object (either directly embedded within itself, or at a separate location addressed via a pointer).

Languages that support classes almost always support inheritance. This allows classes to be arranged in a hierarchy that represents "is-a-type-of" relationships. For example, class Employee might inherit from class Person. All the data and methods available to the parent class also appear in the child class with the same names. For example, class Person might define variables "first_name" and "last_name" with method "make_full_name()". These will also be available in class Employee, which might add the variables "position" and "salary". This technique allows easy re-use of the same procedures and data definitions, in addition to potentially mirroring real-world relationships in an intuitive way. Rather than utilizing database tables and programming subroutines, the developer utilizes objects the user may be more familiar with: objects from their application domain.

Subclasses can override the methods defined by superclasses. Multiple inheritance is allowed in some languages, though this can make resolving overrides complicated. Some languages have special support for mixins, though in any language with multiple inheritance, a mixin is simply a class that does not represent an is-a-type-of relationship. Mixins are typically used to add the same methods to multiple classes. For example, class UnicodeConversionMixin might provide a method unicode to ascii() when included in class FileReader and class WebPageScraper, which don't share a common parent.

Abstract classes cannot be instantiated into objects; they exist only for the purpose of inheritance into other "concrete" classes which can be instantiated. In Java, the final keyword can be used to prevent a class from being subclassed.

The doctrine of composition over inheritance advocates implementing has-a relationships using composition instead of inheritance. For example, instead of inheriting from class Person, class Employee could give each Employee object an internal Person object, which it then has the opportunity to hide from external code even if class Person has many public attributes or methods. Some languages, like Go do not support inheritance at all.

The "open/closed principle" advocates that classes and functions "should be open for extension, but closed for modification".

Delegation is another language feature that can be used as an alternative to inheritance.

Polymorphism

Subtyping - a form of polymorphism - is when calling code can be agnostic as to which class in the supported hierarchy it is operating on - the parent class or one of its descendants. Meanwhile, the same operation name among objects in an inheritance hierarchy may behave differently.

For example, objects of type Circle and Square are derived from a common class called Shape. The Draw function for each type of Shape implements what is necessary to draw itself while calling code can remain indifferent to the particular type of Shape is being drawn.

This is another type of abstraction which simplifies code external to the class hierarchy and enables strong separation of concerns.

Open Recursion

In languages that support open recursion, object methods can call other methods on the same object (including themselves), typically using a special variable or keyword called this or self. This variable is *late-bound*; it allows a method defined in one class to invoke another method that is defined later, in some subclass thereof.

OOP Languages

Simula is generally accepted as being the first language with the primary features of an object-oriented language. It was created for making simulation programs, in which what came to be called objects were the most important information representation. Smalltalk is another early example, and the one with which much of the theory of OOP was developed. Concerning the degree of object orientation, the following distinctions can be made:

- Languages called "pure" OO languages, because everything in them is treated consistently as an object, from primitives such as characters and punctuation, all the way up to whole classes, prototypes, blocks, modules, etc. They were designed specifically to facilitate, even enforce, OO methods. Examples: Python, Ruby, Scala, Smalltalk, Eiffel, Emerald, JADE, Self.

- Languages designed mainly for OO programming, but with some procedural elements. Examples: Java, C++, C#, Delphi/Object Pascal, VB.NET.

- Languages that are historically procedural languages, but have been extended with some OO features. Examples: PHP, Perl, Visual Basic (derived from BASIC), MATLAB, COBOL 2002, Fortran 2003, ABAP, Ada 95, Pascal.

- Languages with most of the features of objects (classes, methods, inheritance), but in a distinctly original form. Examples: Oberon (Oberon-1 or Oberon-2).

- Languages with abstract data type support which may be used to resemble OO programming, but without all features of object-orientation. This includes object-*based* and prototype-based languages. Examples: JavaScript, Lua, Modula-2, CLU.

- Chameleon languages that support multiple paradigms, including OO. Tcl stands out among these for TclOO, a hybrid object system that supports both prototype-based programming and class-based OO.

OOP in Dynamic Languages

In recent years, object-oriented programming has become especially popular in dynamic programming languages. Python, PowerShell, Ruby and Groovy are dynamic languages built on OOP principles, while Perl and PHP have been adding object-oriented features since Perl 5 and PHP 4, and ColdFusion since version 6.

The Document Object Model of HTML, XHTML, and XML documents on the Internet has bindings to the popular JavaScript/ECMAScript language. JavaScript is perhaps the best known prototype-based programming language, which employs cloning from prototypes rather than inheriting from a class (contrast to class-based programming). Another scripting language that takes this approach is Lua.

OOP in a Network Protocol

The messages that flow between computers to request services in a client-server environment can be designed as the linearizations of objects defined by class objects known to both the client and the server. For example, a simple linearized object would consist of a length field, a code point identifying the class, and a data value. A more complex example would be a command consisting of the length and code point of the command and values consisting of linearized objects representing the command's parameters. Each such command must be directed by the server to an object whose class (or superclass) recognizes the command and is able to provide the requested service. Clients and servers are best modeled as complex object-oriented structures. Distributed Data Management Architecture (DDM) took this approach and used class objects to define objects at four levels of a formal hierarchy:

- Fields defining the data values that form messages, such as their length, code point and data values.

- Objects and collections of objects similar to what would be found in a Smalltalk program for messages and parameters.

- Managers similar to AS/400 objects, such as a directory to files and files consisting of metadata and records. Managers conceptually provide memory and processing resources for their contained objects.

- A client or server consisting of all the managers necessary to implement a full processing environment, supporting such aspects as directory services, security and concurrency control.

- The initial version of DDM defined distributed file services. It was later extended to be the foundation of Distributed Relational Database Architecture (DRDA).

Design Patterns

Challenges of object-oriented design are addressed by several approaches. Most common is known as the design patterns codified by Gamma *et al*. More broadly, the term "design patterns" can be used to refer to any general, repeatable, solution pattern to a commonly occurring problem in software design. Some of these commonly occurring problems have implications and solutions particular to object-oriented development.

Inheritance and Behavioral Subtyping

It is intuitive to assume that inheritance creates a semantic "is a" relationship, and thus to infer that objects instantiated from subclasses can always be *safely* used instead of those instantiated from the superclass. This intuition is unfortunately false in most OOP languages, in particular in all those that allow mutable objects. Subtype polymorphism as enforced by the type checker in OOP languages (with mutable objects) cannot guarantee behavioral subtyping in any context. Behavioral subtyping is undecidable in general, so it cannot be implemented by a program (compiler). Class or object hierarchies must be carefully designed, considering possible incorrect uses that cannot be detected syntactically. This issue is known as the Liskov substitution principle.

Gang of Four Design Patterns

Design Patterns: Elements of Reusable Object-Oriented Software is an influential book published in 1994 by Erich Gamma, Richard Helm, Ralph Johnson, and John Vlissides, often referred to humorously as the "Gang of Four". Along with exploring the capabilities and pitfalls of object-oriented programming, it describes 23 common programming problems and patterns for solving them. As of April 2007, the book was in its 36th printing.

The book describes the following patterns:

- Creational patterns: Factory method pattern, Abstract factory pattern, Singleton pattern, Builder pattern, Prototype pattern.

- Structural patterns: Adapter pattern, Bridge pattern, Composite pattern, Decorator pattern, Facade pattern, Flyweight pattern, Proxy pattern.

- Behavioral patterns: Chain-of-responsibility pattern, Command pattern, Interpreter pattern, Iterator pattern, Mediator pattern, Memento pattern, Observer pattern, State pattern, Strategy pattern, Template method pattern, Visitor pattern.

Object-orientation and Databases

Both object-oriented programming and relational database management systems (RDBMSs) are extremely common in software today. Since relational databases don't store objects directly (though some RDBMSs have object-oriented features to approximate this), there is a general need to bridge the two worlds. The problem of bridging object-oriented programming accesses and data patterns with relational databases is known as object-relational impedance mismatch. There are a number of approaches to cope with this problem, but no general solution without downsides. One of the most common approaches is object-relational mapping, as found in IDE languages such as Visual FoxPro and libraries such as Java Data Objects and Ruby on Rails' ActiveRecord.

There are also object databases that can be used to replace RDBMSs, but these have not been as technically and commercially successful as RDBMSs.

Real-world Modeling and Relationships

OOP can be used to associate real-world objects and processes with digital counterparts. However, not everyone agrees that OOP facilitates direct real-world mapping or that real-world mapping is even a worthy goal; Bertrand Meyer argues in Object-Oriented Software Construction that a program is not a model of the world but a model of some part of the world; "Reality is a cousin twice removed". At the same time, some principal limitations of OOP have been noted. For example, the circle-ellipse problem is difficult to handle using OOP's concept of inheritance.

However, Niklaus Wirth (who popularized the adage now known as Wirth's law: "Software is getting slower more rapidly than hardware becomes faster") said of OOP in his paper, "Good Ideas through the Looking Glass", "This paradigm closely reflects the structure of systems 'in the real world', and it is therefore well suited to model complex systems with complex behaviours" (contrast KISS principle).

Steve Yegge and others noted that natural languages lack the OOP approach of strictly prioritizing *things* (objects/nouns) before *actions* (methods/verbs). This problem may cause OOP to suffer more convoluted solutions than procedural programming.

OOP and Control Flow

OOP was developed to increase the reusability and maintainability of source code. Transparent representation of the control flow had no priority and was meant to be handled by a compiler. With the increasing relevance of parallel hardware and multithreaded coding, developing transparent control flow becomes more important, something hard to achieve with OOP.

Responsibility- vs. Data-driven Design

Responsibility-driven design defines classes in terms of a contract, that is, a class should be defined around a responsibility and the information that it shares. This is contrasted by Wirfs-Brock and Wilkerson with data-driven design, where classes are defined around the data-structures that must be held. The authors hold that responsibility-driven design is preferable.

SOLID and GRASP Guidelines

SOLID is a mnemonic invented by Michael Feathers that stands for and advocates five programming practices:

- Single responsibility principle.

- Open/closed principle.

- Liskov substitution principle.

- Interface segregation principle.

- Dependency inversion principle.

GRASP (General Responsibility Assignment Software Patterns) is another set of guidelines advocated by Craig Larman.

Formal Semantics

Objects are the run-time entities in an object-oriented system. They may represent a person, a place, a bank account, a table of data, or any item that the program has to handle.

There have been several attempts at formalizing the concepts used in object-oriented programming. The following concepts and constructs have been used as interpretations of OOP concepts:

- Co algebraic data types.

- Abstract data types (which have existential types) allow the definition of modules but these do not support dynamic dispatch.

- Recursive types.

- Encapsulated state.

- Inheritance.

- Records are basis for understanding objects if function literals can be stored in fields (like in functional-programming languages), but the actual calculi need be considerably more complex to incorporate essential features of OOP. Several extensions of System $F^{<:}$ that deal with mutable objects have been studied; these allow both subtype polymorphism and parametric polymorphism (generics).

Advantages of OOP

Some of the advantages of object-oriented programming include:

Improved software-development productivity: Object-oriented programming is modular, as it provides separation of duties in object-based program development. It is also extensible, as objects can be extended to include new attributes and behaviors. Objects can also be reused within an across applications. Because of these three factors – modularity, extensibility, and reusability – object-oriented programming provides improved software-development productivity over traditional procedure-based programming techniques.

Improved software maintainability: For the reasons mentioned above, object-oriented software is also easier to maintain. Since the design is modular, part of the system can be updated in case of issues without a need to make large-scale changes.

Faster development: Reuse enables faster development. Object-oriented programming languages come with rich libraries of objects, and code developed during projects is also reusable in future projects.

Lower cost of development: The reuse of software also lowers the cost of development. Typically, more effort is put into the object-oriented analysis and design, which lowers the overall cost of development.

Higher-quality software: Faster development of software and lower cost of development allows more time and resources to be used in the verification of the software. Although quality is dependent upon the experience of the teams, object-oriented programming tends to result in higher-quality software.

Some of the disadvantages of object-oriented programming include:

Steep learning curve: The thought process involved in object-oriented programming may not be natural for some people, and it can take time to get used to it. It is complex to create programs based on interaction of objects. Some of the key programming techniques, such as inheritance and polymorphism, can be challenging to comprehend initially.

Larger program size: Object-oriented programs typically involve more lines of code than procedural programs.

Slower programs: Object-oriented programs are typically slower than procedure-based programs, as they typically require more instructions to be executed.

Not suitable for all types of problems: There are problems that lend themselves well to functional-programming style, logic-programming style, or procedure-based programming style, and applying object-oriented programming in those situations will not result in efficient programs.

Structured Programming

Structured programming is a programming paradigm aimed at improving the clarity, quality, and development time of a computer program by making extensive use of the structured control flow constructs of selection (if/then/else) and repetition (while and for), block structures, and subroutines.

Structured programming is most frequently used with deviations that allow for clearer programs in some particular cases, such as when exception handling has to be performed.

Elements

Control Structures

Following the structured program theorem, all programs are seen as composed of control structures:

- "Sequence"; ordered statements or subroutines executed in sequence.

- "Selection"; one or a number of statements is executed depending on the state of the program. This is usually expressed with keywords such as if, then, else, endif.

- "Iteration"; a statement or block is executed until the program reaches a certain state, or operations have been applied to every element of a collection. This is usually expressed with keywords such as while, repeat, for or do, until. Often it is recommended that each loop should only have one entry point (and in the original structural programming, also only one exit point, and a few languages enforce this).

- "Recursion"; a statement is executed by repeatedly calling itself until termination conditions are met. While similar in practice to iterative loops, recursive loops may be more computationally efficient, and are implemented differently as a cascading stack.

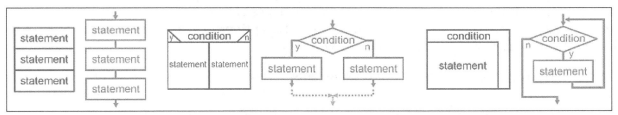

Graphical representation of the three basic patterns — sequence, selection, and repetition — using NS diagrams (blue) and flow charts (green).

Subroutines

Subroutines; callable units such as procedures, functions, methods, or subprograms are used to allow a sequence to be referred to by a single statement.

Blocks

Blocks are used to enable groups of statements to be treated as if they were one statement. Block-structured languages have a syntax for enclosing structures in some formal way, such as an if-statement bracketed by if..fi as in ALGOL 68, or a code section bracketed by BEGIN..END, as in PL/I and Pascal, whitespace indentation as in Python - or the curly braces {...} of C and many later languages.

Structured Programming Languages

It is possible to do structured programming in any programming language, though it is preferable to use something like a procedural programming language. Some of the languages initially used for structured programming include: ALGOL, Pascal, PL/I and Ada, but most new procedural programming languages since that time have included features to encourage structured programming, and sometimes deliberately left out features – notably GOTO – in an effort to make unstructured programming more difficult. Structured programming (sometimes known as modular programming) enforces a logical structure on the program being written to make it more efficient and easier to understand and modify.

Common Deviations

While goto has now largely been replaced by the structured constructs of selection (if/then/else) and repetition (while and for), few languages are purely structured. The most common deviation, found in many languages, is the use of a return statement for early exit from a subroutine. This results in multiple exit points, instead of the single exit point required by structured programming. There are other constructions to handle cases that are awkward in purely structured programming.

Early Exit

The most common deviation from structured programming is early exit from a function or loop. At the level of functions, this is a return statement. At the level of loops, this is a break statement (terminate the loop) or continue statement (terminate the current iteration, proceed with next iteration). In structured programming, these can be replicated by adding additional branches or tests, but for returns from nested code this can add significant complexity. C is an early and prominent example of these constructs. Some newer languages also have "labeled breaks", which allow breaking out of more than just the innermost loop. Exceptions also allow early exit, but have further consequences, and thus are treated below.

Multiple exits can arise for a variety of reasons, most often either that the subroutine has no more work to do (if returning a value, it has completed the calculation), or has encountered "exceptional" circumstances that prevent it from continuing, hence needing exception handling.

The most common problem in early exit is that cleanup or final statements are not executed – for example, allocated memory is not deallocated, or open files are not closed, causing memory leaks or resource leaks. These must be done at each return site, which is brittle and can easily result in bugs. For instance, in later development, a return statement could be overlooked by a developer, and an action which should be performed at the end of a subroutine (e.g., a trace statement) might not be performed in all cases. Languages without a return statement, such as standard Pascal and Seed7, do not have this problem.

Most modern languages provide language-level support to prevent such leaks. Most commonly this is done via unwind protection, which ensures that certain code is guaranteed to be run when execution exits a block; this is a structured alternative to having a cleanup block and a goto. This is most often known as try finally, and considered a part of exception handling. In case of multiple return statements introducing try finally, without exceptions might look strange. Various techniques exist to encapsulate resource management. An alternative approach, found primarily in C++, is Resource acquisition is initialization, which uses normal stack unwinding (variable deallocation) at function exit to call destructors on local variables to deallocate resources.

Kent Beck, Martin Fowler and co-authors have argued in their refactoring books that nested conditionals may be harder to understand than a certain type of flatter structure using multiple exits predicated by guard clauses. Their 2009 book flatly states that "one exit point is really not a useful rule. Clarity is the key principle: If the method is clearer with one exit point, use one exit point; otherwise don't". They offer a cookbook solution for transforming a function consisting only of nested conditionals into a sequence of guarded return (or throw) statements, followed by a single unguarded block, which is intended to contain the code for the common case, while the guarded statements are supposed to deal with the less common ones (or with errors). Herb Sutter and Andrei Alexandrescu also argue in their 2004 C++ tips book that the single-exit point is an obsolete requirement.

In his 2004 textbook, David Watt writes that "single-entry multi-exit control flows are often desirable". Using Tennent's framework notion of sequencer, Watt uniformly describes the control flow constructs found in contemporary programming languages and attempts to explain why certain types of sequencers are preferable to others in the context of multi-exit control flows. Watt writes that unrestricted gotos (jump sequencers) are bad because the destination of the jump is not self-explanatory to the reader of a program until the reader finds and examines the actual label or address that is the target of the jump. In contrast, Watt argues that the conceptual intent of a return sequencer is clear from its own context, without having to examine its destination. Watt writes that a class of sequencers known as *escape sequencers*, defined as a "sequencer that terminates execution of a textually enclosing command or procedure", encompasses both breaks from loops (including multi-level breaks) and return statements. Watt also notes that while jump sequencers (gotos) have been somewhat restricted in languages like C, where the target must be an inside the local block or an encompassing outer block, that restriction alone is not sufficient to make the intent of gotos in C self-describing and so they can still produce "spaghetti code".

In contrast to the above, Bertrand Meyer wrote in his 2009 textbook that instructions like break and continue "are just the old goto in sheep's clothing" and strongly advised against their use.

Exception Handling

Based on the coding error from the Ariane 501 disaster, software developer Jim Bonang argues that any exceptions thrown from a function violate the single-exit paradigm, and proposes that all inter-procedural exceptions should be forbidden. In C++ syntax, this is done by declaring all function signatures as noexcept (since C++11) or throw(). Bonang proposes that all single-exit conforming C++ should be written along the lines of:

```
bool MyCheck1() throw() {

bool success = false;

try {

// Do something that may throw exceptions.

if (!MyCheck2()) {

throw SomeInternalException();

}

// Other code similar to the above.

success = true;

} catch (...) {
```

```
// All exceptions caught and logged.
}

return success;

}
```

Peter Ritchie also notes that, in principle, even a single throw right before the return in a function constitutes a violation of the single-exit principle, but argues that Dijkstra's rules were written in a time before exception handling became a paradigm in programming languages, so he proposes to allow any number of throw points in addition to a single return point. He notes that solutions which wrap exceptions for the sake of creating a single-exit have higher nesting depth and thus are more difficult to comprehend, and even accuses those who propose to apply such solutions to programming languages which support exceptions of engaging in cargo cult thinking.

David Watt also analyzes exception handling in the framework of sequencers. Watt notes that an abnormal situation (generally exemplified with arithmetic overflows or input/output failures like file not found) is a kind of error that "is detected in some low-level program unit, but [for which] a handler is more naturally located in a high-level program unit". For example, a program might contain several calls to read files, but the action to perform when a file is not found depends on the meaning (purpose) of the file in question to the program and thus a handling routine for this abnormal situation cannot be located in low-level system code. Watts further notes that introducing status flags testing in the caller, as single-exit structured programming or even (multi-exit) return sequencers would entail, results in a situation where "the application code tends to get cluttered by tests of status flags" and that "the programmer might forgetfully or lazily omit to test a status flag. In fact, abnormal situations represented by status flags are by default ignored." He notes that in contrast to status flags testing, exceptions have the opposite default behavior, causing the program to terminate unless the programmer explicitly deals with the exception in some way, possibly by adding code to willfully ignore it. Based on these arguments, Watt concludes that jump sequencers or escape sequencers aren't as suitable as a dedicated exception sequencer with the semantics.

The textbook by Louden and Lambert emphasizes that exception handling differs from structured programming constructs like while loops because the transfer of control "is set up at a different point in the program than that where the actual transfer takes place. At the point where the transfer actually occurs, there may be no syntactic indication that control will in fact be transferred." Computer science professor Arvind Kumar Bansal also notes that in languages which implement exception handling, even control structures like for, which have the single-exit property in absence of exceptions, no longer have it in presence of exceptions, because an exception can prematurely cause an early exit in any part of the control structure; for instance if init() throws an exception in for (init(); check(); increm()), then the usual exit point after check() is not reached. Citing multiple prior studies by others and their own results, Westley Weimer and George Necula wrote that a significant problem with exceptions is that they "create hidden control-flow paths that are difficult for programmers to reason about".

The necessity to limit code to single-exit points appears in some contemporary programming environments focused on parallel computing, such as OpenMP. The various parallel constructs from OpenMP, like parallel do, do not allow early exits from inside to the outside of the parallel construct; this restriction includes all manner of exits, from break to C++ exceptions, but all of these are permitted inside the parallel construct if the jump target is also inside it.

Multiple Entry

More rarely, subprograms allow multiple *entry*. This is most commonly only *re*-entry into a coroutine (or generator/semicoroutine), where a subprogram yields control (and possibly a value), but can then be resumed where it left off. There are a number of common uses of such programming, notably for streams (particularly input/output), state machines, and concurrency. From a code execution point of view, yielding from a coroutine is closer to structured programming than returning from a subroutine, as the subprogram has not actually terminated, and will continue when called again – it is not an early exit. However, coroutines mean that multiple subprograms have execution state – rather than a single call stack of subroutines – and thus introduce a different form of complexity.

It is very rare for subprograms to allow entry to an arbitrary position in the subprogram, as in this case the program state (such as variable values) is uninitialized or ambiguous, and this is very similar to a goto.

State Machines

Some programs, particularly parsers and communications protocols, have a number of states that follow each other in a way that is not easily reduced to the basic structures, and some programmers implement the state-changes with a jump to the new state. This type of state-switching is often used in the Linux kernel.

However, it is possible to structure these systems by making each state-change a separate subprogram and using a variable to indicate the active state. Alternatively, these can be implemented via coroutines, which dispense with the trampoline.

Procedure Oriented Programming

Procedural programming is a programming paradigm, derived from structured programming,based on the concept of the *procedure call*. Procedures, also known as routines, subroutines, or functions, simply contain a series of computational steps to be carried out. Any given procedure might be called at any point during a program's execution, including by other procedures or itself. The first major procedural programming languages appeared circa 1957–1964, including Fortran, ALGOL, COBOL, PL/I and BASIC. Pascal and C were published circa 1970–1972.

Computer processors provide hardware support for procedural programming through a stack register and instructions for calling procedures and returning from them. Hardware support for other types of programming is possible, but no attempt was commercially successful (for example Lisp machines or Java processors).

Procedures and Modularity

Modularity is generally desirable, especially in large, complicated programs. Inputs are usually specified syntactically in the form of *arguments* and the outputs delivered as *return values*.

Scoping is another technique that helps keep procedures modular. It prevents the procedure from accessing the variables of other procedures (and vice versa), including previous instances of itself, without explicit authorization.

Less modular procedures, often used in small or quickly written programs, tend to interact with a large number of variables in the execution environment, which other procedures might also modify.

Because of the ability to specify a simple interface, to be self-contained, and to be reused, procedures are a convenient vehicle for making pieces of code written by different people or different groups, including through programming libraries.

Comparison with other Programming Paradigms

Imperative Programming

Procedural programming languages are also imperative languages, because they make explicit references to the state of the execution environment. This could be anything from *variables* (which may correspond to processor registers) to something like the position of the "turtle" in the Logo programming language.

Often, the terms "procedural programming" and "imperative programming" are used synonymously. However, procedural programming relies heavily on blocks and scope, whereas imperative programming as a whole may or may not have such features. As such, procedural languages generally use reserved words that act on blocks, such as if, while, and for, to implement control flow, whereas non-structured imperative languages use goto statements and branch tables for the same purpose.

Object-oriented Programming

The focus of procedural programming is to break down a programming task into a collection of variables, data structures, and subroutines, whereas in object-oriented programming it is to break down a programming task into objects that expose behavior (methods) and data (members or attributes) using interfaces. The most important distinction is that while procedural programming uses procedures to operate on data structures, object-oriented programming bundles the two together, so an "object", which is an instance of a class, operates on its "own" data structure.

Nomenclature varies between the two, although they have similar semantics:

Procedural	Object-oriented
procedure	Method
Record	Object
Module	Class
Procedure call	Message

Functional Programming

The principles of modularity and code reuse in practical functional languages are fundamentally the same as in procedural languages, since they both stem from structured programming. So for example:

- Procedures correspond to functions. Both allow the reuse of the same code in various parts of the programs, and at various points of its execution.

- By the same token, procedure calls correspond to function application.

- Functions and their invocations are modularly separated from each other in the same manner, by the use of function arguments, return values and variable scopes.

The main difference between the styles is that functional programming languages remove or at least deemphasize the imperative elements of procedural programming. The feature set of functional languages is therefore designed to support writing programs as much as possible in terms of pure functions:

- Whereas procedural languages model execution of the program as a sequence of imperative commands that may implicitly alter shared state, functional programming languages model execution as the evaluation of complex expressions that only depend on each other in terms of arguments and return values. For this reason, functional programs can have a free order of code execution, and the languages may offer little control over the order in which various parts of the program are executed. (For example, the arguments to a procedure invocation in Scheme are executed in an arbitrary order).

- Functional programming languages support (and heavily use) first-class functions, anonymous functions and closures, although these concepts are being included in newer procedural languages.

- Functional programming languages tend to rely on tail call optimization and higher-order functions instead of imperative looping constructs.

Many functional languages, however, are in fact impurely functional and offer imperative/procedural constructs that allow the programmer to write programs in procedural style, or in a combination of both styles. It is common for input/output code in functional languages to be written in a procedural style.

There do exist a few esoteric functional languages (like Unlambda) that eschew structured programming precepts for the sake of being difficult to program in (and therefore challenging). These languages are the exception to the common ground between procedural and functional languages.

Logic Programming

In logic programming, a program is a set of premises, and computation is performed by attempting to prove candidate theorems. From this point of view, logic programs are declarative, focusing on what the problem is, rather than on how to solve it.

However, the backward reasoning technique, implemented by SLD resolution, used to solve problems in logic programming languages such as Prolog, treats programs as goal-reduction procedures. Thus clauses of the form:

H :- B1, ..., Bn.

have a dual interpretation, both as procedures

to show/solve H, show/solve B^1 and ... and B^n

and as logical implications:

B^1 and ... and B^n implies H.

Experienced logic programmers use the procedural interpretation to write programs that are effective and efficient, and they use the declarative interpretation to help ensure that programs are correct.

Modular Programming

Modular programming is a software design technique that emphasizes separating the functionality of a program into independent, interchangeable modules, such that each contains everything necessary to execute only one aspect of the desired functionality.

A module interface expresses the elements that are provided and required by the module. The elements defined in the interface are detectable by other modules. The implementation contains the working code that corresponds to the elements declared in the interface. Modular programming is closely related to structured programming and object-oriented programming, all having the same goal of facilitating construction of large software programs and systems by decomposition into smaller pieces, and all originating around the 1960s. While the historical usage of these terms has been inconsistent, "modular programming" now refers to high-level decomposition of the code of an entire program into pieces: structured programming to the low-level code use of structured control flow, and object-oriented programming to the *data* use of objects, a kind of data structure.

In object-oriented programming, the use of interfaces as an architectural pattern to construct modules is known as interface-based programming.

Language Support

Languages that formally support the module concept include Ada, Algol, BlitzMax, C#, Clojure, COBOL, D, Dart, eC, Erlang, Elixir, F, F#, Fortran, Go, Haskell, IBM/360 Assembler, IBM i Control Language (CL), IBM RPG, Java, MATLAB, ML, Modula, Modula-2, Modula-3, Morpho, NEWP, Oberon, Oberon-2, Objective-C, OCaml, several derivatives of Pascal (Component Pascal, Object Pascal, Turbo Pascal, UCSD Pascal), Perl, PL/I, PureBasic, Python, Ruby, Rust, JavaScript, Visual Basic .NET and WebDNA.

Conspicuous examples of languages that lack support for modules are C, C++, and Pascal (in its original form). As of 2014, modules have been proposed for C++; modules were added to Objective-C in iOS 7 (2013); and Pascal was superseded by Modula and Oberon, which included modules from the start, and various derivatives that included modules. JavaScript has had native modules since ECMAScript 2015.

Modular programming can be performed even where the programming language lacks explicit syntactic features to support named modules, like, for example, in C. This is done by using existing language features, together with, for example, coding conventions, programming idioms and the physical code structure. The IBM System i also uses modules when programming in the Integrated Language Environment (ILE).

Key Aspects

With modular programming, concerns are separated such that modules perform logically discrete functions, interacting through well-defined interfaces. Often modules form a directed acyclic graph (DAG); in this case a cyclic dependency between modules is seen as indicating that these should be a single module. In the case where modules do form a DAG they can be arranged as a hierarchy, where the lowest-level modules are independent, depending on no other modules, and higher-level modules depend on lower-level ones. A particular program or library is a top-level module of its own hierarchy, but can in turn be seen as a lower-level module of a higher-level program, library, or system.

When creating a modular system, instead of creating a monolithic application (where the smallest component is the whole), several smaller modules are written separately so when they are composed together, they construct the executable application program. Typically these are also compiled separately, via separate compilation, and then linked by a linker. A just-in-time compiler may perform some of this construction "on-the-fly" at run time.

This makes modular designed systems, if built correctly, far more reusable than a traditional monolithic design, since all (or many) of these modules may then be reused (without change) in other projects. This also facilitates the "breaking down" of projects into several smaller projects. Theoretically, a modularized software project will be more easily assembled by large teams, since no team members are creating the whole system, or even need to know about the system as a whole. They can focus just on the assigned smaller task (this, it is claimed, counters the key assumption of The Mythical Man Month, making it actually possible to add more developers to a late software project without making it later still).

Application Software

The software is a kind of programs that enable a user to perform some specific task or used to operate a computer. It directs all the peripheral devices on a computer system - what to do and how to perform work. Without Software, we can't operate hardware and perform any calculations. A computer system can be divided into three components: the hardware, the software and the users. The software can be further divided into mainly two parts: Application software and System Software. Bare use of hardware is not easy, so to make it easy software is created.

System Software: System Software (a type of computer program) provides a platform to run computer's hardware and computer application to utilize system resources and solve their computation problem. It is written in a low-level language, like assembly language so it can easily interact with hardware with basic level. It controls working of peripheral devices. System software acts as a scheduler for the execution of the processes and arrange the sequence according to their priority and I/O devices requirement and creation of the process. The best-known example of system software is the operating system (OS). It responsible for manages all the other programs on a computer.

Application Software: Applications software is capable of dealing with user inputs and helps the user to complete the task. It is also called end-user programs or only an app. It resides above system software. First user deal with system software after that he/she deals with application software. The end user uses applications software for a specific purpose. It programmed for simple as well as complex tasks. It either be installed or access online. It can be a single program or a group of small programs that referred to as an application suite. Some examples of Application Software are Word processing software, Spreadsheets Software, Presentation, Graphics, CAD/CAM, Sending email etc.

Types of Application Software: According to the need of users it is categorized into following types.

1. Presentation Software: Presentation program is a program to show the information in the form of slides. We can add text, graphics video and images to slides to make them more informative.

The software has three components:

1. Text editor for inputting and formatting text.

2. Inserting graphics, text, video and other multimedia files.

3. Slideshow to display the information.

Presentation software helps the presenter to present their ideas with ease and visual information easy to understand. Example of presentation software: Microsoft's PowerPoint and Apple's Keynote.

2. Spreadsheet Software: Spreadsheet software is used to perform manipulate and calculations. In spreadsheet software data is stored in intersection row and column. The intersection of row and column is known as a cell. The cell labeled with the row and column label like A1, A2 etc. While entering data into the cell, we can also define the data value like text, date, time, number. It provides many formula and function to perform calculations like arithmetic operations, logical operations, text operation etc. It provides charts, graphs to display data graphically. For example Microsoft Excel, lotus 1-2-3 for windows and number for MAC OS.

3. Database Software: Database is a collection of data related to any applications. Today is environment every application has some database where data regarding users stored. For this purpose, we used database software. When we operate the application data is accessed from the database, and after manipulation, it gets back stored in the database.

Database Management System (DBMS) software tool used for storing, modifying extracting and searching for information within a database. MySQL, MS Access, Microsoft SQL Server and Oracle are the example of database application Software.

4. Multimedia Software: Multimedia is a combination of text, graphics, audio and Multimedia software used in the editing of video, audio and text. Multimedia software used in the growth of business, educations, information, remote system and entertainment.

Entertainment: This area deal with the general public, media and telecommunication. With the growth entertainment mode, many applications are available for mobile phone as well as the system. Like Music and video entertainment app, navigation app, social networking application, news and weather application, educational apps and e-book reader's app for preparation of any type of exams.

5. Simulation Software: Simulation is an imitation of real world and environment. The simulation creates a physical environment of the real world to represent the similar behavior, function and key nature of the selected topic. Simulation is technology for education, engineering, testing, training, video games and for scientific modeling of natural systems to gain insight into their functioning. The simulation used in the area of the real world where the real system cannot be accessible or may be dangerous or unacceptable. Area of technology: flight, economics, automobiles, Robotics, digital lifecycle, Space Shuttle Navigation, weather.

6. Word Processing Software: Word Processing software is used to manipulate, format the text, to create memos, letters, faxes and documents. Processing Software is used to format and beautify the text. It provides a list of features. Like thesaurus, the option provides synonyms, antonyms and related words for chosen word or phrase. Find and replace feature enables users to scan and replace selected words or phrases in the document. Font option provides font color, font style, font effect, font size to modify the txt. Word Art option to modify or animated titles, hyphens, columns and text boxes in documents. Grammar and Spelling check option available for checking errors. Many more option is listed here in software.

For example Microsoft Word, Lotus Word Pro, Word pad and Corel WordPerfect.

References

- Stallings, william (2008). Computer organization & architecture. New delhi: prentice-hall of india private limited. P. 267. Isbn 978-81-203-2962-1

- Software, definition: techterms.com, Retrieved 29 March, 2019

- "desktop operating system market share worldwide | statcounter global stats". Statcounter global stats. Retrieved 18 december 2017

- System-software, disk-operating-system, fundamental: ecomputernotes.com, Retrieved 16 January, 2019

- Peter van-roy; seif haridi (2004). Concepts, techniques, and models of computer programming. Mit press. Isbn 978-0-262-22069-9

- What-is-software-programming: learn.org, Retrieved 25 February, 2019

- Ali, junade (28 september 2016). Mastering php design patterns | packt books (1 ed.). Birmingham, england, uk: packt publishing limited. P. 11. Isbn 978-1-78588-713-0. Retrieved 11 december 2017

- Application-software, disk-operating-system, fundamental: ecomputernotes.com, Retrieved 13 May, 2019

- Neward, ted (26 june 2006). "the vietnam of computer science". Interoperability happens. Archived from the original on 4 july 2006. Retrieved 2 june 2010

Computer Networking 5

- **Computer Network**
- **Basics of Computer Networking**
- **Network Topology**
- **Network Nodes**
- **Network Security**
- **Network Performance**

A group of computers connected with each other for sharing information and other resources is defined as a computer network. Network topology, network nodes, network security and network performance are studied under computer networking. This chapter delves into the subject of computer networking to provide an in-depth understanding of it.

Computer Network

A computer network is a system in which multiple computers are connected to each other to share information and resources.

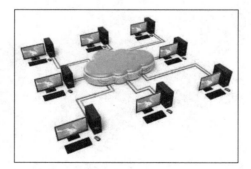

Characteristics of a Computer Network

- Share resources from one computer to another.
- Create files and store them in one computer, access those files from the other computer(s) connected over the network.

- Connect a printer, scanner, or a fax machine to one computer within the network and let other computers of the network use the machines available over the network.

Following is the list of hardware's required to set up a computer network:

- Network Cables.
- Distributors.
- Routers.
- Internal Network Cards.
- External Network Cards.

Network Cables

Network cables are used to connect computers. The most commonly used cable is Category 5 cable RJ-45.

Distributors

A computer can be connected to another one via a serial port but if we need to connect many computers to produce a network, this serial connection will not work.

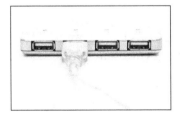

The solution is to use a central body to which other computers, printers, scanners, etc. can be connected and then this body will manage or distribute network traffic.

Router

A router is a type of device which acts as the central point among computers and other devices that are a part of the network. It is equipped with holes called ports. Computers and other devices are connected to a router using network cables. Now-a-days router comes in wireless modes using which computers can be connected without any physical cable.

Network Card

Network card is a necessary component of a computer without which a computer cannot be connected over a network. It is also known as the network adapter or Network Interface Card (NIC). Most branded computers have network card pre-installed. Network cards are of two types: Internal and External Network Cards.

Internal Network Cards

Motherboard has a slot for internal network card where it is to be inserted. Internal network cards are of two types in which the first type uses Peripheral Component Interconnect (PCI) connection, while the second type uses Industry Standard Architecture (ISA). Network cables are required to provide network access.

External Network Cards

External network cards are of two types: Wireless and USB based. Wireless network card needs to be inserted into the motherboard, however no network cable is required to connect to the network.

Universal Serial Bus (USB)

USB card is easy to use and connects via USB port. Computers automatically detect USB card and can install the drivers required to support the USB network card automatically.

Basics of Computer Networking

Open System

A system which is connected to the network and is ready for communication.

Closed System

A system which is not connected to the network and can't be communicated with.

Computer Network

It is the interconnection of multiple devices, generally termed as Hosts connected using multiple paths for the purpose of sending/receiving data or media. There are also multiple devices or mediums which helps in the communication between two different devices which are known as Network devices. Ex: Router, Switch, Hub, Bridge.

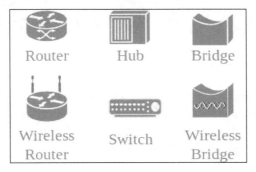

The layout pattern using which devices are interconnected is called as network topology. Such as Bus, Star, Mesh, Ring, Daisy chain.

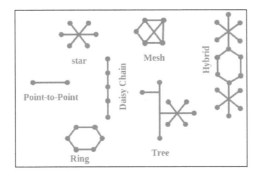

OSI

OSI stands for Open Systems Interconnection. It is a reference model that specifies standards for communications protocols and also the functionalities of each layer.

Protocol

A protocol is the set of rules or algorithms which define the way how two entities can communicate across the network and there exists different protocol defined at each layer of the OSI model. Few of such protocols are TCP, IP, UDP, ARP, DHCP, FTP and so on.

Unique Identifiers of Network

Host Name

Each device in the network is associated with a unique device name known as Hostname. Type "hostname" in the command prompt and press 'Enter', this displays the hostname of your machine.

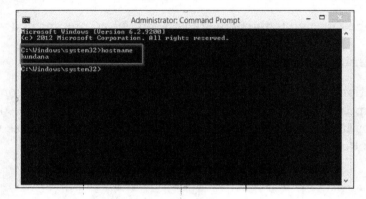

IP Address (Internet Protocol Address)

Also, known as the Logical Address, is the network address of the system across the network. To identify each device in the world-wide-web, Internet Assigned Numbers Authority (IANA) assigns IPV4 (Version 4) address as a unique identifier for each device on the Internet. Length of the IP address is 32-bits. (Hence we have 2^{32} IP addresses available.) Type "ipconfig" in the command prompt and press 'Enter', this gives us the IP address of the device.

MAC Address (Media Access Control Address)

Also known as physical address, is the unique identifier of each host and is associated with the NIC (Network Interface Card). MAC address is assigned to the NIC at the time of manufacturing. Length of the MAC address is : 12-nibble/ 6 bytes/ 48 bits Type "ipconfig/all" in the command prompt and press 'Enter', this gives us the MAC address.

Port

Port can be referred as a logical channel through which data can be sent/received to an application. Any host may have multiple applications running, and each of this application is identified using the port number on which they are running. Port number is a 16-bit integer, hence we have 2^{16} ports available which are categorized as shown below:

PORT TYPES	RANGE
Well known Ports	0 – 1023
Registered Ports	1024 – 49151
Ephemeral Ports	49152 – 65535

Number of ports: 65,536

Range: 0 – 65535

Type "netstat -a" in the command prompt and press 'Enter', this lists all the ports being used.

Socket

The unique combination of IP address and Port number together are termed as Socket.

Few more Concepts

DNS Server

DNS stands for Domain Name system. DNS is basically a server which translates web addresses or URL (ex: www.google.com) into their corresponding IP addresses. We don't have to remember all the IP addresses of each and every website. The command 'nslookup' gives you the IP address of the domain you are looking for. This also provides the information of our DNS Server.

ARP

ARP stands for Address Resolution Protocol. It is used to convert the IP address to its corresponding Physical Address(i.e.MAC Address). ARP is used by the Data Link Layer to identify the MAC address of the Receiver's machine.

RARP

RARP stands for Reverse Address Resolution Protocol. As the name suggests, it provides the IP address of the device given a physical address as input.

Network Topology

Network topology is the arrangement of the elements (links, nodes, etc.) of a communication network. Network topology can be used to define or describe the arrangement of various types of telecommunication networks, including command and control radio networks, industrial fieldbusses and computer networks.

Network topology is the topological structure of a network and may be depicted physically or logically. It is an application of graph theory wherein communicating devices are modeled as nodes and the connections between the devices are modeled as links or lines between the nodes. Physical topology is the placement of the various components of a network (e.g., device location and cable installation), while logical topology illustrates how data flows within a network. Distances between nodes, physical interconnections, transmission rates, or signal types may differ between two different networks, yet their topologies may be identical. A network's physical topology is a particular concern of the physical layer of the OSI model.

Examples of network topologies are found in local area networks (LAN), a common computer network installation. Any given node in the LAN has one or more physical links to other devices in the network; graphically mapping these links results in a geometric shape that can be used to describe the physical topology of the network. A wide variety of physical topologies have been used in LANs, including ring, bus, mesh and star. Conversely, mapping the data flow between the components determines the logical topology of the network. In comparison, Controller Area Networks, common in vehicles, are primarily distributed control system networks of one or more controllers interconnected with sensors and actuators over, invariably, a physical bus topology.

Topologies

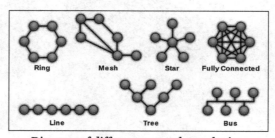

Diagram of different network topologies.

Two basic categories of network topologies exist, physical topologies and logical topologies.

The transmission medium layout used to link devices is the physical topology of the network. For conductive or fiber optical mediums, this refers to the layout of cabling, the locations of nodes, and the links between the nodes and the cabling. The physical topology of a network is determined by the capabilities of the network access devices and media, the level of control or fault tolerance desired, and the cost associated with cabling or telecommunication circuits.

In contrast, logical topology is the way that the signals act on the network media, or the way that the data passes through the network from one device to the next without regard to the physical interconnection of the devices. A network's logical topology is not necessarily the same as its physical topology. For example, the original twisted pair Ethernet using repeater hubs was a logical bus topology carried on a physical star topology. Token ring is a logical ring topology, but is wired as a physical star from the media access unit. Physically, AFDX can be a cascaded star topology of multiple dual redundant Ethernet switches; however, the AFDX Virtual links are modeled as time-switched single-transmitter bus connections, thus following the safety model of a single-transmitter bus topology previously used in aircraft. Logical topologies are often closely associated with media access control methods and protocols. Some networks are able to dynamically change their logical topology through configuration changes to their routers and switches.

Links

The transmission media (often referred to in the literature as the physical media) used to link devices to form a computer network include electrical cables (Ethernet, HomePNA, power line communication, G.hn), optical fiber (fiber-optic communication), and radio waves (wireless networking). In the OSI model, these are defined at layers 1 and 2 — the physical layer and the data link layer.

A widely adopted family of transmission media used in local area network (LAN) technology is collectively known as Ethernet. The media and protocol standards that enable communication between networked devices over Ethernet are defined by IEEE 802.3. Ethernet transmits data over both copper and fiber cables. Wireless LAN standards (e.g. those defined by IEEE 802.11) use radio waves, or others use infrared signals as a transmission medium. Power line communication uses a building's power cabling to transmit data.

Wired Technologies

Fiber optic cables are used to transmit light from
one computer/network node to another.

The orders of the following wired technologies are, roughly, from slowest to fastest transmission speed:

- Coaxial cable is widely used for cable television systems, office buildings, and other work-sites for local area networks. The cables consist of copper or aluminum wire surrounded by an insulating layer (typically a flexible material with a high dielectric constant), which itself is surrounded by a conductive layer. The insulation helps minimize interference and distortion. Transmission speed ranges from 200 million bits per second to more than 500 million bits per second.

- ITU-T G.hn technology uses existing home wiring (coaxial cable, phone lines and power lines) to create a high-speed (up to 1 Gigabit/s) local area network.

- Signal traces on printed circuit boards are common for board-level serial communication, particularly between certain types integrated circuits, a common example being SPI.

- Ribbon cable (untwisted and possibly unshielded) has been a cost-effective media for serial protocols, especially within metallic enclosures or rolled within copper braid or foil, over short distances, or at lower data rates. Several serial network protocols can be deployed without shielded or twisted pair cabling, that is, with "flat" or "ribbon" cable, or a hybrid flat/twisted ribbon cable, should EMC, length, and bandwidth constraints permit: RS-232, RS-422, RS-485, CAN, GPIB, SCSI, etc.

- Twisted pair wire is the most widely used medium for all telecommunication. Twisted-pair cabling consist of copper wires that are twisted into pairs. Ordinary telephone wires consist of two insulated copper wires twisted into pairs. Computer network cabling (wired Ethernet as defined by IEEE 802.3) consists of 4 pairs of copper cabling that can be utilized for both voice and data transmission. The use of two wires twisted together helps to reduce crosstalk and electromagnetic induction. The transmission speed ranges from 2 million bits per second to 10 billion bits per second. Twisted pair cabling comes in two forms: unshielded twisted pair (UTP) and shielded twisted-pair (STP). Each form comes in several category ratings, designed for use in various scenarios.

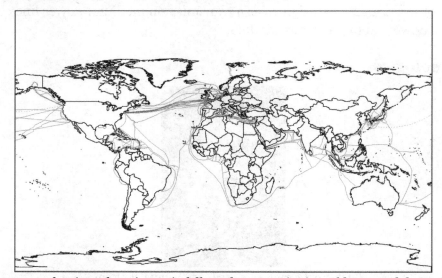

2007 map showing submarine optical fiber telecommunication cables around the world.

- An optical fiber is a glass fiber. It carries pulses of light that represent data. Some advantages of optical fibers over metal wires are very low transmission loss and immunity from electrical interference. Optical fibers can simultaneously carry multiple wavelengths of light, which greatly increases the rate that data can be sent, and helps enable data rates of up to trillions of bits per second. Optic fibers can be used for long runs of cable carrying very high data rates, and are used for undersea cables to interconnect continents.

Price is a main factor distinguishing wired- and wireless-technology options in a business. Wireless options command a price premium that can make purchasing wired computers, printers and other devices a financial benefit. Before making the decision to purchase hardwired technology products, a review of the restrictions and limitations of the selections is necessary. Business and employee needs may override any cost considerations.

Wireless Technologies

Personal computers are very often connected to networks using wireless links.

- Terrestrial microwave: Terrestrial microwave communication uses Earth-based transmitters and receivers resembling satellite dishes. Terrestrial microwaves are in the low gigahertz range, which limits all communications to line-of-sight. Relay stations are spaced approximately 50 km (30 mi) apart.

- Communications satellites: Satellites communicate via microwave radio waves, which are not deflected by the Earth's atmosphere. The satellites are stationed in space, typically in geostationary orbit 35,786 km (22,236 mi) above the equator. These Earth-orbiting systems are capable of receiving and relaying voice, data, and TV signals.

- Cellular and PCS systems use several radio communications technologies. The systems divide the region covered into multiple geographic areas. Each area has a low-power transmitter or radio relay antenna device to relay calls from one area to the next area.

- Radio and spread spectrum technologies: Wireless local area networks use a high-frequency radio technology similar to digital cellular and a low-frequency radio technology. Wireless LANs use spread spectrum technology to enable communication between multiple devices in a limited area. IEEE 802.11 defines a common flavor of open-standards wireless radio-wave technology known as Wi-Fi.

- Free-space optical communication uses visible or invisible light for communications. In most cases, line-of-sight propagation is used, which limits the physical positioning of communicating devices.

Exotic Technologies

There have been various attempts at transporting data over exotic media:

- IP over Avian Carriers was a humorous April fool's Request for Comments, issued as RFC 1149. It was implemented in real life in 2001.

- Extending the Internet to interplanetary dimensions via radio waves, the Interplanetary Internet.

Both cases have a large round-trip delay time, which gives slow two-way communication, but doesn't prevent sending large amounts of information.

Nodes

Network nodes are the points of connection of the transmission medium to transmitters and receivers of the electrical, optical, or radio signals carried in the medium. Nodes may be associated with a computer, but certain types may have only a microcontroller at a node or possibly no programmable device at all. In the simplest of serial arrangements, one RS-232 transmitter can be connected by a pair of wires to one receiver, forming two nodes on one link, or a Point-to-Point topology. Some protocols permit a single node to only either transmit or receive (e.g., ARINC 429). Other protocols have nodes that can both transmit and receive into a single channel (e.g., CAN can have many transceivers connected to a single bus). While the conventional system building blocks of a computer network include network interface controllers (NICs), repeaters, hubs, bridges, switches, routers, modems, gateways, and firewalls, most address network concerns beyond the physical network topology and may be represented as single nodes on a particular physical network topology.

Network Interfaces

An ATM network interface in the form of an accessory card. A lot of network interfaces are built-in.

A network interface controller (NIC) is computer hardware that provides a computer with the ability to access the transmission media, and has the ability to process low-level network information. For example, the NIC may have a connector for accepting a cable, or an aerial for wireless transmission and reception, and the associated circuitry.

The NIC responds to traffic addressed to a network address for either the NIC or the computer as a whole.

In Ethernet networks, each network interface controller has a unique Media Access Control (MAC) address—usually stored in the controller's permanent memory. To avoid address conflicts between network devices, the Institute of Electrical and Electronics Engineers (IEEE) maintains and administers MAC address uniqueness. The size of an Ethernet MAC address is six octets. The three most significant octets are reserved to identify NIC manufacturers. These manufacturers, using only their assigned prefixes, uniquely assign the three least-significant octets of every Ethernet interface they produce.

Repeaters and Hubs

A repeater is an electronic device that receives a network signal, cleans it of unnecessary noise and regenerates it. The signal may be reformed or retransmitted at a higher power level, to the other side of an obstruction possibly using a different transmission medium, so that the signal can cover longer distances without degradation. Commercial repeaters have extended RS-232 segments from 15 meters to over a kilometer. In most twisted pair Ethernet configurations, repeaters are required for cable that runs longer than 100 meters. With fiber optics, repeaters can be tens or even hundreds of kilometers apart.

Repeaters work within the physical layer of the OSI model, that is, there is no end-to-end change in the physical protocol across the repeater, or repeater pair, even if a different physical layer may be used between the ends of the repeater, or repeater pair. Repeaters require a small amount of time to regenerate the signal. This can cause a propagation delay that affects network performance and may affect proper function. As a result, many network architectures limit the number of repeaters that can be used in a row, e.g., the Ethernet 5-4-3 rule.

A repeater with multiple ports is known as hub, an Ethernet hub in Ethernet networks, a USB hub in USB networks.

- USB networks use hubs to form tiered-star topologies.

- Ethernet hubs and repeaters in LANs have been mostly obsoleted by modern switches.

Bridges

A network bridge connects and filters traffic between two network segments at the data link layer (layer 2) of the OSI model to form a single network. This breaks the network's collision domain but maintains a unified broadcast domain. Network segmentation breaks down a large, congested network into an aggregation of smaller, more efficient networks.

Bridges come in three basic types:

- Local bridges: Directly connect LANs.

- Remote bridges: Can be used to create a wide area network (WAN) link between LANs. Remote bridges, where the connecting link is slower than the end networks, largely have been replaced with routers.

- Wireless bridges: Can be used to join LANs or connect remote devices to LANs.

Switches

A network switch is a device that forwards and filters OSI layer 2 datagrams (frames) between ports based on the destination MAC address in each frame. A switch is distinct from a hub in that it only forwards the frames to the physical ports involved in the communication rather than all ports connected. It can be thought of as a multi-port bridge. It learns to associate physical ports to MAC addresses by examining the source addresses of received frames. If an unknown destination is targeted, the switch broadcasts to all ports but the source. Switches normally have numerous ports, facilitating a star topology for devices, and cascading additional switches.

Multi-layer switches are capable of routing based on layer 3 addressing or additional logical levels. The term *switch* is often used loosely to include devices such as routers and bridges, as well as devices that may distribute traffic based on load or based on application content (e.g., a Web URL identifier).

Routers

A typical home or small office router showing the
ADSL telephone line and Ethernet network cable connections.

A router is an internetworking device that forwards packets between networks by processing the routing information included in the packet or datagram (Internet protocol information from layer 3). The routing information is often processed in conjunction with the routing table (or forwarding table). A router uses its routing table to determine where to forward packets. A destination in a routing table can include a "null" interface, also known as the "black hole" interface because data can go into it, however, no further processing is done for said data, i.e. the packets are dropped.

Modems

Modems (Modulator-Demodulator) are used to connect network nodes via wire not originally designed for digital network traffic, or for wireless. To do this one or more carrier signals are modulated by the digital signal to produce an analog signal that can be tailored to give the required properties for transmission. Modems are commonly used for telephone lines, using a digital subscriber line technology.

Firewalls

A firewall is a network device for controlling network security and access rules. Firewalls are typically configured to reject access requests from unrecognized sources while allowing actions from recognized ones. The vital role firewalls play in network security grows in parallel with the constant increase in cyber attacks.

Classification

The study of network topology recognizes eight basic topologies: point-to-point, bus, star, ring or circular, mesh, tree, hybrid, or daisy chain.

Point-to-point

The simplest topology with a dedicated link between two endpoints. Easiest to understand, of the variations of point-to-point topology, is a point-to-point communication channel that appears, to the user, to be permanently associated with the two endpoints. A child's tin can telephone is one example of a physical dedicated channel.

Using circuit-switching or packet-switching technologies, a point-to-point circuit can be set up dynamically and dropped when no longer needed. Switched point-to-point topologies are the basic model of conventional telephony.

The value of a permanent point-to-point network is unimpeded communications between the two endpoints. The value of an on-demand point-to-point connection is proportional to the number of potential pairs of subscribers and has been expressed as Metcalfe's Law.

Daisy Chain

Daisy chaining is accomplished by connecting each computer in series to the next. If a message is intended for a computer partway down the line, each system bounces it along in sequence until it reaches the destination. A daisy-chained network can take two basic forms: linear and ring.

- A linear topology puts a two-way link between one computer and the next. However, this was expensive in the early days of computing, since each computer (except for the ones at each end) required two receivers and two transmitters.

- By connecting the computers at each end of the chain, a ring topology can be formed. When a node sends a message, the message is processed by each computer in the ring. An advantage of the ring is that the number of transmitters and receivers can be cut in half. Since a message will eventually loop all of the way around, transmission does not need to go both directions. Alternatively, the ring can be used to improve fault tolerance. If the ring breaks at a particular link then the transmission can be sent via the reverse path thereby ensuring that all nodes are always connected in the case of a single failure.

Bus

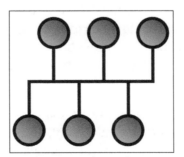

Bus network topology.

In local area networks using bus topology, each node is connected by interface connectors to a single central cable. This is the 'bus', also referred to as the backbone, or trunk) – all data transmitted between nodes in the network is transmitted over this common transmission medium and is able to be received by all nodes in the network simultaneously.

A signal containing the address of the intended receiving machine travels from a source machine in both directions to all machines connected to the bus until it finds the intended recipient, which then accepts the data. If the machine address does not match the intended address for the data, the data portion of the signal is ignored. Since the bus topology consists of only one wire it is less expensive to implement than other topologies, but the savings are offset by the higher cost of managing the network. Additionally, since the network is dependent on the single cable, it can be the single point of failure of the network. In this topology data being transferred may be accessed by any node.

Linear Bus

In a linear bus network, all of the nodes of the network are connected to a common transmission medium which has just two endpoints. When the electrical signal reaches the end of the bus, the signal is reflected back down the line, causing unwanted interference. To prevent this, the two endpoints of the bus are normally terminated with a device called a terminator.

Distributed Bus

In a distributed bus network, all of the nodes of the network are connected to a common transmission medium with more than two endpoints, created by adding branches to the main section of the transmission medium – the physical distributed bus topology functions in exactly the same fashion as the physical linear bus topology because all nodes share a common transmission medium.

Star

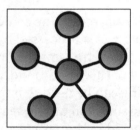

Star network topology.

In star topology, every peripheral node (computer workstation or any other peripheral) is connected to a central node called a hub or switch. The hub is the server and the peripherals are the clients. The network does not necessarily have to resemble a star to be classified as a star network, but all of the peripheral nodes on the network must be connected to one central hub. All traffic that traverses the network passes through the central hub, which acts as a signal repeater.

The star topology is considered the easiest topology to design and implement. One advantage of the star topology is the simplicity of adding additional nodes. The primary disadvantage of the star topology is that the hub represents a single point of failure. Also, since all peripheral communication must flow through the central hub, the aggregate central bandwidth forms a network bottleneck for large clusters.

Extended Star

The extended star network topology extends a physical star topology by one or more repeaters between the central node and the peripheral (or 'spoke') nodes. The repeaters are used to extend the maximum transmission distance of the physical layer, the point-to-point distance between the central node and the peripheral nodes. Repeaters allow greater transmission distance, further than would be possible using just the transmitting power of the central node. The use of repeaters can also overcome limitations from the standard upon which the physical layer is based.

A physical extended star topology in which repeaters are replaced with hubs or switches is a type of hybrid network topology and is referred to as a physical hierarchical star topology, although some texts make no distinction between the two topologies.

A physical hierarchical star topology can also be referred as a tier-star topology, this topology differs from a tree topology in the way star networks are connected together. A tier-star topology uses a central node, while a tree topology uses a central bus and can also be referred as a star-bus network.

Distributed Star

A distributed star is a network topology that is composed of individual networks that are based upon the physical star topology connected in a linear fashion – i.e., 'daisy-chained' – with no central or top level connection point (e.g., two or more 'stacked' hubs, along with their associated star connected nodes or 'spokes').

Ring

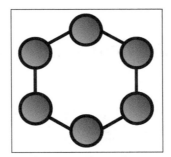

Ring network topology.

A ring topology is a bus topology in a closed loop. Data travels around the ring in one direction. When one node sends data to another, the data passes through each intermediate node on the ring until it reaches its destination. The intermediate nodes repeat (re transmit) the data to keep the signal strong. Every node is a peer; there is no hierarchical relationship of clients and servers. If one node is unable to re transmit data, it severs communication between the nodes before and after it in the bus.

Advantages

- When the load on the network increases, its performance is better than bus topology.

- There is no need of network server to control the connectivity between workstations.

Disadvantages

- Aggregate network bandwidth is bottlenecked by the weakest link between two nodes.

Mesh

The value of fully meshed networks is proportional to the exponent of the number of subscribers, assuming that communicating groups of any two endpoints, up to and including all the endpoints, is approximated by Reed's Law.

Fully Connected Network

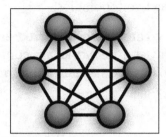

Fully connected mesh topology.

In a fully connected network, all nodes are interconnected. (In graph theory this is called a complete graph.) The simplest fully connected network is a two-node network. A fully connected network doesn't need to use packet switching or broadcasting. However, since the number of connections grows quadratically with the number of nodes:

$$c = \frac{n(n-1)}{2}.$$

This makes it impractical for large networks. This kind of topology does not trip and affect other nodes in the network.

Partially Connected Network

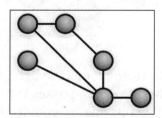

Partially connected mesh topology.

In a partially connected network, certain nodes are connected to exactly one other node; but some nodes are connected to two or more other nodes with a point-to-point link. This makes it possible to make use of some of the redundancy of mesh topology that is physically fully connected, without the expense and complexity required for a connection between every node in the network.

Hybrid

Hybrid topology is also known as hybrid network.Hybrid networks combine two or more topologies in such a way that the resulting network does not exhibit one of the standard topologies (e.g., bus, star, ring, etc.). For example, a tree network (or star-bus network) is a hybrid topology in which star networks are interconnected via bus networks. However, a tree network connected to another tree network is still topologically a tree network, not a distinct network type. A hybrid topology is always produced when two different basic network topologies are connected.

A star-ring network consists of two or more ring networks connected using a multistation access unit (MAU) as a centralized hub.

Snowflake topology is a star network of star networks.

Two other hybrid network types are hybrid mesh and hierarchical star.

Centralization

The star topology reduces the probability of a network failure by connecting all of the peripheral nodes (computers, etc.) to a central node. When the physical star topology is applied to a logical bus network such as Ethernet, this central node (traditionally a hub) rebroadcasts all transmissions received from any peripheral node to all peripheral nodes on the network, sometimes including the originating node. All peripheral nodes may thus communicate with all others by transmitting to, and receiving from, the central node only. The failure of a transmission line linking any peripheral node to the central node will result in the isolation of that peripheral node from all others, but the remaining peripheral nodes will be unaffected. However, the disadvantage is that the failure of the central node will cause the failure of all of the peripheral nodes.

If the central node is *passive*, the originating node must be able to tolerate the reception of an echo of its own transmission, delayed by the two-way round trip transmission time (i.e. to and from the central node) plus any delay generated in the central node. An *active* star network has an active central node that usually has the means to prevent echo-related problems.

A tree topology (a.k.a. hierarchical topology) can be viewed as a collection of star networks arranged in a hierarchy. This tree has individual peripheral nodes (e.g. leaves) which are required to transmit to and receive from one other node only and are not required to act as repeaters or regenerators. Unlike the star network, the functionality of the central node may be distributed.

As in the conventional star network, individual nodes may thus still be isolated from the network by a single-point failure of a transmission path to the node. If a link connecting a leaf fails, that leaf is isolated; if a connection to a non-leaf node fails, an entire section of the network becomes isolated from the rest.

To alleviate the amount of network traffic that comes from broadcasting all signals to all nodes, more advanced central nodes were developed that are able to keep track of the identities of the nodes that are connected to the network. These network switches will "learn" the layout of the network by "listening" on each port during normal data transmission, examining the data packets and recording the address/ identifier of each connected node and which port it is connected to in a lookup table held in memory. This lookup table then allows future transmissions to be forwarded to the intended destination only.

Decentralization

In a partially connected mesh topology, there are at least two nodes with two or more paths between them to provide redundant paths in case the link providing one of the paths fails.

Decentralization is often used to compensate for the single-point-failure disadvantage that is present when using a single device as a central node (e.g., in star and tree networks). A special kind of mesh, limiting the number of hops between two nodes, is a hypercube. The number of arbitrary forks in mesh networks makes them more difficult to design and implement, but their decentralized nature makes them very useful. In 2012 the Institute of Electrical and Electronics Engineers (IEEE) published the Shortest Path Bridging protocol to ease configuration tasks and allows all paths to be active which increases bandwidth and redundancy between all devices.

This is similar in some ways to a grid network, where a linear or ring topology is used to connect systems in multiple directions. A multidimensional ring has a toroidal topology, for instance.

A fully connected network, complete topology, or full mesh topology is a network topology in which there is a direct link between all pairs of nodes. In a fully connected network with n nodes, there are n(n-1)/2 direct links. Networks designed with this topology are usually very expensive to set up, but provide a high degree of reliability due to the multiple paths for data that are provided by the large number of redundant links between nodes. This topology is mostly seen in military applications.

Network Nodes

A node is any physical device within a network of other tools that's able to send, receive, or forward information. A personal computer is the most common node. It's called the computer node or internet node.

Modems, switches, hubs, bridges, servers, and printers are also nodes, as are other devices that connect over Wi-Fi or Ethernet. For example, a network connecting three computers and one printer, along with two more wireless devices, has six total nodes.

Nodes within a computer network must have some form of identification, like an IP address or MAC address, for other network devices to recognize it. A node without this information, or one that's offline, no longer functions as a node.

Principle of Network Node

Network nodes are the physical pieces that make up a network. They usually include any device that both receives and then communicates information. But they might receive and store the data, relay the information elsewhere, or create and send data instead.

For example, a computer node might back up files online or send an email, but it can also stream videos and download other files. A network printer can receive print requests from other devices on the network, while a scanner can send images back to the computer. A router determines which data goes to which devices that request file downloads within a system, but it can also send requests out to the public internet.

Other Types of Nodes

In a fiber-based cable TV network, nodes are the homes or businesses that connect to the same fiber optic receiver.

Another example of a node is a device that provides intelligent network service within a cellular network, like a base station controller (BSC) or Gateway GPRS Support Node (GGSN). In other words, the mobile node is what provides the software controls behind the equipment, like the structure with antennas that transmit signals to all the devices within a network.

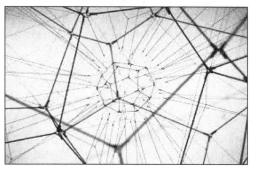

William Bout on Unsplash.

A supernode is a node within a peer-to-peer network that functions not only as a regular node but also as a proxy server and the device that relays information to other users within the P2P system. Because of this, supernodes require more CPU and bandwidth than regular nodes.

End-node Problem

The term "end node problem" refers to the security risk that comes with users connecting their computers or other devices to a sensitive network, either physically (like at work) or through the cloud (from anywhere), while at the same time using that same device to perform unsecured activities.

Some examples include an end user who takes their work laptop home but then checks their email on an unsecured network like at a coffee shop or a user who connects their personal computer or phone to the company's Wi-Fi network.

One of the most significant risks to a corporate network is a compromised personal device that someone uses on that network. The problem is pretty clear: mixing a potentially unsecured network and a business network that likely contains sensitive data.

The end user's device might be malware-infested with things like keyloggers or file transfer programs that extract sensitive information or move malware to the private network once it logs in.

VPNs and two-factor authentication can help fix this problem. So can special bootable client software that can only use specific remote access programs.

However, another method is to educate users on how to secure their device correctly. Personal laptops can use an antivirus program to keep their files protected from malware, and smartphones can use a similar antimalware app to catch viruses and other threats before they cause any harm.

Routers

A router is a networking device that forwards data packets between computer networks. Routers perform the traffic directing functions on the Internet. Data sent through the internet, such as a web page or email, is in the form of data packets. A packet is typically forwarded from one router to another router through the networks that constitute an internetwork (e.g. the Internet) until it reaches its destination node.

A router is connected to two or more data lines from different IP networks. When a data packet comes in on one of the lines, the router reads the network address information in the packet header to determine the ultimate destination. Then, using information in its routing table or routing policy, it directs the packet to the next network on its journey.

The most familiar type of IP routers are home and small office routers that simply forward IP packets between the home computers and the Internet. An example of a router would be the owner's cable or DSL router, which connects to the Internet through an Internet service provider (ISP). More sophisticated routers, such as enterprise routers, connect large business or ISP networks up to the powerful core routers that forward data at high speed along the optical fiber lines of the Internet backbone.

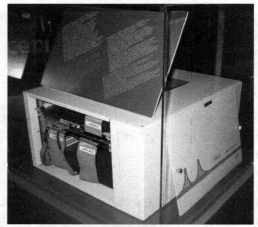

A Cisco ASM/2-32EM router deployed at CERN in 1987.

Operation

When multiple routers are used in interconnected networks, the routers can exchange information about destination addresses using a routing protocol. Each router builds up a routing table listing the preferred routes between any two computer systems on the interconnected networks.

A router has two types of network element components organized onto separate processing planes:

- Control plane: A router maintains a routing table that lists which route should be used to forward a data packet, and through which physical interface connection. It does this using internal preconfigured directives, called static routes, or by learning routes dynamically using a routing protocol. Static and dynamic routes are stored in the routing table. The control-plane logic then strips non-essential directives from the table and builds a forwarding information base (FIB) to be used by the forwarding plane.

- Forwarding plane: The router forwards data packets between incoming and outgoing interface connections. It forwards them to the correct network type using information that the packet header contains matched to entries in the FIB supplied by the control plane.

Applications

A typical home or small office DSL router showing the telephone socket *(left, white)* to connect it to
the internet using ADSL, and Ethernet jacks *(right, yellow)* to connect it to home computers and printers.

A router may have interfaces for different types of physical layer connections, such as copper cables, fiber optic, or wireless transmission. It can also support different network layer transmission standards. Each network interface is used to enable data packets to be forwarded from one transmission system to another. Routers may also be used to connect two or more logical groups of computer devices known as subnets, each with a different network prefix.

Routers may provide connectivity within enterprises, between enterprises and the Internet, or between internet service providers' (ISPs') networks. The largest routers (such as the Cisco CRS-1 or Juniper PTX) interconnect the various ISPs, or may be used in large enterprise networks. Smaller routers usually provide connectivity for typical home and office networks.

All sizes of routers may be found inside enterprises. The most powerful routers are usually found in ISPs, academic and research facilities. Large businesses may also need more powerful routers to cope with ever-increasing demands of intranet data traffic. A hierarchical internetworking model for interconnecting routers in large networks is in common use.

Access, Core and Distribution

A screenshot of the LuCI web interface used by OpenWrt.
This page configures Dynamic DNS.

Access routers, including small office/home office (SOHO) models, are located at home and customer sites such as branch offices that do not need hierarchical routing of their own. Typically, they are optimized for low cost. Some SOHO routers are capable of running alternative free Linux-based firmware like Tomato, OpenWrt or DD-WRT.

Distribution routers aggregate traffic from multiple access routers. Distribution routers are often responsible for enforcing quality of service across a wide area network (WAN), so they may have considerable memory installed, multiple WAN interface connections, and substantial onboard data processing routines. They may also provide connectivity to groups of file servers or other external networks.

In enterprises, a core router may provide a collapsed backbone interconnecting the distribution tier routers from multiple buildings of a campus, or large enterprise locations. They tend to be optimized for high bandwidth, but lack some of the features of edge routers.

Security

External networks must be carefully considered as part of the overall security strategy of the local network. A router may include a firewall, VPN handling, and other security functions, or these may be handled by separate devices. Routers also commonly perform network address translation which restricts connections initiated from external connections but is not recognised as a security feature by all experts. Some experts argue that open source routers are more secure and reliable than closed source routers because open source routers allow mistakes to be quickly found and corrected.

Routing Different Networks

Routers are also often distinguished on the basis of the network in which they operate. A router in a local area network (LAN) of a single organisation is called an interior router. A router that is operated in the Internet backbone is described as exterior router. While a router that connects a LAN with the Internet or a wide area network (WAN) is called a border router, or gateway router.

Internet Connectivity and Internal Use

Routers intended for ISP and major enterprise connectivity usually exchange routing information using the Border Gateway Protocol (BGP). RFC 4098 defines the types of BGP routers according to their functions:

- Edge router: Also called a provider edge router, is placed at the edge of an ISP network. The router uses Exterior Border Gateway Protocol (EBGP) to routers at other ISPs or large enterprise autonomous systems.

- Subscriber edge router: Also called a customer edge router, is located at the edge of the subscriber's network, it also uses EBGP to its provider's autonomous system. It is typically used in an (enterprise) organization.

- Inter-provider border router: Interconnecting ISPs, is a BGP router that maintains BGP sessions with other BGP routers in ISP Autonomous Systems.

- Core router: A core router resides within an Autonomous System as a back bone to carry traffic between edge routers.

- Within an ISP: In the ISP's Autonomous System, a router uses internal BGP to communicate with other ISP edge routers, other intranet core routers, or the ISP's intranet provider border routers.

- "Internet backbone:" The Internet no longer has a clearly identifiable backbone, unlike its predecessor networks. The major ISPs' system routers make up what could be considered to be the current Internet backbone core. ISPs operate all four types of the BGP routers. An ISP "core" router is used to interconnect its edge and border routers. Core routers may also have specialized functions in virtual private networks based on a combination of BGP and Multi-Protocol Label Switching protocols.

- Port forwarding: Routers are also used for port forwarding between private Internet-connected servers.

- Voice/Data/Fax/Video Processing Routers: Commonly referred to as access servers or gateways, these devices are used to route and process voice, data, video and fax traffic on the Internet. Since 2005, most long-distance phone calls have been processed as IP traffic (VOIP) through a voice gateway. Use of access server type routers expanded with the advent of the Internet, first with dial-up access and another resurgence with voice phone service.

- Larger networks commonly use multilayer switches, with layer 3 devices being used to simply interconnect multiple subnets within the same security zone, and higher layer switches when filtering, translation, load balancing or other higher level functions are required, especially between zones.

Forwarding

The main purpose of a router is to connect multiple networks and forward packets destined either for its own networks or other networks. A router is considered a layer-3 device because its primary forwarding decision is based on the information in the layer-3 IP packet, specifically the destination IP address. When a router receives a packet, it searches its routing table to find the best match between the destination IP address of the packet and one of the addresses in the routing table. Once a match is found, the packet is encapsulated in the layer-2 data link frame for the outgoing interface indicated in the table entry. A router typically does not look into the packet payload, but only at the layer-3 addresses to make a forwarding decision, plus optionally other information in the header for hints on, for example, quality of service (QoS). For pure IP forwarding, a router is designed to minimize the state information associated with individual packets. Once a packet is forwarded, the router does not retain any historical information about the packet.

The routing table itself can contain information derived from a variety of sources, such as a default or static routes that are configured manually, or dynamic routing protocols where the router learns routes from other routers. A default route is one that is used to route all traffic whose destination does not otherwise appear in the routing table; this is common – even necessary – in small networks, such as a home or small business where the default route simply sends all non-local traffic to the Internet service provider. The default route can be manually configured (as a static route), or learned by dynamic routing protocols, or be obtained by DHCP.

A router can run more than one routing protocol at a time, particularly if it serves as an autonomous system border router between parts of a network that run different routing protocols; if it does so, then redistribution may be used (usually selectively) to share information between the different protocols running on the same router.

Besides making a decision as to which interface a packet is forwarded to, which is handled primarily via the routing table, a router also has to manage congestion when packets arrive at a rate higher than the router can process. Three policies commonly used in the Internet are tail drop, random early detection (RED), and weighted random early detection (WRED). Tail drop is the simplest and most easily implemented; the router simply drops new incoming packets once the length of the queue exceeds the size of the buffers in the router. RED probabilistically drops datagrams early when the queue exceeds a pre-configured portion of the buffer, until a pre-determined max, when it becomes tail drop. WRED requires a weight on the average queue size to act upon when the traffic is about to exceed the pre-configured size, so that short bursts will not trigger random drops.

Another function a router performs is to decide which packet should be processed first when multiple queues exist. This is managed through QoS, which is critical when Voice over IP is deployed, so as not to introduce excessive latency.

Yet another function a router performs is called policy-based routing where special rules are constructed to override the rules derived from the routing table when a packet forwarding decision is made.

Router functions may be performed through the same internal paths that the packets travel inside the router. Some of the functions may be performed through an application-specific integrated circuit (ASIC) to avoid overhead of scheduling CPU time to process the packets. Others may have to be performed through the CPU as these packets need special attention that cannot be handled by an ASIC.

Modems

Modem is short for "Modulator-Demodulator." It is a hardwarecomponent that allows a computeror another device, such as a router or switch, to connect to the Internet. It converts or "modulates" an analogsignal from a telephone or cable wire to digital data (1s and 0s) that a computer can recognize. Similarly, it converts digital data from a computer or other device into an analog signal that can be sent over standard telephone lines.

The first modems were "dial-up," meaning they had to dial a phone number to connect to an ISP. These modems operated over standard analog phone lines and used the same frequencies as telephone calls, which limited their maximum data transfer rate to 56 Kbps. Dial-up modems also required full use of the local telephone line, meaning voice calls would interrupt the Internet connection.

Modern modems are typically DSL or cable modems, which are considered "broadband" devices. DSL modems operate over standard telephone lines, but use a wider frequency range. This allows for higher data transfer rates than dial-up modems and enables them to not interfere with phone calls. Cable modems send and receive data over standard cable television lines, which are typically coaxial cables. Most modern cable modems support DOCSIS (Data Over Cable Service

Interface Specification), which provides an efficient way of transmitting TV, cable Internet, and digital phone signals over the same cable line.

Firewalls

In computing, a firewall is a network security system that monitors and controls incoming and outgoing network traffic based on predetermined security rules. A firewall typically establishes a barrier between a trusted internal network and untrusted external network, such as the Internet.

Firewalls are often categorized as either network firewalls or host-based firewalls. Network firewalls filter traffic between two or more networks and run on network hardware. Host-based firewalls run on host computers and control network traffic in and out of those machines.

Types

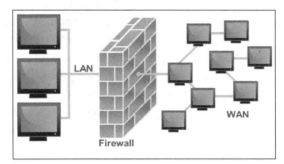

An illustration of where a firewall would be located in a network.

Firewalls are generally categorized as network-based or host-based. Network-based firewalls are positioned on the gateway computers of LANs, WANs and intranets. They are either software appliances running on general-purpose hardware, or hardware-based firewall computer appliances. Firewall appliances may also offer other functionality to the internal network they protect, such as acting as a DHCP or VPN server for that network. Host-based firewalls are positioned on the host itself and control network traffic in and out of those machines. The host-based firewall may be a daemon or service as a part of the operating system or an agent application such as endpoint security or protection. Each has advantages and disadvantages. However, each has a role in layered security.

Firewalls also vary in type depending on where communication originates, where it is intercepted, and the state of communication being traced.

Network Layer or Packet Filters

Network layer firewalls, also called packet filters, operate at a relatively low level of the TCP/IP stack, blocking packets unless they match the established rule set. The firewall administrator may define the rules; or default rules may apply.

Network layer firewalls generally fall into two sub-categories, stateful and stateless.

Commonly used packet filters on various versions of Unix are ipfirewall (FreeBSD, Mac OS X (< 10.7)), NPF (NetBSD), PF (Mac OS X (> 10.4), OpenBSD, and some other BSDs), iptables/ipchains (Linux) and IPFilter.

Application-layer

Application-layer firewalls work on the application level of the TCP/IP stack (i.e., all browser traffic, or all telnet or FTP traffic), and may intercept all packets traveling to or from an application.

Application firewalls function by determining whether a process should accept any given connection. Application firewalls accomplish their function by hooking into socket calls to filter the connections between the application layer and the lower layers of the OSI model. Application firewalls that hook into socket calls are also referred to as socket filters. Application firewalls work much like a packet filter but application filters apply filtering rules (allow/block) on a per process basis instead of filtering connections on a per port basis. Generally, prompts are used to define rules for processes that have not yet received a connection. It is rare to find application firewalls not combined or used in conjunction with a packet filter.

Also, application firewalls further filter connections by examining the process ID of data packets against a rule set for the local process involved in the data transmission. The extent of the filtering that occurs is defined by the provided rule set. Given the variety of software that exists, application firewalls only have more complex rule sets for the standard services, such as sharing services. These per-process rule sets have limited efficacy in filtering every possible association that may occur with other processes. Also, these per-process rule sets cannot defend against modification of the process via exploitation, such as memory corruption exploits. Because of these limitations, application firewalls are beginning to be supplanted by a new generation of application firewalls that rely on mandatory access control (MAC), also referred to as sandboxing, to protect vulnerable services.

Proxies

A proxy server (running either on dedicated hardware or as software on a general-purpose machine) may act as a firewall by responding to input packets (connection requests, for example) in the manner of an application, while blocking other packets. A proxy server is a gateway from one network to another for a specific network application, in the sense that it functions as a proxy on behalf of the network user.

Proxies make tampering with an internal system from the external network more difficult, so that misuse of one internal system would not necessarily cause a security breach exploitable from outside the firewall (as long as the application proxy remains intact and properly configured). Conversely, intruders may hijack a publicly reachable system and use it as a proxy for their own purposes; the proxy then masquerades as that system to other internal machines. While use of internal address spaces enhances security, crackers may still employ methods such as IP spoofing to attempt to pass packets to a target network.

Network Address Translation

Firewalls often have network address translation (NAT) functionality, and the hosts protected behind a firewall commonly have addresses in the "private address range", as defined in RFC 1918. Firewalls often have such functionality to hide the true address of computer which is connected to the network. Originally, the NAT function was developed to address the limited number of IPv4 routable addresses that could be used or assigned to companies or individuals as well as reduce both the amount and therefore cost of obtaining enough public addresses for every computer in an organization. Although NAT on its own is not considered a security feature, hiding the addresses of protected devices has become an often used defense against network reconnaissance.

Network Security

Network security consists of the policies and practices adopted to prevent and monitor unauthorized access, misuse, modification, or denial of a computer network and network-accessible resources. Network security involves the authorization of access to data in a network, which is controlled by the network administrator. Users choose or are assigned an ID and password or other authenticating information that allows them access to information and programs within their authority. Network security covers a variety of computer networks, both public and private, that are used in everyday jobs; conducting transactions and communications among businesses, government agencies and individuals. Networks can be private, such as within a company, and others which might be open to public access. Network security is involved in organizations, enterprises, and other types of institutions. It does as its title explains: it secures the network, as well as protecting and overseeing operations being done. The most common and simple way of protecting a network resource is by assigning it a unique name and a corresponding password.

Network Security Concept

Network security starts with authentication, commonly with a username and a password. Since this requires just one detail authenticating the user name—i.e., the password—this is sometimes termed one-factor authentication. With two-factor authentication, something the user 'has' is also used (e.g., a security token or 'dongle', an ATM card, or a mobile phone); and with three-factor authentication, something the user 'is' is also used (e.g., a fingerprint or retinal scan).

Once authenticated, a firewall enforces access policies such as what services are allowed to be accessed by the network users. Though effective to prevent unauthorized access, this component may fail to check potentially harmful content such as computer worms or Trojans being transmitted over the network. Anti-virus software or an intrusion prevention system (IPS) help detect and inhibit the action of such malware. An anomaly-based intrusion detection system may also monitor the network like wireshark traffic and may be logged for audit purposes and for later high-level analysis. Newer systems combining unsupervised machine learning with full network traffic analysis can detect active network attackers from malicious insiders or targeted external attackers that have compromised a user machine or account.

Communication between two hosts using a network may be encrypted to maintain privacy.

Honeypots, essentially decoy network-accessible resources, may be deployed in a network as surveillance and early-warning tools, as the honeypots are not normally accessed for legitimate purposes. Techniques used by the attackers that attempt to compromise these decoy resources are studied during and after an attack to keep an eye on new exploitation techniques. Such analysis may be used to further tighten security of the actual network being protected by the honeypot. A honeypot can also direct an attacker's attention away from legitimate servers. A honeypot encourages attackers to spend their time and energy on the decoy server while distracting their attention from the data on the real server. Similar to a honeypot, a honeynet is a network set up with intentional vulnerabilities. Its purpose is also to invite attacks so that the attacker's methods can be studied and that information can be used to increase network security. A honeynet typically contains one or more honeypots.

Security Management

Security management for networks is different for all kinds of situations. A home or small office may only require basic security while large businesses may require high-maintenance and advanced software and hardware to prevent malicious attacks from hacking and spamming. In order to minimize susceptibility to malicious attacks from external threats to the network, corporations often employ tools which carry out network security verifications.

Types of Attacks

Networks are subject to attacks from malicious sources. Attacks can be from two categories: "Passive" when a network intruder intercepts data traveling through the network, and "Active" in which an intruder initiates commands to disrupt the network's normal operation or to conduct reconnaissance and lateral movements to find and gain access to assets available via the network.

Types of attacks include:

- Passive
  - Network
    - Wiretapping
    - Port scanner
    - Idle scan
    - Encryption
    - Traffic analysis
- Active
  - Virus
  - Eavesdropping
  - Data modification
  - Denial-of-service attack
  - DNS spoofing
  - Man in the middle
  - ARP poisoning
  - VLAN hopping

- ◦ Smurf attack

- ◦ Buffer overflow

- ◦ Heap overflow

- ◦ Format string attack

- ◦ SQL injection

- ◦ Phishing

- ◦ Cross-site scripting

- ◦ CSRF

- ◦ Cyber-attack

Network Performance

Network performance is defined by the overall quality of service provided by a network. This encompasses numerous parameters and metrics that must be analyzed collectively to assess a given network.

Network performance measurement is therefore defined as the overall set of processes and tools that can be used to quantitatively and qualitatively assess network performance and provide actionable data to remediate any network performance issues.

Measuring Network Performance

The demands on networks are increasing every day, and the need for proper network performance measurement is more important than ever before. Effective network performance translates into improved user satisfaction, whether that be internal employee efficiencies, or customer-facing network components such as an e-commerce website, making the business rationale for performance testing and monitoring self-evident.

When delivering services and applications to users, bandwidth issues, network down time, and bottlenecks can quickly escalate into IT crisis mode. Proactive network performance management solutions that detect and diagnose performance issues are the best way to guarantee ongoing user satisfaction.

The performance of a network can never be fully modeled, so measuring network performance before, during, and after updates are made and monitoring performance on an ongoing basis are the only valid methods to fully ensure network quality. While measuring and monitoring network performance parameters are essential, the interpretation and actions stemming from these metrics are equally important.

Network Performance Measurement Tools

Network performance measurement tools can be broadly categorized into two types - passive and active. Passive network measurement tools monitor (or measure) existing applications on the network to gather data on performance metrics. This category of tool minimizes network disruption, since no additional traffic is introduced by the tool itself. In addition, by measuring network performance using actual applications, a realistic assessment of the user experience may be obtained.

Active networking performance measurement tools generate data that can be tailored to baseline performance using pre-set routines. This testing requires an additive level of data traffic by nature, so it must be scheduled appropriately to minimize impact on existing network traffic.

The continuous improvement of network performance monitoring tools has enabled IT professionals to stay one step ahead of the game. Advanced tools provide cutting edge data packet capture analytics, software solutions that integrate user experience data into effective root cause analysis and trending, and large-scale network performance measurement dashboards with remote diagnostic capabilities.

Network Performance Measurement Parameters

To ensure optimized network performance, the most important metrics should be selected for measurement. Many of the parameters included in a comprehensive network performance management system focus on data speed and data quality. Both of these broad categories can significantly impact end user experience and are influenced by several factors.

Latency

With regards to network performance measurement, latency is simply the amount of time it takes for data to travel from one defined location to another. This parameter is sometimes referred to as delay. Ideally, the latency of a network is as close to zero as possible. The absolute limit or governing factor for latency is the speed of light, but packet queuing in switched networks and the refractive index of fiber optic cabling are examples of variables that can increase latency.

Packet Loss

With regards to network performance measurement, packet loss refers to the number of packets transmitted from one destination to another that fail to transmit. This metric can be quantified by capturing traffic data on both ends, then identifying missing packets and/or retransmission of packets. Packet loss can be caused by network congestion, router performance and software issues, among other factors.

The end effects will be detected by users in the form of voice and streaming interruptions, or incomplete transmission of files. Since retransmission is a method utilized by network protocols to compensate for packet loss, the network congestion that initially led to the issue can sometimes be exacerbated by the increased volume caused by retransmission.

To minimize the impact of packet loss and other network performance problems, it is important to develop and utilize tools and processes that identify and alleviate the true source of problems quickly. By analyzing response time to end user requests, the system or component that is at the root of the issue can be identified. Data packet capture analytics tools can be used to review response time for TCP connections, which in turn can pinpoint which applications are contributing to the bottleneck.

Transmission Control Protocol (TCP) is a standard for network conversation through which applications exchange data, which works in conjunction with the Internet Protocol (IP) to define how packets of data are sent from one computer to another. The successive steps in a TCP session correspond to time intervals that can be analyzed to detect excessive latency in connection or round trip times.

Throughput and Bandwidth

Throughput is a metric often associated with the manufacturing industry and is most commonly defined as the amount of material or items passing through a particular system or process. A common question in the manufacturing industry is how many of product X were produced today, and did this number meet expectations. For network performance measurement, throughput is defined in terms of the amount of data or number of data packets that can be delivered in a pre-defined time frame.

Bandwidth, usually measured in bits per second, is a characterization of the amount of data that can be transferred over a given time period. Bandwidth is therefore a measure of capacity rather than speed. For example, a bus may be capable of carrying 100 passengers (bandwidth), but the bus may actually only transport 85 passengers (throughput).

Jitter

Jitter is defined as the variation in time delay for the data packets sent over a network. This variable represents an identified disruption in the normal sequencing of data packets. Jitter is related to latency, since the jitter manifests itself in increased or uneven latency between data packets, which can disrupt network performance and lead to packet loss and network congestion. Although some level of jitter is to be expected and can usually be tolerated, quantifying network jitter is an important aspect of comprehensive network performance measurement.

Latency vs. Throughput

While the concepts of throughput and bandwidth are sometimes misunderstood, the same confusion is common between the terms latency and throughput. Although these parameters are closely related, it is important to understand the difference between the two.

In relation to network performance measurement, throughput is a measurement of actual system performance, quantified in terms of data transfer over a given time.

Latency is a measurement of the delay in transfer time, meaning it will directly impact the throughput, but is not synonymous with it. The latency might be thought of as an unavoidable bottleneck on an assembly line, such as a test process, measured in units of time. Throughput, on the other hand, is measured in units completed which is inherently influenced by this latency.

Factors Affecting Network Performance

Network performance management includes monitoring and optimization practices for key network performance metrics such as application down time and packet loss. Increased network availability and minimized response time when problems occur are two of the logical outputs for a successful network management program. A holistic approach to network performance management must consider all of the essential categories through which problems may be manifested.

Infrastructure

The overall network infrastructure includes network hardware, such as routers, switches and cables, networking software, including security and operating systems as well as network services such as IP addressing and wireless protocols. From the infrastructure perspective, it is important to characterize the overall traffic and bandwidth patterns on the network. This network performance measurement will provide insight into which flows are most congested over time and could become potential problem areas.

Identifying the over-capacity elements of the infrastructure can lead to proactive corrections or upgrades that can minimize future downtime rather than simply responding to any performance crisis that may arise.

Network Issues

Performance limitations inherent to the network itself are often a source of significant emphasis. Multiple facets of the network can contribute to performance, and deficiencies in any of these areas can lead to systemic problems. Since hardware requirements are essential to capacity planning, these elements should be designed to meet all anticipated system demands. For example, an inadequate bus size on the network backplane or insufficient available memory might in turn lead to an increase in packet loss or otherwise decreased network performance. Network congestion, on either the active devices or physical links (cabling) of the network can lead to decreased speeds, if packets are queued, or packet loss if no queuing system is in place.

Applications

While network hardware and infrastructure issues can directly impact user experience for a given application, it is important to consider the impact of the applications themselves as important cogs in the overall network architecture. Poor performing applications can over-consume bandwidth and diminish user experience. As applications become more complex over time, diagnosing and monitoring application performance gains importance. Window sizes and keep-alives are examples of application characteristics that impact network performance and capacity.

Whenever possible, applications should be designed with their intended network environment in mind, using real-world networks for testing rather than simulation labs. Ultimately, the variety of network conditions an application is exposed to cannot be fully anticipated, but improvements in development practices can lead to a decrease in network performance degradation due to application issues. Applications contributing to poor network performance can be identified using analytics to identify slow response time, while correcting these design limitations post-release can become a formidable task.

Security Issues

Network security is intended to protect privacy, intellectual property, and data integrity. Managing and mitigating network security issues requires device scanning, data encryption, virus protection, authentication and intrusion detection, all of which consume valuable network bandwidth and can impact performance.

Security breaches and downtime due to viruses are among the most costly performance problems encountered, so any degradation induced by security products should be carefully weighed against the potential downtime or data integrity disasters they prevent. With these constraints in mind, an invaluable element of network performance monitoring with respect to security is the strategic use of network security forensics. By recording, capturing and analyzing network data, the source of intrusions and anomalous traffic such as malware may be identified. Captured network traffic can utilized retrospectively for investigative purposes by reassembling transferred files.

Full Packet Capture (FPC) is one such technique used for after-the-fact security investigations. Rather than monitoring incoming traffic for known malicious signatures, FPC provides constant storage of unmodified network traffic and the ability to replay previous traffic through new detection signatures. Given the high volume of data packet transfer inherent to a modern network, the storage requirements associated with FPC can be formidable. By defining the mean time to detect (MTTD) based on previous incident metrics, a logical minimum time for packet data storage can be established. In some cases, packet filtering may be a viable method to selectively monitor high risk traffic and lessen the storage demands. To facilitate forensic analysis capabilities, FPC software must enable accurate time and date stamping of stored packets for search and investigation purposes.

Network Performance Measurement Challenges

The potential culprits leading to diminished network performance become actionable with an observable drop off in speed or quality. Network performance measurement solutions should be designed with the user in mind. Slight degradation in latency, for example, may not be perceptible. Finding these acceptable limits is the key to establishing relevant testing and monitoring.

With performance demands constantly increasing, novel solutions to common performance issues have emerged. Packet shaping is a method used to prioritize package delivery for different applications. This allows adequate bandwidth to be consistently allocated to the most important categories. File compression is another innovation that decreases the bandwidth and memory consumed.

Perhaps the most important component in maintaining network performance is the implementation of effective network performance measurement and oversight practices. If problems with servers, routing, delivery or bandwidth can be detected in real time, expedient solutions and preventative strategies are the logical byproducts.

References

- Computer-networking, computer-fundamentals: tutorialspoint.com, Retrieved 8 January, 2019

- M. Afshar alam; tamanna siddiqui; k. R. Seeja (2013). Recent developments in computing and its applications. I. K. International pvt ltd. P. 513. Isbn 978-93-80026-78-7

- Basics-computer-networking: geeksforgeeks.org, Retrieved 21 May, 2019

- Bradley, ray. Understanding computer science (for advanced level): the study guide. Cheltenham: nelson thornes. P. 244. Isbn 978-0-7487-6147-0. Oclc 47869750. Retrieved 2016-03-26

- What-is-a-node: lifewire.com, Retrieved 19 April, 2019

- Overview of key routing protocol concepts: architectures, protocol types, algorithms and metrics". Tcpipguide. com. Archived from the original on 20 december 2010. Retrieved 15 january 2011

- Canavan, john e. (2001). Fundamentals of network security (1st ed.). Boston, ma: artech house. P. 212. Isbn 9781580531764

PERMISSIONS

We would like to thank the editorial team for lending their expertise to make the book truly unique. They have played a crucial role in the development of this book. Without their invaluable contributions this book wouldn't have been possible. They have made vital efforts to compile up to date information on the varied aspects of this subject to make this book a valuable addition to the collection of many professionals and students.

This book was conceptualized with the vision of imparting up-to-date and integrated information in this field. To ensure the same, a matchless editorial board was set up. Every individual on the board went through rigorous rounds of assessment to prove their worth. After which they invested a large part of their time researching and compiling the most relevant data for our readers.

The editorial board has been involved in producing this book since its inception. They have spent rigorous hours researching and exploring the diverse topics which have resulted in the successful publishing of this book. They have passed on their knowledge of decades through this book. To expedite this challenging task, the publisher supported the team at every step. A small team of assistant editors was also appointed to further simplify the editing procedure and attain best results for the readers.

Apart from the editorial board, the designing team has also invested a significant amount of their time in understanding the subject and creating the most relevant covers. They scrutinized every image to scout for the most suitable representation of the subject and create an appropriate cover for the book.

The publishing team has been an ardent support to the editorial, designing and production team. Their endless efforts to recruit the best for this project, has resulted in the accomplishment of this book. They are a veteran in the field of academics and their pool of knowledge is as vast as their experience in printing. Their expertise and guidance has proved useful at every step. Their uncompromising quality standards have made this book an exceptional effort. Their encouragement from time to time has been an inspiration for everyone.

The publisher and the editorial board hope that this book will prove to be a valuable piece of knowledge for students, practitioners and scholars across the globe.

INDEX